Gulf of St. Lawrence

Ste. Anne
des Monts

△ Mont Jacques
Cartier (4300 ft.)

National Park

△ Mont Albert
(3700 ft.)

Cap
Des Rosiers
Cap Bon A

Gaspé

G A S P É

Percé

I.
Bonaventure

Port Daniel

Cascapedia

St.
Siméon

Pte. de Paspébiac

Baie des Chaleurs

N. S W I C H

# GASPÉ

*Land of History and Romance*

by
BLODWEN DAVIES

AMBASSADOR BOOKS LIMITED
TORONTO                CANADA

PRINTED IN CANADA
BY THE HUNTER·ROSE CO. LIMITED

# GASPÉ

*Land of History and Romance*

**By Blodwen Davies**

STORIED STREETS OF QUEBEC

THE CHARM OF OTTAWA

RUFFLES AND RAPIERS

STORIED YORK

SAGUENAY

ROMANTIC QUEBEC

TOM THOMSON

PLANETARY DEMOCRACY
   (with Oliver L. Reiser)

YOUTH SPEAKS ITS MIND

# Acknowledgments

It is with pleasure that I acknowledge my indebtedness to the people and the government of the Province of Quebec for the help they have given me in the preparation of *Gaspé*. My special thanks and appreciation are due to Georges Levéillé, Secretary to the Prime Minister, for his interest in the project and for making available the fine camera studies of George Driscoll, ARSP, as illustrations for the book. When Mr. Levéillé proposed Mr. Driscoll as the illustrator of the Gaspé story, he proved his wisdom in selecting a creative photographer whose love of Gaspé qualified him to do a skillful and sympathetic study of the great peninsula.

My thanks are also due to L. P. Gagnon, General Superintendent of Parks for Quebec, who provided information on the parks of Gaspé and made possible a memorable buggy ride to Cape Gaspé along the narrow Forillon road. To many friends in my native province, friends old and new, French speaking and English speaking, I am grateful for helpfulness and hospitality and for those many intangible graces that characterize the citizens of the old province and charm the traveller.

Nor must I forget to acknowledge all that I owe to those old Gaspésian ghosts who haunt the harbours and the hills of Gaspé and who seem to come to life again in the imagination of those who love the sea-washed and wind-swept land, the lusty Vikings, the bluff mariner, Jacques Cartier, the dreamer, Samuel de Champlain, the stern and lonely Charles Robin, the privateer, Duval, the scientist, Logan, and many more, men and women, celebrated and obscure, a strangely assorted company indeed. Without their help, *Gaspé* would not have been written, for they were my companions on the Gaspé Road, pointing out to me the courage of the fisher folk, the tragedy of legendary shipwrecks, the sidelights of history, through centuries gone by.

BLODWEN DAVIES.

The Clearing,
Cedar Grove, Ontario.

# Contents

# Introduction

Gaspé has been many times discovered. Beautiful Viking ships, with the battle shields of their fighting men, bright with color and design, hung over the gunwales and with fierce, beautiful women among the explorers, sailed to Gaspé nearly a thousand years ago as some of their ancient sagas tell us. Then, through the grey mists of unrecorded history, we see those cockle shells of fishing ships out of Normandy and Britanny, and Cornwall, braving the unknown with incredible courage. In those times no high admiral of the king knew there was land in the west or that a continent lay half way round the world between Europe and China.

In those far off days spices took the place of our oils and gold mines and industrial goods. The men of wealth struggled over trading rights in pepper and cinnamon and all the rich spices Europe wanted to make its food palatable. But the fishermen of Europe wanted cod,—millions of cod which were to be found not in the waters that led to the spice islands, but in those cold, grey-green seas to the west, the unknown seas, out of which came only legend and secretly whispered tales of fish that lay in such uncounted millions that they seemed like a silver floor down in the jade depths of water, off the unnamed rocky shores of land on the other side of the Atlantic.

And so the "little men" of the west coast of Europe, the fishing folk, entered into a conspiracy of silence about their fishing grounds and for hundreds of years they sailed away each spring and sailed home again each autumn, and brought to the markets the dried cod upon which so many Europeans depended for food, for generations before North America was "discovered".

It was to Gaspé that hundreds of these little boats sailed in the unrecorded years. It was here that these men of simple and unbelievable courage came for the harvest of cod. Now we marvel when some solitary airman sets out on a record breaking journey. Yet this land knew literally tens of thousands of fishing men, throughout the legendary centuries, each one of whom had courage immeasurable to face the Atlantic in their little ships.

When the dawn of the new learning,—the Renaissance,—came to Europe, thoughtful men became curious about the fishermen's tales, those strange legends of lands across the sea. The men of the fifteenth and sixteenth centuries were very "modern" in their views, they had revolutionary "know-how" about many things and they had the compass. Every new type of transportation has brought revolutionary changes to our way of life, every improvement in an old type of transportation has opened up new opportunities to men and women endowed with the divine sense of curiosity. And so North America was discovered, the shores explored and claimed by rival nations in Europe, and our history,—our recorded history,—began.

In the twentieth century the motor car made every man and woman a potential explorer, searching for new roads to ride, roads leading to natural beauty of landscape and seascape, to communities with older ways of living and working, to at least a nodding acquaintance with people still quaint or unusual in their manners and customs. It seemed as though the more modern and sophisticated and gadget-minded the city dweller became, the more urgent was his desire to move backward in his thoughts to other days, to see how other people lived in older traditions, to collect handicrafts and antiques and to gaze in wonderment at ancient towns and picturesque villages, contrasting so vividly with the glass and cement efficiency of the contemporary industrial city.

So the twentieth century explorers discovered Gaspé. Here they found not only a highway into a land of sea-washed hills, not merely a road to Gaspé, or through Gaspé, but an encircling road that embraces the whole of the humor and history and romance of the peninsula and its people. Upon the Gaspé Road the villages are strung like beads upon a rosary, beads that the travellers tell one by one as the way leads from sea shore to mountain crest, from fishing cove to shadowy forest aisles.

Officially the length of the Gaspé Road is 558 miles, but actually the journey is not measurable in time and space. It runs through centuries long gone by. It moves through the thoughts and dreams and memories of a people at once near to us and yet remote, by reason of their tongue, their traditions and their ways of life. Near enough to be neighbors yet strange enough to be the goal of our pilgrimage are these Gaspésians, gallant, romantic, weatherbeaten folks.

Here cod is still king and the symbols of his rule are everywhere along the Gaspé Road. It is very good cod, the best in all the world, so they say. This is the cod that swam through many pages of religious strife and national jealousies. Now, in our day, when it has lost its fierce religious and political significance, it still plays a large part in international trade as a primary food supply for Catholic countries in Europe and South America.

So Gaspé has a large and dramatic background for the simple life of its own people. For centuries the settlers of Gaspé were poor and exploited people, their struggles for livelihood making a moving contrast against the natural wealth of the peninsula. But those days are past, better education, more enlightened economic conditions, easier communication with the rest of the world, have brought promise of better things to the patient, home-loving Gaspésians to whom love, labor and religion are still the chief factors of life.

The country is rich also in the lure of the unknown. Even geologically it is mysterious. By stepping aside along the road at almost any point the scientist, the prospector, the explorer, the hunter, the fisherman or the artist may come across strange things.

Gaspé has been a hard land to conquer, and its North Shore hardest of all. From the days of that rugged old Gaspésian, Nicholas Denys, fishermen who developed the sedentary fisheries have insinuated themselves into the little coves and set up their toy villages, clearing the meagre acres around them with hope and persistence. There was no rich invitation here to the settler and colonizer. The man with the heart to make Gaspé his home had to be content with small things for himself and his children. All that Nature would give him was a toe-hold on some gravelly beach in a crevice between hills sloping rashly to the sea. In the waters off the coast was his harvest of fish. In the tiny fields he might, with infinite patience, grow roots and grains for food. It has taken literally centuries of this slow and plodding pace to bring Gaspé under cultivation and settlement. Even today the habitations of Gaspé are all set out along the shores like fringe upon a shawl. Nowhere in the peninsula has cultivation penetrated more than ten miles and that only in the Baie des Chaleurs.

Gaspé is the southern lip of the mouth of the St. Lawrence. It is a peninsula one hundred and seventy miles long. On the west it is bounded by the Valley of the Matapédia, on the north by the River St. Lawrence, on the east by the Gulf and on the south by the Baie des Chaleurs. Only within very recent years has it become possible to drive all around Gaspé. Today the road is one of the best in America, the special pride of the government of the old Province of Quebec. With that instinct for the spectacle which is inherent in the heart of the French Canadian, the government has banned the use of billboards and so the panorama of native life is unspoiled.

Gaspé has some sophisticated resorts and many good hotels. There are plenty of small local hotels and modest inns and pensions, as well as cabin camps. The stopping places in Gaspé are nearly always scrupulously clean, for they are closely scrutinized by the paternal government, jealous of the reputation of the Gaspé Road. In any event, the convent-trained women of Quebec are good housekeepers without the prompting of any government inspector. So the Gaspé traveller can be comfortably housed in no matter what part of the peninsula he finds himself as evening falls. The government information bureaus provide the traveller with excellent literature and lists of stopping places.

Let us hope Gaspé will never be too fashionable and that it will always attract those with a capacity for natural pleasure, those who look for beauty and not just prettiness. There is delight in Gaspé for those who can feel joy in the hills and in rocks etched in sun and shadow, in natural forms, whether they be mountain ranges, the movement of waves breaking against cliffs, or in the swift, sure flight of seabirds.

To enjoy Gaspé most the traveller must adopt the tempo of the country, leisurely and contemplative as it is. He should make frequent stops to explore, for the country invites him to climb its hills, to follow its streams and to brood and bask upon its beaches. And in these places off the highway he will make friends with the kindly and responsive Gaspésians who will give him welcome to their land.

The country will not reveal itself childishly at first glance, but it will repay an effort at acquaintance. Those who make the effort will find that the heart of Gaspé is warm and friendly and that it seems to breathe the massive strength of its hills and their peace.

To us the age between the Vikings and ourselves seems quite a long one. To these high Shickshocks that have stood as race succeeded race and civilizations waxed and waned, that saw the ice age drift by into oblivion, our little life upon the Gaspé Road is as insubstantial as a morning's mist. Yet, in his brief span of human life, modern man has not only the qualities of heart and mind to seek out what is strange and beautiful, but he has given himself the mechanical means and social framework by which he can travel the world in search of what he wants,—and one of these things is the journey around the Gaspé Road.

# 1

## *The Road to Gaspé*

THERE are many routes to Gaspé by road,—from the Maritimes, from the New England States and from Quebec and Montreal. It can also be reached by sea from ports on the Upper St. Lawrence or the Maritimes; moreover it is possible to travel by river steamer or by road to St. Simeon and then cross the St. Lawrence by ferry to Rivière du Loup. These ferries carry thirty cars across the forty-odd miles of river from the North Shore to the South Shore.

Having reached Rivière du Loup by whatever route he chooses, the Gaspé visitor finds himself on what we shall now call the North Shore. In the Upper St. Lawrence country, Canadians speak of the North Shore when they mean the northern shores of the St. Lawrence River, since the great river divides the province east of Montreal into two great regions. But when Gaspésians speak of the North Shore they mean the bold coast of the Gaspé Peninsula which forms the out-thrust lower lip of the St. Lawrence as it nears the Gulf. The South Shore of Gaspé is the area around Baie des Chaleurs.

From Rivière du Loup to Ste. Flavie we drive through eighty-five miles of prosperous agricultural country. The town of Rivière du Loup itself is a port with a population of ten thousand or more. The town and its neighborhood depend largely on timber which provides both lumber and pulpwood. Sailing ships from many nearby villages carry pulpwood to Rivière du Loup where there is a pulp mill, and tramp steamers and small freighters dock here for the lumber that goes to Europe, as well as to home markets.

1

The town has a history of two hundred and fifty years but its traditions go farther back still. Champlain dropped anchor in its harbor and named the river for a tribe of Indians that were camped on its banks and whose totem was a wolf. In the French régime three seigneuries were granted here and after the Cession of New France, one of General Wolfe's Scottish officers, Alexander Fraser, became the lord of the manor and called the little town Fraserville. With the French-Canadian genius for absorption, the Frasers and all their Scottish settlers were taken into the heart and life of the community and by the time of the First Great War even the name had disappeared and Rivière du Loup had become complacently French Canadian again.

Cacouna is another river town with an Indian name meaning "the home of the porcupine". Here the Indians came to gather porcupine quills for their embroideries and in times of poor hunting, the queer little animals, so easily caught, provided emergency rations for the red men.

Ile Vert is a town, not an island, but it takes its name from the low-lying islands out in the bay. After a history dating from 1713 its chief claim to fame rests with its fine potatoes.

Trois Pistoles is a twin settlement, founded at the same time as Ile Vert, although it was granted in seigneurial tenure in the seventeenth century to Sieur de Vitre, a brother of Nicholas Denys, whom we shall meet so often down in Gaspé. There is a beautiful view looking back from the village along the shore and up the river valley which we crossed to enter Trois Pistoles. This is a good place to learn the lesson that by looking ahead all the time you may miss much of the flavor of Gaspé. If, Janus-like, we could only look two ways at once as we travel the North Shore, the delights of Gaspé would be doubled for us.

These little villages are typically French Canadian in their air of sociable living. The houses are usually as close to the road as the property rights permit and every house has a verandah running from end to end, and every verandah its row of rocking chairs. The highway is, and always has been, the moving picture of life to these gregarious Quebecers, ever since this highway was a trail or a sleigh road from parish to parish in the early days of settlement. There is no chance of slipping along a side street unnoticed. All the neighborly visiting moves up and down past the rocking chairs. All the courting, all the weddings, all the priestly visits for the last rites for the dying, pass to and fro, so that the life of the village is an open book for one and all.

As the road winds out of Trois Pistoles it brings us to a curious stretch of mountain farmlands. Between the fox-breeding village of St. Simon and quiet St. Fabien lies a dramatic valley between broken crests of hills. One little range of hills cuts off our view of the St. Lawrence for several miles. The ingenious way the colonists have contrived to create prosperous and beautiful farms in this broken country will intrigue the traveller no less than the views from the highway. As we run along the sloping walls of one range of hills, they suddenly open out and we are faced with a wedge of hill and on the other side of it we are in another little valley equally beautiful. Then again the walls close in on us and we are enclosed in another fold of hills only to come, at the end of it, to another beak-like intrusion, another gate into another amphitheater, until we realize that the whole district is one long series of interlocking hilly ranges with numerous beautiful habitable and unsuspected valleys lying among them.

Across these valleys, from slope to slope, the settlers have laid out their fields, carved them acre by acre from the woods, the remnants of which still fringe the fields and cover the crests of the hills, leaving patterns of trees, dark in summer but ablaze with color in autumn. Every field is well defined with rail fences that run like brown threads, working out an intricate design, filled in with fields of wheat and oats and barley, green pastures and crops of heavy headed buckwheat where the bees hum over the nectar cups. There are rare views along the road and sometimes as we pass one of those

3

beaks of hills we can see two valleys at once, one running inland on each side of a wooded crest.

The miniature valleys seem to be snared in vast networks of fences, nets that will draw in everything the habitant needs, even to his "tabac Canadien". Not least of the memories we will carry away from these hills will be those of whitewashed houses with sloping roofs and thick chimneys, tidy barns, snow white and rose red, silhouetted against the sky line.

The French Canadians have an instinct for pageantry and these farmers of the St. Lawrence like to sit on their verandahs, when the day's work is done, and look down into their valleys, disappearing softy into the grey veils of dusk, and across to their neighbors' rooftrees, knowing that peace and contentment and simple faith are common to them all. Here is something that hints at "the greatness and dignity and peace" which the common man should know when we learn to live together in a sense of community.

When we travel out of this area the road descends into a fashionable resort, the town of Bic, where city people retreat for the summer months to refresh themselves by living among the farmers and fisher folk. Everywhere on the St. Lawrence the church broods over the life of the people. Here at Bic, on a hill top, is a great cross that bears on its black arms the gilded body of a dying Christ.

The curious formations of rock and hill at Bic gave birth to an ancient legend. The story goes that when the world was created one of the angels was entrusted with the placing of all the mountains. She gathered them up in her draperies and eagerly set out to fulfil her appointed task. But mountain building is wearisome work even for an angel and by the end of the day she was very tired. Perhaps, too, she had lost her enthusiasm for mountains. She had planned to arrange a nice little series of hills at Bic but by the time she got there her hands were tired holding up her big pockets. So when she came to a pause she just opened her hands and let her draperies slip away. Out tumbled all that remained of her supply of mountains and they fell, helter-skelter, all over the shores of Bic. There was nothing more that could be done about it and so there they are to this day.

Of course the practical scientist dismisses the weary angel with an impatient gesture of his hand. The hills, he says, came not from above but from below, heaved up by some titanic thrust of nature. The highest of them is Mount St. Louis, around which the town clusters. The angel dropped some of her hills into the water and so we have Cap Enrage, Ile au Massacre, Ile Brulee, and farther out, Bic Island, now haunted by the ghosts of two drowned lighthouse keepers.

Bic Island was the shelter behind which the first pilots of the Lower St. Lawrence anchored as they waited to pick up ships bound for Quebec. Most of them were farmers and eked out their livelihood by piloting. They competed for customers, tossing around in open boats until they spied a passing ship signalling for pilotage. Many a man was lost in the storms that raged up and down the river, while he waited off Bic for incoming ships.

In a cave on Ile au Massacre, a band of Micmacs, two hundred strong, once hid from their enemies, the Iroquois. They filled the mouth of the cave with brushwood and so thought themselves safe from discovery. They all went off to sleep. The Iroquois traced them to the cave and just set fire to the brushwood. Wakened by the glare and the crackle of burning wood, the Micmacs tried to rush out of the trap and went straight into the massacre awaiting them. The bones of the unfortunates were still to be seen, strewn about the cave, until the middle of the last century.

The narrow ridges of hills, running parallel to the coast, gave Bic the derivation of its name, since so many "beaks" were found there. Its harbor was famous among the early explorers of New France. Governor d'Avougour and the great engineer, Vauban, planned to fortify Bic in the seventeenth century and make it the outer gateway to the colony. Instead Charles, Sieur de Vitre, a descendant of the first seigneur, was captured here by Saunders in 1759 and forced to pilot the British fleet up to Quebec.

A hundred years ago Bic was the loneliest kind of wilderness. The North Shore Road stopped four miles to the east of it and beyond was "a trackless waste of desert without a single habitation on the banks of the Metis and of Little Matane Rivers". There was a dreadful inn near Bic, kept by a ghoulish woman called Madame Petit. Tired travellers who passed the night under her roof might never come out again if the old crone happened to know that they carried gold or jewels. Many a strange tale is still told in the countryside about this creature and her inn.

Near Bic are two small towns that are important points in the navigation of the St. Lawrence—Rimouski and Father Point, or Pointe au Père, as the French call it.

Rimousky was first settled in 1663 by a venturesome colonist named Lepage. His son, Rene Lepage, was granted seigneurial rights to the land some years later. Off Rimousky lies St. Barnabe Island, a spot for picnics today, but once associated with a tragic love story. In 1723 on a ship bound from France to Quebec there travelled a young man named Toussaint Cartier and his bride. They were emigrating to New France, full of hope and dreams and romance. Off St. Barnabe Island the ship was wrecked and most of the passengers and crew lost. Toussaint saw his bride go down before his eyes. Cursing his fate, he found himself safe on shore on what turned out to be St. Barnabe Island. Nothing could persuade him to leave the spot where the girl had disappeared, so he built himself a cabin and lived there, a hermit, until his death forty-four years later. Toussaint left her this lasting memorial in the form of a legend and sanctified the island with a tale of human love. If the bridal pair had reached their farmlands and lived happily ever afterwards, we would never have heard of them.

Rimousky, the county town and educational center, is also the landing place of the mail planes that connect with the ocean liners.

Six miles farther on is Pointe au Père with its beautiful

6

lighthouse, the most notable on the river. There is a shrine at Pointe au Père to Ste. Anne, the patron saint of sailors.

Pointe au Père is famous as the headquarters of the pilot services of the St. Lawrence. When the government took over the administration of pilotage, the pilots who fought for ships in such haphazard and dangerous fashion became employees of the state. It was imperative that pilotage become socialized when the state acknowledged responsibility for the ships entering Canada and the lives and welfare of the river pilots. All the pilotage services were concentrated here, the old lighthouse was converted into offices, homes built for the staff and on the water's edge was built the great octagonal concrete tower that holds the light ninety-one feet above the river. This lovely bit of modern architecture is one of the best known landmarks of the river route and has been painted many times by artists in search of the significant.

The river never freezes over completely here but navigation does not open until the last week in April and closes the last week in November. The pilots operate between Pointe au Père and Quebec. Trim little government vessels lie along side the long quay and when an ocean going liner is signalled one of them will dart out to meet it, carrying pilot and customs officers. At this point the sea captain must be ready to hand over his papers in good order.

About six miles east of Pointe au Père the Empress of Ireland went down at the end of May in 1914. The river was wrapped in a heavy fog. The pilot had just been dropped at Pointe au Père. The ship was going full speed ahead when it was rammed by a little vessel that had lost its way in the fog. The famous liner sank in fifteen minutes and eleven hundred and forty lives were lost.

A special cemetery was laid out at Pointe au Père for the unidentified dead and a monument was put up to their tragic memory. A tablet along the roadside calls attention to the place where they lie.

# 2

## Sea Villages

WHEN we reach Ste. Flavie we are really in Gaspé, the land of lighthouses and fishing boats. For two hundred miles of precipitous coast our way lies among some of the most quaintly insular people in North America. Many of them have never seen a train or a moving picture, but they are accustomed to airplanes overhead and to cars from every part of the continent. So far as they are concerned the modern problem novel might as well be written in Sanscrit. Only a people content with the small change of economic life would make their homes on this wild coast, people with no fear of loneliness, or of nature gaunt and naked. Their tiny villages are set jewel-like, wide-spaced, along the deeply incised moulding, the high relief, of a peninsula where the mountains are married to the sea. Only a people in some ways primitive enough to preserve a religious faith that has dissolved before the realities of industrial life, could be happy here, men and women who still believe in the almost forgotten saints and their concern for human welfare. The big names of international politics that explode daily in our newspaper headings mean less to these people than the names of Ste. Anne and St. Joseph, St. Francis and St. Peter or even St. Yvon or Ste. Félicité.

The war years have indeed brought changes to parts of Gaspé, partly because of the prosperity the war economy brought to the region, the demand for lumber and pulpwood, the building of airports and manning depots, the development of tourism. A great many Gaspésians enlisted in the armed services of Canada and more went into war industry in the industrial areas. They brought home new ideas and new ways of looking at things. Nevertheless many of the fishing villages live as they always did and there is still poverty or near-poverty in many places. But it is poverty with decency, not the poverty of industrial slums.

Gaspé continued prosperous after the war and the building that has been done or is in process testifies to the freer flow of money among the people. The thousands of tourists who make the Gaspé trip every year leave behind them considerable sums of money in the hands of those who cater to their needs in hotels, camps, stores and in the handicraft field. Now many of the fishermen are abandoning their nets to work for the companies exploring for oil in the interior.

But Gaspé has been so long in the making that it will not change very much for years to come. In summer the highway seems like a pleasant holiday country, dramatic and picturesque. Before this highway was built the people lived season after season with only rare travellers to break the monotony of village life. Here in the shadowy coves, cut off on the one side by the mountains and on the other by the sea, their lives went their little rounds from cradle to coffin, through the tragedy and comedy of life, through hope and love, grief, pain, success and defeat, on the tiny stage that destiny had allotted them. One might think that Anatole France had looked at Gaspé when he wrote: "Be the earth great or small, what matter is that to mankind? It is always great enough provided it gives us a stage for suffering and for love. To suffer and to love, these are the twin sources of its inexhaustible beauty. Suffering,—pain,—how divine it is, how misunderstood. To it we owe all that is good in us, all that makes life worth living. To it we owe pity and courage and all the virtues."

"Pity and courage and all the virtues!" Surely these are to be found in plenty along the Gaspé coast. If they had not courage, they would have been overcome long since by the terror of the sea. But they wait its moods. When it lashes itself into furies too awful to look upon, tossing its white passion against the shores and cliffs, they quietly wait for it to subside, to draw itself sobbing back into the outer depths. They repair the damage to their little boats, renovate the landing places, haul up their sails and set off to make up for lost time on the fishing banks. The business of living takes courage in Gaspé. When disaster strikes at a village it seldom strikes once. If a boat goes down, two or three men go with it. If a storm strikes at the fishing fleet while it is at sea two or three or four boats may go down together. They have learned to be pitiful, to share their meagre goods among the stricken and the bereaved, and to pray for the souls of the dead.

The North Shore owes most of its settlement to the period after 1713 when France lost everything else in the Gulf but little St. Pierre and Miquelon. Gaspé became important to the French fisheries so king and governor encouraged settlement of fishermen wherever there was room for them to build their cabins and spread their cod to dry.

By the middle of last century there were only 25,000 people in all Gaspé, including the settlements along the Baie des Chaleurs. Between Cap Chat and Cap des Rosiers on the North Shore there was "a barren tract having only three or four houses throughout the whole district, besides a small settlement of a few families at Mont Louis, in the vicinity of which there happens to be some land fit for cultivation". There were several seigneurial grants within the same area, but no one attempted to carry out their seigneurial duties.

In 1857 John Lovell of Montreal, who published a Canada Directory, sent an agent to gather information on the Gaspé Peninsula. He was three months away from Montreal and when he returned all he had to report was that the roads were impassable and that he had spent all his time in vain attempts to penetrate that remote corner of the province and nothing was accomplished.

About that time the young men of Quebec became restless. The province was over-crowded with big families and the old farms had been cut to their utmost ribbon-like subdivisions and could support no more. Twenty thousand young French Canadians migrated to New England but some who could

10

not wrench themselves away from the altars of Quebec, compromised by spreading down the river and filling up the beaches of Gaspé. They took with them the untutored graces of their ancestral life on the Upper St. Lawrence and in our contacts with the Gaspésians as we travel through their country we will meet with little courtesies and gracious gestures that have come down the centuries in New France.

Every year four or five hundred men had been accustomed to going down from Quebec for the summer fishing but as more and more families settled down to colonizing there was less need for the transients, until at last Gaspé had sufficient of her own people to man the fisheries.

All the habitable land in Gaspé is on raised beaches. Ste. Flavie is an excellent example of a Gaspé town. It lies on what is called Micmac Beach, which stretches all along the North Shore to Cap des Rosiers. At Ste. Flavie it is twenty feet above sea level. Ste. Flavie is chiefly notable as the spot where the Gaspé Road begins and ends. Here you may turn aside into the road through the Matapédia Valley, or go straight ahead along the North Shore. Most motorists prefer taking the North Shore so that they keep the inside of the road, though it is merely a matter of choice, for there is no danger anywhere along the Gaspé Road, for a competent and careful driver with a good car. It is not a trip to make in a car of dubious condition or with an absent-minded or reckless driver. As recently as 1930 anyone who took the route from the South Shore to the North Shore was considered reckless, so accustomed were Gaspésians to regarding the passing of two vehicles as a dangerous business. Up until 1925 there was no continuous road around Gaspé that could be travelled by car. Now the Gaspé Road is one of the best touring routes in America with roads wide, well-built, well-defined and carefully marked throughout for the guidance of the driver. But when the guide posts say "caution, attention and danger", then caution and attention are definitely indicated as a means of averting danger. When the signs say narrow bridge, or steep hill or low gear, the driver would be wise to do the keepers

11

of the road the courtesy of accepting their warnings in good faith. The only serious accidents recorded in Gaspé are due to deliberate disregard for warnings or for the laws of the road.

There is only one disadvantage to the North Shore approach to Gaspé. The traveller is likely to gorge himself on the exciting landscapes and race from point to point, from summit to water level, as though the road was an inexhaustible panorama. The North Shore is the most spectacular section of the road. Parts of it are indescribably magnificent. Words lose their potency where nature seems to have spent its ingenuity in composing a very symphony of sea and mountains. Don't hurry over the North Shore. The traveller hasn't been in Gaspé long enough to overcome his lust for speed. He should carefully discard it at Ste. Flavie and drop into the tempo of Gaspésian life, if he would enjoy this sea-girdled land and its people.

The most completely satisfying spot in Gaspé is Percé. The South Shore suffers in comparison with the North Shore but it has several spots that demand time and the loitering spirit. Throughout Gaspé the wise traveller moves slowly not only for safety but also for satisfaction.

It is a good general rule to spend several nights along the North Shore stopping at sunset to enjoy the color of the evening light on the countryside, and walking about in the morning getting acquainted with the fishing villages. There are a great many good small hotels and cabin camps along the way where Gaspésians will serve native foods, not only cod and salmon and lobster, but bread baked in the outdoor ovens, clear golden maple syrup and home-made doughnuts, and other traditional dishes. By moving slowly along the North Shore the visitor can take sea trips. Fishermen will usually be willing to arrange a run along the coast for those who take the time to see Gaspé from the sea.

Metis-sur-Mer is another example of a Scottish colony engulfed by the French. About a hundred years ago or a little more, Seigneur MacNider brought out a hundred families and settled them on his lands in this vicinity. In the course of time many of them moved away and most of the remainder married into French Canadian families and only their names recall the colonizing families. It is not at all uncommon to run into some one by the name of Fraser, for instance, who speaks not a word of English.

Metis was one of the mail towns of the last century when letters were carried along the North Shore on foot every two weeks. It is now a fashionable summer resort. The opposite shore of the St. Lawrence is forty miles away and usually seems only a faint smoky line on the horizon, except on very bright days when the rounded forms of the hills lie purple in the sun. Metis is the Indian word for birch. Here the Indians found a plentiful supply of bark for their canoes and tepees. Today it is a pleasant and comfortable place to stay for boating and bathing and hiking. There is fishing for salmon and trout in the inland waters and porpoise hunting in the St. Lawrence.

Matane stands at the end of the railway. To reach it we drive through Baie des Sables, once called Sandy Bay, by the Scots, and through St. Ulric, cut in two by the uneasy waters of the Rivière Blanche. Near the village is Pointe au Naufrage. In the late fall of 1806 a coal carrier was wrecked on the reef near the point and although the ship was helpless it drifted long enough to give its crew time to dump the cargo overboard in an effort to save it. At low tide the villagers went out with carts and carried away six hundred loads of coal. That was a winter never to be forgotten. St. Ulric is in the seigneurial area of Matane and its proper name is St. Ulric de Matane.

The little town that stands at the mouth of the Matane River has appropriated the name for its own use. The river was discovered and named by Champlain and the land granted in seigneurial tenure as long ago as 1662. It has an excellent harbor and ferries ply from it to the north shore of the St. Lawrence. Matane is a little industrial town of more than five thousand people, the largest in Gaspé Peninsula. Once

13

we pass Matane we are in a region reached only by steamer and highway and we begin to get the real flavor of Gaspé.

The character of the country has changed. The beaches are no longer sandy. The shore is rocky and strewn with many boulders. The land grows bolder and more rugged. We have left the land of summer homes behind us.

From now on we discover what an infinite variety of angles there can be along the Gaspé Road. It has had to accommodate itself to the contours of the country and so we are either turning to the right to turning to the left, or climbing up only to drop again on the other side of the hill. The sharper the angles and the longer the climbs, the more picturesque the scenery becomes. A traveller in Gaspé, writing many years ago, described the Peninsula as a vast sea of frozen mountains. The thought goes with us as we soar and dip and wind our way along. Geographically we are now at the beginning of the Shickshock range of the Appalachians. The next sixty-odd miles of road will lie along the flanks of their hills and at the narrow beaches at their feet.

The first town in this area is a delightful little grey settlement called Ste. Félicité. It lies strewn along a rocky beach, grey houses against grey cliffs, with little gardens won by love and toil from the gravelly soil. Here and there is a pink pig nosing its way about in the grass by the roadside. Many of the little homes are of unpainted shingles, beaten by the winds to tones of hammered silver. In place of rail fences about the houses they have walls of firewood drawn from the woods in the winter, cut into stove lengths in the summer and in autumn neatly stacked to fence height around the gardens. All winter long they will nibble at the walls, armful by armful, until by spring the good man of the house will have to begin all over again building up the fences of firewood.

Off shore lie the seine nets, of woven willows, to catch the fish that come in with the tides and get caught when it ebbs again.

The pretty name of Ste. Félicité is a recent one, for the

settlement used to be known as Pointe au Massacre, refer-
ring not to a massacre but to a wreck, since the French word
may mean wreck or destruction. The frigate that fell foul
of this point was one of Sir Hovendon Walker's ill-fated
fleet of 1711. Fishermen who came here to dry their fish,
long before there was a settlement, often found human bones
and rusty weapons along the shore. There may have been
other wrecks besides that of the English ship for this was a
treacherous coast in the days before lighthouses and fog
signals.

After leaving Ste. Félicité, pause along the road to look
back at the cove and the settlement along the beach, and at
the curious rocks that give it its character. The bay is strewn
with the boulders deposited here by the glaciers in the ice
age. In the fading light, when eerie things may happen to
a landscape, they look like so many giant toads and so the
Gaspésians call it Great Toad Cove or Anse du Gros Crapaud.
Whale Cape, or to give it its proper French name, Cap à la
Baleine, got its name either from the fact that a whale was
washed up at its base, or, as the legend says, that a whale
was deposited right on top of the cape by an angry sea. Or
perhaps the whale just had a strong evolutionary urge to
become a land animal.

This is a good place to pause. There are local curiosities
such as caves and queer rocks to be seen, and perhaps you
can find a fisherman who will rent his boat for an expedition
along the coast.

A last glance back into the great scoop in the hills in which
the village lies, its fantastic rocks and promontories and we
have dipped out of sight. The road is growing steeper in its
ascents and descents. Every one seems to climb a little higher
than the last one. No one seems to have taken the trouble to
calculate the total of the ascents we make on the Gaspé Road,
but it might be interesting to know how high we would go if
we were not forever dipping down again absolutely to sea
level, ready for the next take-off. The hills seem to arch
their necks towards the sea so that there is no possible way

of getting by, except by going over them. The road is always in flight, upwards or downwards.

One of the mysteries of Gaspé is just how these mountain roads were ever discovered and created. Time after time the traveller will marvel as he mounts around a mountain or spirals his way through a pass, how anyone ever discovered the way through this country. Perhaps most of the roads were Indian trails to begin with and may date back hundreds of years before ever white men came to North America. Certainly some of them follow ancient Indian trails but modern engineering must be given a good deal of credit for what we have today. Nevertheless the traveller cannot resist the imaginative journey back to the days of the narrow mocassin trails that first established the routes we travel.

The first village after Ste. Félicité is Mechins, a fishing village, but not wholly dependent on fish for a livelihood. Curiously enough one of its chief industries is cutting a certain kind of wood which is made into special lengths, for export to England where it is used to make bobbins, spools and reels for the thread and yarn trades. Along the roadways lie these great piles of fragrant, yellow wood, awaiting shipment. "Bois de Fuseau" is the local name for this product of the Gaspé hills.

Five miles of roadway run through the hills to bring us out at St. Paul des Capucins. Long ago there were two lonely rocks on the shore, each so carved by the storms that they suggested Capuchin monks to the fanciful settlers. One of the Capucins is gone and now only one cowled figure remains in the little harbor. The village has a charming grey church and the houses flock together in a recess against the hills, and are of every imaginable tone of grey. Even the crooked crosses in the little churchyard play this game of subtle color. Little Mechins seen against a blue St. Lawrence stands out in quaint relief.

Along the road are countless scenes that reveal the life of Gaspé. Here, far below the road is a tiny settlement that seems to have been cast up by the sea and forgotten. Here, as we cross a bridge, is the carcase of some old fishing vessel, forlornly breaking up, its bones sinking into the sand. But there is nothing forlorn about the people. They have zest and small things can bring them pleasure. In each little house there is usually a glittering nickle trimmed range, dear to the heart of the housewife and it stands in the place of honor just as the bed of state once stood in the great hall of the castle. In many of these houses there are also looms, for lengths of catalogne hang over the verandah rails to catch the eye of the tourist, side by side with the hooked rugs worked on winter days.

From way down the river, for twenty-five miles or so, sailors inward bound recognize the familiar contour of Cap Chat. Although the headland that thrusts itself out here is not a particularly lofty one, it bulks large and dominating, even in a land of bold forelands. Cap Chat is some five hundred feet high but it is surrounded for some distance by comparatively level land and so its contours are clean cut against the sky and sea. It is one of the best known landmarks in Gaspé.

A curious thing has happened to the name of this cape. Champlain on his first voyage of discovery up the river named two points, close together on this coast, for two of his friends and patrons. One of these he called Pointe de Monts in honor of Sieur de Monts, the Huguenot merchant who was supporting the project to colonize New France. This distinctive spot he called Cap de Chaste, in honor of Eymard de Chaste, Knight of Malta and Governor of Dieppe. With the cramped handwriting of that day and the delightful diversity that seventeenth century folks allowed themselves in spelling, the transition from Chaste to Chatte, and thence to Chat was the easiest thing imaginable. Presently travellers were being told as they passed Cap "Chat" that it was so called because it looked like a sleeping cat, and everyone agreed, none wishing to be accused of lack of imagination. So in common usage it became Cap Chat and the Governor of Dieppe was forgotten.

The little mountain lies on our left as we run into the

town of Cap Chat. The town is a bit too big and sprawling to be picturesque and yet it has a certain dramatic quality.

From Cap Chat to Cap de Rosiers is a coast line of about a hundred and seventeen miles "free from dangers and destitute of harbor," as the St. Lawrence Pilot puts it so graphically, so every little river mouth has to be used to provide shelter for the fishing boats. Cap Chat harbor is characteristically Gaspésian. There is a long low beach, a gravel bar like a gate across the entrance to the river, and a little channel through the bar admitting fishing boats to shelter within the curve of the stream.

The town stands principally on a little rise of land west of the river and the road drops from this height to the waterside. The covered bridge across the Cap Chat River is the longest in Gaspé, twelve hundred feet. These elongated, barnlike structures over the wooden bridges are intended to protect the bridge itself against the heavy snowfalls.

The Cap Chat River is the route that leads into the Shickshocks but hereabouts there is a stretch of meadow lands between the sea and the hills. So while Cap Chat is a fishing town it is also the heart of a good farming district and there is an excellent experimental farm in the vicinity, which welcomes visitors. Also the Cap Chat River is a famous salmon stream and its fishing rights are rented to individuals or groups of individuals who have fishing lodges along its banks. There is fishing within a few minutes ride up the river from Cap Chat, but its famous pools lie hidden in the farther reaches where its banks are high.

There is a great cross above the town, for the Gaspésian likes to proclaim his faith. His church has been faithful to him, following him into the remotest fishing villages, to consecrate his great moments, living and dying, and to him the cross set up upon the hills seems to spread its great arms in beneficent shadows over everything he does. There is a church here, too, poised high above the water and a lighthouse on the tip of Cap Chat. The keeper of the light and

the curé know their duties well,—to guide wayfarers safely
to their journey's end.

The road out of Cap Chat crosses the long bridge onto
the gravel bar that lies between the meandering river and
the sea. The bay is beautifully rounded and its grey stoney
beach lies like a sickle, bearing a single row of little homes
and fishing sheds.

One of the remarkable things about Gaspé is the disposi-
tion of its small population. It is hard to realize how few
people there really are in Gaspé, in comparison with its great
territory, because the road seems one long procession of settlements. The entire population of the Peninsula seems to be
there for our inspection and this is almost literally true. It
is a traditional social trait, this habit of the French Canadian
of living close to the road, but it is doubly stressed here not
merely because the surveys of the French regime laid out
the land in strips from the water way, but because the habitable land in Gaspé is so narrow that, geographically the Gaspésian has little choice but to set his house facing the road.
And so Gaspé never seems to be a lonely place. There are
some parts of the North Shore where even the ingenuity of
the French Canadian has been outwitted and there are no
roadside homes, but generally speaking the Gaspésians have
spread themselves hand to hand along the coast. Every settlement is a ribbon, all length and no breadth, for the fishermen needs his patch of beach in front and his patch of garden
behind his house and as much farmland beyond that as he
can extract from the hilly slopes.

So, along the beach at Cap Chat are these little homes.
Here and there a great iron soap pot bubbles over an outdoor
fire. Long lines of washing flap lazily in the wind and innumerable little Gaspesians play barefooted around the over-
turned boats and in and out among the drying nets.

We are still on the St. Lawrence but unconsciously we think
and speak about it as the sea. The immensity of the river
is nowhere more emphatically declared than here where the
eyes strain themselves to see the dim northern shore. Here

we can imagine the awe of the explorers as they realized that this was the entrance not to another sea but to a river flowing out of some unknown land. How their imaginations must have worked as they sailed west, creating pictures of what might be ahead. There was not a river in Europe that could compare with this. The senses hesitated, at a loss to conceive a land worthy of this majesty. If it wasn't a land of milk and honey, it was at least a land of cod and fur, of timber and of virgin soil. If we could only call back some of the scenes that have been played on this river, since the days of the fair Vikings with their horned headdresses and carved ships, what a pageant it would be! These little lads, amusing themselves among their fathers' nets, are heirs of all the sea rovers of the St. Lawrence, and in spite of what the rest of the world may think or do, most of them will be fishermen, as their forefathers were before them.

# 3

## *Mountains of Gaspé*

THE Appalachian mountains that lie along the eastern coastal district of North America curve up into Canada from Vermont and then reach out along the southern shore of the St. Lawrence. They come to an end in the great peninsula and taper off at last in a thin finger of limestone at Cape Gaspé. This limestone finger is only half a mile wide where it emerges from the mainland and it stands like a high stone wall rising out of the sea, a spectacular climax to the mountain system.

Gaspé is, then a part of the Appalachian mountains, surrounded on three sides by water. From the Matapédia Valley to Cape Gaspé is a hundred and seventy miles. The Valley is a pass from the St. Lawrence to the Baie des Chaleurs, a deep indentation between two ranges, the Notre Dame Mountains to the west and the Shickshocks to the east.

The Shickshocks give Gaspé its character, a land of glorious hills, steep and craggy cliffs and little coves on the sea shore. If the motor tour could be combined with a trip by boat a few miles off the North Shore, from Gaspé to Cap Chat, the traveller would see Gaspé in another dimension. Those who have the leisure should try to spend a few days on one of the steamers that call at Gaspé ports. Winding along the roads, under overhanging precipices, through mountain gorges, dipping down into the coves, the traveller can scarcely visualize the entirely different pictures of Gaspé that present themselves to the seafarer.

From a ship at sea Gaspé is incredible, a great stage set designed by some vast Imagination, with wonder heaped on wonder. The immensity of it all is impressively dramatic.

21

Everything is molded on an heroic scale and where the mountains part in deep crevices they shape the shadowy valleys of Gaspé. In these valleys the vistas reveal the folds of the distant hills, interlocking at their roots, tucked one behind the other until their planes of light and shade are lost in the distance. Down in the deepest trenches of these valleys the mountain streams tumble, white and frothy, from level to level, until at last they wander out, a little more decorously, in the coves that indent the shore. And in these niches at the water line are the villages. From the deck of a passing ship the houses look like toys set by the sea to give scale to the scene, toys so quaint that they seem theatrical. White specks set here and there on grey rocks turn out to be lighthouses.

As hour after hour the ship sails past this panorama of ancient hills and little fishing villages, it seems as though Gaspé was speaking some message, offering some symbolic idea, as enigmatic and as challenging as the Sphinx on the Nile.

These mountains of Gaspé, since Europeans first began sailing up the Gulf, have been the most familiar hills in Canada. Yet, even today, very little is known of them, except to scientists. They can be crossed only on foot. Not a single road has crossed the peninsula from north to south. The first white man to cross the Shickshocks was Sir William Logan, the founder of the geological survey of Canada. This mountain wall, wrapped in mystery and solitude, was a challenge to him. Gaspé presented him with the first problem he set out to solve for Canada.

The western end of the Shickshock range begins in the vicinity of Cap Chat, and some ten or twelve miles back from the shore of the river. When the young geologist started out from Cap Chat through its deeply carved valley in the summer of 1844, his object was to make a cross section of the geological formation of the peninsula. He had already made the whole journey around Gaspé, and in those days that alone was a considerable adventure. It's a question whether anyone before him had deliberately attempted the same journey. After the survey he turned back to Cap Chat, having decided it was the best approach to the interior. There is no true pass through the Shickshocks, only a dip in the ridge where the Cap Chat and the Ste. Anne Rivers have carved their way through canyons to the sea. In some places these canyons are twenty-five hundred feet deep.

Logan's party went up the Cap Chat River in canoes until they were forced to abandon them. Then they broke trail with their packs on their backs. One of the peaks they discovered, more than four thousand feet high, his staff insisted, in spite of his protests, on naming in his honor. Mount Logan commemorates that historic journey.

The party made its way slowly but safely through and over the hills and came at last to the headwaters of the Cascapédia and so, descending it, Logan and his associates came at last to the Baie des Chaleurs. It was forty years before the Shickshocks were crossed again.

It was in 1883 that A. P. Low made the trip up the Ste. Anne River, which he mapped for the first time. He also climbed Mount Albert. From its summit he sketched the parade of mountain tops against the horizon and made a record of the beauty which so few have ever seen. He also reached the headwaters of the Cascapédia and descended it to the Baie des Chaleurs.

It was not until after the First World War that the glacial mysteries of Gaspé were probed, by A. P. Coleman of the Royal Ontario Museum. He realized that even at that late day there was no record of the elevation of the Shickshocks, the highest mountains in eastern Canada. In the course of his scientific work he realized that these mountains were never covered by the ice fields that enveloped so much of the continent and that ground down the Laurentians to the low and rounded roots of the mountains they once were. The peaks of the Shickshocks stood like islands in the sea of ice and cherished on their rocky tops the flora and the fauna of the pre-glacial world. They must have looked like parts of the

Arctic look today, solitary and bleak, sentinels of living matter in a great white world that had crushed out all sentient things under its glittering mantle. These hill tops were the only part of eastern Canada to escape the ice.

The Shickshocks were formed in the titanic growing pains of the earth, pushed up from the floor of the sea uncountable ages ago. In the tumult, fissures burst and molten rock from the earth's interior poured out into the crevices. Today the hills are eaten and rubbed by weather and winds, and worn down to the bare granite ribs that give them shape.

As the great Labrador ice sheet came down over the Laurentians of the North Shore of the St. Lawrence, it parted into two streams. One forced its way out through the St. Lawrence Valley to the sea. The other moved down the Matapédia Valley to the Baie des Chaleurs. Consequently the Peninsula of Gaspé was spared the pent up force that transformed the Laurentians. Fragments of glaciers, half a mile deep, filled up the valleys of the Shickshocks and on the southern slopes moved like pre-historic bulldozers creating the habitable lands around the Baie des Chaleurs. Because they could not force themselves completely over the hill tops, Arctic flowers and mosses lived on there and Arctic animals roamed the rocks until, little by little, as age succeeded age, the ice crept away again and made room for a richer vegetation. In time forests and meadowlands were ready for new animals and for man.

Today, twenty million acres of Gaspé are still virgin forest and hills too rugged ever to be put to the plough. Twenty-five hundred miles of the Shickshock country has been set aside as a National Park, a heritage of the people for all time. In time parts of this Park will be opened up for hunting and fishing camps, and camps for those who neither fish or hunt, but find in the primeval wilderness the sense of awe that opens up the secret places of the heart and provides an antidote for the tensions of modern civilization.

The usual approach to the Shickshocks now is from Ste. Anne des Monts. Twenty-five miles up the river is The Forks.

The river journey there is made in special Gaspé canoes, about twenty-four feet long, very heavy and narrow and stoutly built. The river is so swift that the canoes must be poled by the Indian guides all the way.

From The Forks the rest of the ascent is on foot. The most accessible of the Shickshock peaks is Mount Albert. There is also a trail leading into the Mount Richardson country, a nice test for ambitious mountain climbers. The Hogsback Ridge is a thin granite ridge nearly three thousand feet high, bare of trees, but from it there are magnificent views down the Valley of Ste. Anne, with Mount Albert to the west, a lake glittering in its flank, and to the south Mount Lyall and Sterling Mountain.

Mount Albert is 3669 feet high. The ascent of three thousand feet is through a deep forest and ends in a short climb over rocks to an open tableland. Tabletop lies eight miles away across the Valley of Ste. Anne and it is nearly four thousand feet high. Some of the little lakes that gleam from the velvet of the forest would be famous if they were not quite so difficult of access.

Tabletop is much more difficult to climb and gets its name from the thirty square miles or more of rolling country on its summit, with lakes and hills and dales of its own. It is a little world, remote and beautiful, with Arctic vegetation, creeping plants with blue and scarlet berries, and colorful mosses everywhere on its ancient rocks.

The highest mountain hereabouts was renamed not many years ago for Jacques Cartier. It was Botanist Dome, because of the discovery there of a cairn left by an expedition of adventurous botanists who climbed it long ago. It is 4350 feet high.

The Shickshocks were originally a mighty range, at least twice as high as they are now, and rivalling the Rockies. Now they are so weather worn that only the geologist can imagine their former glories or conceive of the immensity of time that lies between their origins and today.

The only mine in Gaspé is on the south side of the Shick-shocks, The Federal Lead and Zinc Mine. Mining claims were staked hereabouts in 1910 and when investors had acquired sufficient mineral rights, the mine was opened. It looks down Berry Mountain Valley to Big Berry Mountain. An old lumber road up the Cascapédia was extended to reach the mine.

At Percé there is a dramatic demonstration of the fate of the Shickshocks, for there we can see what the weathering of the hills can do.

The Gaspé Peninsula is only beginning to reveal itself. It is as though Nature had reserved this pleasant surprise for the people of America, for a time when their sophistication had reached a point that required tempering by some mighty revelation of primeval strength and peace. Here where the hills and the sea contend and where man seems so infinitesimal when he is measured against this background, there are lessons to be learned by thoughtful visitors from the crowded cities where Nature has no place but in the little parks where growing things are displayed just as the animals are shown in the zoo.

# 4

## *Land of Ancient Songs*

STE. ANNE DE MONTS lies on a fine stretch of raised sea beach, between the hills and the water's edge. At Cap Chat there are ten of these terraces, stretching back into the mountains. At Ste. Anne's there are fourteen of them to be discovered at various heights from a few feet above water level to some four hundred feet above, far back in the hills.

The thrifty French Canadians have cultivated this part of the North Shore very thoroughly. As usual all the homes are close to the river and behind them the land looks like a great patchwork quilt, marked off with fences into little squares and oblongs, each a different note of color.

The mountains behind Ste. Anne des Monts are so high that they can be seen for eighty or ninety miles at sea on a clear day. The Shickshocks were important landmarks for sailors of the French regime and when ships passed by about here they had the custom of initiating newcomers in much the same fashion that those who cross the equator for the first time are introduced to Neptune.

There is a long covered bridge at Ste. Anne's, one of many encountered on the Gaspé Road. There is a typical barachois at the mouth of the river and the town itself lies east of the river, with a great long quay at which the passenger ships to Gaspé tie up. There was also a large church, the only one in Gaspé with twin spires. It was burned to the ground in 1938.

The church of Ste. Anne des Monts was notable for other things. It was built of beautiful granite, hewn into blocks from what are called locally, beach stones. These are among

Gaspé's geological riddles. All along the shore the great boulders lie strewn in great profusion. They give the beaches their characteristic Gaspé contours. Geologists say that the stones do not belong to Gaspé but came here from the country north of the St. Lawrence with the Labrador ice sheets uncountable ages ago. They are found in the hills also on those sea beaches which lie at many levels along the Gaspé shore. They are of beautiful granite and when cut they make a fine building material.

Ste. Anne des Monts owes its name to another of those corruptions of historical names of which Cap Chat is an example. The place where the little town began was named Pointe de Monts by Sieur de Champlain, in honor of his Huguenot patron, Sieur de Monts. Obviously Champlain would not have called this, of all places in Gaspé, The Point of the Mountains when it is one of the few places without even a hillock to break its long beach. The change from Pointe de Monts to Pointe des Monts was simple and natural, and Ste. Anne of the Mountains followed in due course. Unfortunately it means that a man who did so much for New France has been forgotten where Champlain intended that he should be long remembered.

English, French and Basque had traded along this coast before 1600, but in 1602 Henry of Navarre gave his old friend and supporter, Pierre du Guast, Sieur de Monts, a monopoly of the fur trade in all Acadia, which included Gaspé, as a reward for his contribution to getting Henry on the throne of France. He issued a proclamation to the traders of Calais, Picardy, Normandy, Brittany, Guyenne and the Biscay ports, warning them to stay out of their old trading grounds on the St. Lawrence and to go no farther west than the Forillon at Gaspé. Their resentment was bitter when they pictured Sieur de Monts getting all the beavers and martens and black fox they had formerly traded in so profitably. There was a tremendous row in France about it, with the traders, the parliamentarians and the king all vigorously involved.

Eight years later, in 1610, the king rescinded the monopoly and declared for free trade.

Meantime Champlain had founded a colony in New France with headquarters in the little settlement at Quebec. After watching the free traders at work in the St. Lawrence country, Champlain organized a company comprised of the chief and most reliable of the traders. They were to have certain trading privileges in New France in return for promises made to colonize the shores of the St. Lawrence and to supply Champlain with men every summer for exploration and for war against the Iroquois. Sieur de Monts was one of this selected company and part of his trade privileges concerned Gaspé fish. Sieur de Monts was always a friend of the colony and of its devoted Governor. It is too bad to think that Champlain's intention to commemorate his friend here at Pointe de Monts should have been frustrated by a little twist of the tongue.

The church at Ste. Anne's was beloved by sea-faring folk because among its treasure was a tiny bone from one of the fingers of Ste. Anne. Every year there is, nevertheless, a pilgrimage of fishermen from all over Gaspé who come to ask her blessing and protection, even though the relic was destroyed.

Until the Gaspé Road began to take shape as a government project, Ste. Anne's was the end of the passable highway. Those who fared forth to reach the settlements between Ste. Anne's and Gaspé town went part way by boat from cove to cove, part way on foot and sometimes made use of horses on the better stretches of the trail. There are plenty still living who recall that state of affairs.

It may be your good fortune to see here something of the war waged against the porpoises, those lazy white whales who are interesting to watch but so very destructive. Porpoise fishing used to be one of the profitable industries of New France and even now when the fishermen choose to hunt porpoises they can make money out of it, for their skin is tanned into leather and they yield huge quantities of oil. But porpoise fishing has gone out of fashion and now they are a menace, consuming such quantities of fish that they endangered the north shore fisheries. The government declared war on them, equipped motor boats with small guns and engaged fishermen with rifles to hunt and destroy them. There are still plenty of porpoises in the St. Lawrence and sometimes they can actually be seen from the trains between Rivière du Loup and Mt. Joli. Whether any other railway can equal that claim remains to be proved.

Just west of Ste. Anne des Monts—at a road sign marked Mt. Albert—there is a road turning inland into an area of Gaspé still known to few people. This is the way into an unexpected and rewarding journey and no visitor to Gaspé should miss it. It will not be long before this side trip becomes an integral part of the Gaspé tour, but those who discover it for themselves before it becomes famous will have something to boast about in days to come. This is the road that is being extended into the Gaspésian National Park, which begins about twenty miles from the coast. Unless the traveller is watchful he may ride past this unobtrusive sideroad but if he finds it and turns aside he will, within minutes, find himself in the mountains of Gaspé.

Today it is little more than a good colonization road, for it was built in order to open up new lands for clearing and settlement. Before the traveller is more than two or three miles from the highway he will find himself deep in the heart of a mountain range with magnificent scenery on every side. That is especially true if he drives through Gaspé in September or October for he will find in this Mt. Albert road a countryside steeped in all the dyes of rose and gold, scarlet and crimson, if the hardwoods are touched with frost. This good country road winds and dips along the slopes of the valleys that have been so patiently cleared by the French folk of Gaspé, sons of overcrowded farmlands in the older parts of the province. History comes alive before our

30

very eyes when we see here every step in the process of pioneer settlement. We can imagine what this continent looked like in other centuries as the newcomers moved slowly inland spreading over the new colonies in days that are now pages in our history. Here the little homes and the sturdy barns bespeak a love of the land which prompted these families to take up the burdens of colonization in a forest territory rather than move into the cities to work in factories. The timber cut on the colonists' crown grants was the first harvest. Along the way there are still to be seen the sites of temporary mills set up to make the timber marketable in the war years.

Against the skyline run the ridges of the Shickshocks. They look to the visitor like unconquerable hills but beside the roadside are the evidences of what determined men will do to create homes even in a country that seems to be a kingdom for hunters and fishermen alone.

This is indeed a sportsman's country and before too long the Gaspésian National Park will be opened to visitors. Doubtless there will be good camps and inns made available so that the people of the east will be able to enjoy here many of the recreations, such as mountain climbing, exploration and high altitude hunting and fishing, for which they now go to the Pacific coast. Many of these mountains are four thousand feet or more high. Twenty-five hundred square miles have been set aside for this new park.

Well along the road into the heart of the Shickshocks we shall come upon the little settlement of St. Bernard du Lac. Perched on the side of a hill is the parish church, with its presbytery nearby, for the settlement has already been organized as a parish and a curé makes his home among the colonists.

The road leads directly to the foot of Mt. Albert. It will not be many years before artists and photographers make this dramatic country familiar everywhere among the lovers of travel.

There are as yet no camps or tea rooms in the Gaspésian National and those who intend to spend any time in the park should carry lunches with them. The ascent of Mt. Albert can be made if visitors make the necessary arrangements. Permission should be obtained from the Park Inspector who lives in Ste. Anne des Monts, as visitors making the ascent must be accompanied by one of the park wardens.

The rest of the North Shore after we leave Ste. Anne des Monts is one long series of ups and downs. The chief characteristics of the Gaspé highway are the abrupt descents to the sea and the coves that lie between the paws of the great mountains and the equally abrupt ascent into the hills when the cove is passed. The road never becomes monotonous, for when the road is not over the mountains it is under them. In places the roadbed has been blasted out of the rock and what has been taken away has been used to build up cribwork on which the highway lies.

The little village of St. Joachim de Tourelle is one of the picturesque settlements in one of those secret coves. The road dips steeply into it and down below lies the picture of a village on its gravel beach, a single street of little houses, for these settlements have no contrasting communities of rich and poor. In some villages they are all poor. In some, in recent years, many have acquired an air of prosperity entirely new to Gaspé fishermen. But there is little wealth to be found among the Gaspésians and life in the fishing villages we shall see along this North Shore is simple and frugal, even in good times. St. Joachim is one of these. On the other side of the cove, a spur of a mountain slopes gently to the sea and on a lower level of it the people of St. Joachim have built their church. The home of God in the Gaspé villages is always finer than the home of any man, for no matter how poor the fisher folk their church is always sumptuous in comparison with the actualities of their life. They are content that the church vigilant will always represent something to which they can never quite aspire.

The village takes its descriptive name from a "tourelle" or tower-like rock that stands on the beach not far from the village. St. Joachim de Tourelle is famous for something quite different from cod and herring. A few years ago Marius Barbeau, who has done so much for the arts in Canada, went to St. Joachim in search of folk songs. Already it was realized that the habitants of the Upper St. Lawrence had preserved a rich heritage of songs from old France. Thousands of them had been recorded by Dr. Barbeau and filed away at the Victoria Museum in Ottawa. Yielding to a conviction that there might be other songs tucked away in the remote villages of Gaspé, Marius Barbeau picked upon St. Joachim as a likely place to work. He has described in some of his writing very beautifully his acquaintance with the folk-singers among the fishermen. There was one patriarchal man of over eighty, dignified by "the habit of suffering". The old man sang him songs the Gaspésians once sang baiting their lines, or hauling the silvery hordes into their boats, work songs contrived to speed up their labor with rhythms which fitted their actions. Times have changed. But the artist had discovered the real Gaspé. "I had found its voice, strange and wild, yet tender and appealing." The old man was born at Anse Pleureuse while his parents were there seeking salvage from a wreck. Born to the sea and bred to its ways, he had learned innumerable old songs by the Gaspésians in their seafast coves. He sang scores of them for his new friend, songs of medieval miracles, of adventures of the crusades, songs of princesses in distress and knights in search of honor and great deeds. There were others too who recall a great wealth of song. In two months among them Marius Barbeau had collected the words and music of eight hundred folk songs!

So when you pity these fisher folk for their meagre ways of living and the scantiness of their rewards for lives of skilled labor, think of the treasures they have preserved in song and story. Around the fires in the evenings generation after generation, this heritage of folk culture has been handed on. Like ancient bards and raconteurs the old Gaspésians have poured out their tales of chivalrous tradition and courtly life, to leaven the harsh every day facts of existence on the fishing coast. Is it any wonder they have an inborn grace, a natural courtesy, these simple folks who dream of knights and princesses? Romance will not die in Gaspé as long as the old songs live.

# 5

## *The North Shore*

THIS next stretch of road from St. Joachim to Cap des Rosiers, about a hundred and twenty-five miles of driving, is a long, dramatic unfolding of this fiercely beautiful land. This is also the part of the road where the traveller is most apt to make mistakes in timing which he will regret. Too many travel offices in distant cities, obsessed with speed, route the traveller through from Rivière du Loup to Gaspé in one day,—an offense which should be punishable by a long term of solitary confinement and time to repent. Three hundred odd miles in a day's drive may not seem out of the way across the middle states of the American republic, but three hundred miles on the Gaspé coast is something to take at leisure, gathering up along the way memories that will never be forgotten. Gaspé hotel keepers are both amused and horrified by American tourists who hammer on the dining room door at six o'clock in the morning, demanding breakfast so that they can be off in frantic haste to catch up with their next reservation hundreds of miles away. They seldom have time to enjoy the unexpected, the unplanned side trips into Gaspé valleys, the little sea journeys that would bring them such pleasure and such curious experiences, and the friendly encounters with Gaspésians both French and English who are prepared to reveal to the travellers something of the human side of Gaspé. Two or three days at the least spent along this shore will yield dividends of relaxation and insights and memories to the wise visitor.

The road should be taken slowly for several good reasons. One of them is the fact that there are no long stretches of this road on which to "make time". As one of the government publications quaintly puts it "it is elementary wisdom to give due warning" when you are about to take a hairpin turn or to start down a long hill in this kaleidoscopic country. Although it violates every Roman principle of the straight line road,—the speedways of chariot days,—yet it is a road of which they would have felt proud. But for the wisdom of safety and the love of beauty, drive slowly on the North Shore.

This land belongs to the fishermen and is as primitive as any twentieth century community can be. Here men contrive against all sorts of handicaps, limitations of space, hard work, meagre returns, and in spite of all seem to live their humble lives happily. Little as they seem to have even today, the ordinary fisherman of Gaspé knows a little more of security and comfort now than he has known in all the history of the Gaspé fisheries. Little by little legislation and public opinion have brought him conditions which have raised the mantle of fear and brought him better returns for his work, better schools for his children, better means of communication with the outside world. As social and economic conditions improve, the old picturesque primitiveness recedes and perhaps some day we shall find Gaspé has set aside a typical small fishing village complete with boats and barachois, flaking platforms and fishingroom as a museum piece. But for the present we shall find the old Gaspé waiting for us along this coast.

For part of the way we ride along a narrow strip of land raised sixty feet above the water with hills hanging over it that rise twenty-three hundred feet high. At one place the road lies on the face of a cliff that rises a sheer eight hundred feet. These are merely incidents along this coast of wonders. Everything along this shore is so precipitous that the population is very sparse even for Gaspé. The next three villages are all missions of the same parish which is fifteen miles long. There are less than four hundred people throughout its length and breadth.

The first of these tiny villages is called St. Francois du Cap aux Renards. It lies near a deeply cut valley through which flows Ruisseau Vallée. At this point the Gaspé Road rises to a height of twenty-six hundred feet above the water.

When we come down to the shore again we crawl along the foot of the cliffs until at Ruisseau Sorel a thin veil of water drips over the face of the precipice with a faint musical song. Somehow, this delicate, lacey waterfall coming out of the black rocks, starkly forbidding, makes such a contrast that the effect is startling as well as pleasing and we shall find ourselves remembering this single note of beauty and treasuring it among all the mighty pictures of the North Shore.

Our next village is Rivière à la Marte. The lighthouse and the church share the cape beside the village.

There is a choice of two roads in this vicinity for in 1939 a new road was opened that clings to the shore of the river. It shortens the distance but it deprives the traveller of some of the best scenery in Gaspé. If, as one Quebec publication puts it, "local information" assures the traveller that the old road is in good condition, then the visitor should by all means take the old road for one of the finest experiences in Gaspé.

The old highway leaves the shore at Rivière à la Marte and for two and a half miles runs through a tableland a thousand feet above the river, a protected valley enclosed by mountain tops. The highway emerges into the flanks of the hills, climbs to a height of two thousand feet and then, as though regretting having been so long away from the shore, plunges back down into the next cove and the last of the three mission villages, Marsouins.

On that inland road there is another colonization project and we can see the little homes of French Canadians who are as patiently winning their acres from the wilderness as did Louis Hebert on the Rock at Quebec. The French Canadian would rather toil here in the crevices between the hills, with no prospect of ever getting more than a meagre living for his work, than go into the west away from his ancestral hearths and altars. Tell him of golden acres lying out there waiting to be tilled and he will flash you a brilliant smile and shake his dark head, but he will go on cutting and clearing and planting and reaping with the patient contentment of the real habitant. Leaders of cultural thought today are trying to teach through the community centers and adult education projects that the *process* of the thing the individual does with his leisure, painting or modelling, handicrafts or little theatre work, amateur research or whatever it may be, is the matter of most importance, that it is not the created thing, the product of the effort that matters nearly as much as the long, careful effort to create, the acquisition of skills; that, in short, the important thing is what our work does to us as personalities, not what we get out of it in profit. But this is what the French Canadian accepts as the A.B.C. of life. The get-rich-quick era has passed him by. He has not sold his birthright for a mess of potage. He has retained his *joie de vie* and while the modern world went through its age of grasping anxiety, its worship of gadgets, its mental and emotional tensions, Jean Baptiste clung to his traditions of family life and community relationships.

Today Jean Baptiste is waking up. He wants more education and better education, he wants co-operation social and economic, he wants an open door to the social sciences. He is like a patient man that has quietly endured all that was necessary to live through bad times, but now he is bringing his strength and his determination to bear upon a modernization of his life. He has much to bring to the common council table, many things that the restless and aggressive modern has lost, his songs and his handicrafts, his gaiety and his capacity for pleasure in small things, his friendliness and his love of family and neighbors. When we talk of tariffs and dividends, mass production and gadgetry, we do not talk a common language with Jean Baptiste, but when we talk about singing and dancing and making things with our hands, about our common pioneering history and a peaceful nativism, then we are coming nearer to a common understanding of modern life in personal terms. It is not the stock market that will unite the Canadian people but the community center and the exchange from province to province of examples of the cultural contributions that each region makes to the common life. The very spirit that brings young men and women to homesteads in country like this, to build homes together, is an invaluable ingredient in the national culture. When those whose work it is to express this spirit, to make articulate the power that moves us, the painters and poets and novelists, can relate life of this kind to the life of the whole nation, then we shall find more and more common ground with the homesteaders and the fishermen of Gaspé.

Quebec was the only successful colony of France and it was successful in spite of her. Those she brought here in the seventeenth century took root tenaciously and developed characteristics of their own, not least of which was a simple and passionate attachment to the soil on which they were born. There is nothing abstract about the French Canadians' citizenship. Their loyalty begins with the farm, moves on to the parish, and then to the province, before it becomes national. The English speaking Canadian works the other way. He is always conscious of Canada as a whole, of confederation and its implications, of the need for national unity and integrity; his loyalty to his province comes next and is oftentimes a little vague. The parish is even less an entity, and even his love of the land on which he was born is far more detached than that of the more emotionally exuberant French Canadian. Consequently Quebec remains French, in spite of nearly two hundred years of British law and English speaking neighbors, and in spite of the fact that a "Frenchman from France" is as much a stranger to Quebec people as a Londoner. When France became restless and radical, Quebec retreated into conservatism; while France bemoans its race suicide, Quebec is prolific, while France grows more pessimistic, Quebec clings to the things of the spirit, while France is divided and politically unstable, Quebec remains simple and unshakeable. But Quebec is awakening and even Gaspé is changing.

Now that the whole world has been shocked into a revaluation of its social fabric and men and women everywhere are looking for new values and new objectives, Gaspé will have something to say to every visitor. Gaspé's role today is to pour out beauty and a sense of strength on a restless and unhappy world. Thousands will race around the Gaspé world and learn nothing, but many more will take home with them questions and ideas to mull over in the months that follow. Even in the poorest of these little villages in the coves of the North Shore, facing the seasons of heat and cold, of snow and of harvest, human life goes on, love and hate and fear and hope and all the derivatives of these basic emotions weave themselves into life patterns just as surely as they do Toronto or New York, Vancouver or San Francisco. Gadgets are not the essentials of life; human relationships are the essentials.

The hills to the west of Marsuoins are so high that the descent into the village is one of the longest and steepest on the road and while we are still descending we can spy the ribbon of road that mounts again on the other side of the cove through the green of the forest. Here in this pocket in the hills lies the village and its church.

These little churches along the Gaspé coast have an air of brooding tenderness as though they knew how fishermen and their fish have played so large a part in Christian history, in the symbolism of the church and in the very terminology of the faith. The church is not a thing apart to be used on Sunday. To the children who grow up in these isolated coves all they know of beauty, other than natural beauty, comes from the church. To them the gilded statues, the crowned plaster saints, the lace trimmed altar cloths, the carved and painted candle sticks, the ancient liturgy, are all that they may ever know of art. The church is their theater, picture gallery and concert hall, playing to these twentieth century Canadians the role that the medieval church played in Europe, with its story book windows and rituals. The curé is the most learned and worldly-wise man in the parish. When

40

life's complications involve more than nets and bait, the villages turn to him for advice. So, along with the light-houses, the churches of Gaspé are among its significant characteristics.

Yet the exuberance of these Gaspésians is not restrained by the multiplicity of their churches and wayside shrines and crosses planted on every headland. In the little homes and hotels of the peninsula the visitor will see decorative cards, shining with tinsel, begging the people to restrain their profanity, and the fishermen's co-operatives adopt resolutions concerning not only research and marketing, education and construction, but also on morality, deploring the "sinister consequences" of infractions of the moral law.

There are tales of buried treasure hereabouts and the ghostly visitations of a restless Protestant, drowned off the coast and buried in the village churchyard, whose heretical spirit could not lie at ease in a Catholic grave, and so, most ungratefully, he comes to haunt the villagers.

We climb a mere thirteen hundred and fifty feet on our way through the hills before we descend to the next village at Ruisseau Arbour, where there is a pretty beach and a little mill.

These little coves make only the slightest indentations on the coast. As the St. Lawrence Pilot puts it, they cannot be "distinguished with facility" from the sea. The water off the shore is so deep that soundings give ships no warning of their approach to land and before the confused mariner knows where he is, in the fog, he has run onto the rocks. The saw-toothed greywackè rips an unlucky ship to pieces. "And such is the nature of the country," proceeds the Pilot, "that those who might succeed in landing run a risk of perishing from want before they could reach a settlement." That is not literally true, now, but indeed there are parts of Gaspé that would offer a most inhospitable welcome to a wrecked sailor, but fortunately as the Gaspésians increase in numbers and spread into every available nook and corner of the sea beaches, there is more hope of succor for those whom the seas might toss up on this storm wracked coast.

Rivière à Claude is at our roadside in the next cove, a lovely rounded bay, encircled with grey cabins and cod flakes. This is another poor village, so poor that even its church, perched on a bluff overlooking the water, is extremely simple, even as Gaspé churches go, and so, extremely beautiful. It has fine proportions and is set solidly upon the rock so that it seems to spring from it of its own accord. The broad steps are well balanced and spaced and draw the eye up to its little tower and steeple. They were probably so poor that they had to put their native ingenuity into contriving it, for a little more money and a little more advice would probably have ruined it. The church stands alone upon its splendid perch and the road winds past it and down into the valley where the Rivière à Claude winds its lonely way at the feet of the mountains. The village lies beyond the river at the base of a hill. Four miles before Rivière à Claude lies one of the loveliest spots in Gaspé awaiting us.

The village of Mont St. Pierre lies at the end of a great cove enclosed by two majestic peaks. No other word describes the sombre beauty, the magnificent modelling of the two capes. Ask a fisherman which of the two is Mont St. Pierre and he will tell you, with a charming smile, that either of them is Mont St. Pierre. One of them is eighteen hundred feet high, the other sixteen hundred. They are covered with forests except for patches swept clean here and there by landslides, and for the splendid brow of the eastern hill that is so deeply furrowed and carved that it takes on the impression of a fine piece of sculpture.

It would be worth the trouble of timing your arrival at Mont St. Pierre for sunset and to linger at the western entrance to the bay until the light has played out its drama of color over this ancient stage so superbly set for it. There are experiences so rare and so fleeting, as time goes, and yet so substantial in memory, that they exist as entities in themselves. Sunset at Mont St. Pierre is one of them. Over the bay lies some peculiar magic, at any hour of the day, but at sunset it culminates in a beauty so powerful as to seem tangible.

Behind the rounded beach the valley opens up into a long succession of interlocking hills. The valley floor is wider than we generally find in Gaspé and much of it is cultivated. Here and there along the way stand little white farmhouses. Along the sea shore is a single row of houses. The beach is dotted with upturned boats and in the bay the fishing fleet lies reflected at its buoys in the evening light. As the light grows richer in color, the shadows gather in the valley. The bay glows with the deep emerald green that the reflected forests cast upon it. On the hillsides the light lies slantingly across the trees. Suddenly the great rocky hill on the east of the cove seems to come alive in color. Every ridge throws a purple shadow, the twisting patterns in the rock are touched with rose in unbelievable nuances of color. It is hard to believe that the glow and warmth come from the setting sun, hard to believe that the rock has not exuded suddenly this vehemence from some deep passion within.

If you catch the sunset colors on the mountains, you are not likely to pass Mont St. Pierre that night. When the light draws within itself and the rocks are grey and dark again, you will feel a reverence as though you had been at some mystic rite. So you will sleep in the shadow of these magic hills and next morning prowl about the village in quest of something of its spirit and its history. In the white light of morning the hills show the patterns in their naked rocks only like faint tracings of what you saw in the rose and purple sunset. The bay is blue and the silvery houses are merely grey and white. But by day it has a charm of its own and there is always another sunset. There has been an endless succession of them with no human eye to see them and there will be many more when perhaps again man has gone his little way.

This is one of the few villages in Gaspé without a church. Perhaps the fisherfolk thought their cove so cathedral-like in its natural state that they left church building to their neighbors. Certainly there is peace and repose unlimited in Mont St. Pierre.

It is a pleasant beach to linger on although it is a poor anchorage. There is no shelter from the squalls that blow down the valley nor from the heavy seas that roll in from the gulf. But here the spirit of Gaspé seems incarnate, in the quietude of the hills and the restlessness of the sea. It is strange how the mobility of the sea breathes a kind of peace, too. Its vastness and its obedience to natural laws seem to give a sense of spaciousness to the tired human mind. It seems to say that all our little frets and disappointments and disillusionments are no more than the breaking of waves on the shores of experience. The seas roll in, crested and force-ful, to break protestingly and scatter into oblivion on the stones. It is only in the sum total of their effects that they are important. At the long last they wear down mountains and wash up beaches and make such lands as Gaspé ready for human habitation. Human experience is something the same. The sum total of our little lives prepares the way for those who come after us. The land of Gaspé is full of sym-bolism for those who seek it, or recognize it when they see it. Nothing here is immutable. It is the weathering of the hill tops that give them their beauty, the gnawing of the sea that shapes the lovely curves of long beaches. Those black boats, sailing against the silvery sheen of the morning sea, the gulls that wheel in wide-winged ecstasy against the sky, the fisher-men at their lines, all come and go in endless succession, century after century, as slowly Nature works out her pro-cesses.

But we too must proceed and the next village we reach is Mont Louis, one of the oldest villages on the North Shore. Wolfe sent ships and men from Gaspé to sack it in the sum-mer of 1758 for it was even then one of the most important fishing stations in the peninsula.

Although all the fisher folk were dispersed, some carried off as prisoners, some to hiding places in the woods, yet eventually Mont Louis came to life again and went back

to its work of catching and curing cod. The village is impressively situated at the foot of a green hill that makes a
velvet setting for its little white houses. The church stands
here right in the middle of the town, with something of an
old monastic air for it gathered around it convent and presbytery and graveyard, all about the village square. There
is a long quay here and ships call for fish for the ports of
France and Italy and Spain.

Mont Louis bay is considered good anchorage only in
good weather for there is not much room to work out and
it is a dangerous spot for sailing ships with an offshore wind.

Sixteen miles to the southwestward is the highest peak
in the Shickshocks, Mont Jacques Cartier, towering four
thousand four hundred and fifty feet high. The coast is
everywhere along here precipitous, rising behind narrow
beaches into mountains two or three thousand feet high. The
rock formation is very striking, even fantastic. The laminated
shale has been twisted and turned in the slow process of
time until it is all sharp edges, broken and ragged and
tormented. The cliffs are naked to the tops and as the road
runs along the water's edge between walls of stone and the
sea, it seems as though the rocks are all sharp teeth waiting
for their prey, ready to rip and tear any frail vessel that
drifts their way.

The next village along the road is Anse Pleureuse, or Weeping Cove, appropriately enough, it would seem, to those who
feel the grimness of this coast. But, curiously enough, the
name comes from a legend and not from any disaster, as one
might suppose.

When the cove was first settled by fishermen, at the end
of the eighteenth century, the people were frequently alarmed
by a strange weeping that they heard in the nearby woods.
Women crossed themselves in fear and said a prayer, for it
seemed as if some soul in torment was crying out for solace
from some remote world of pain. The men, listening to the
moaning as they hurried home through the dusk, resolved to
be more circumspect and cast a thought of pity on the suffer-

45

ing creature. From year to year the villagers repeated their encounters and with every telling of the tale the fear and superstition grew worse. Then, in 1814, a missionary on his way home to Quebec, after a trip through the mission stations, stopped at Anse Pleureuse to hear confessions, christen the young and marry the romantic. Sitting around the fire in the evening he talked to the fisher folk and they poured out all their tales to his willing ear. Among other things they told him about the mysterious weeper who haunted the village. Now this missionary was a very practical young man. His name is recorded. He was Reverend Father Charles Francois Painchaud. He did not like the superstitious dread of ghosts and on the other hand he wanted to lift the mantle of fear that had settled down on this settlement. He decided to investigate. He stayed until a day when the weeping could be heard and then he wandered off into the woods to see what he could see. Sure enough there was the plaintive moaning acting as a guide. But he noticed that he heard it only when the wind was in a certain quarter. So, being a man of imagination, he seized the opportunity to clear up a mystery. One morning he armed himself with an axe, and tucking his long robes up around his waist he set off, as he assured them, to lay the ghost. He found the weeper, for in a little clearing in the woods there were two big trees that had grown at an angle to one another, each of them leaning towards the other. When the wind blew from a certain direction their trunks touched. The harder the wind blew the louder they "groaned" and the more the villagers shivered and prayed. Father Painchaud smiled to himself, swung his axe like the good woodsman that he was and cut down one of the trees. The weeping was over in Anse Pleureuse.

Meantime the villagers were suffering agonies of apprehension. Probably some of them were blaming themselves for letting the priest go alone and women were bemoaning the fate of a fine young man. At last he came out of the woods, weary and disheveled so that they were sure he had been in single combat with the devil himself. But Father

Painchaud smiled and reassured them and told them confidently that the weeper would never come back again.

Although it is an old settlement it is scarcely even a village. Its little beach has a "tickle" on the western side leading into a river that is as crooked as a corkscrew and winds through farmlands that seem, all told, not much bigger than a pocket handkerchief. Just a very short distance from the village, the valley opens up into a beautiful lake, one of the most inviting spots in Gaspé, all broken shoreline. It is two and a half miles long and lies between cliffs that are from eight hundred to a thousand feet high. This is one of the few lakes on the North Shore.

Of course we have to climb to get out of Anse Pleureuse, and there is another drop to the sea on the other side. We are coming now to what is perhaps the climax of the North Shore. For sheer savage grandeur, of mass and form, it would be hard to excel Cap du Gros Morne. Dark and sharp-ridged, it overhangs the road, the spirit of this untamed mountain-coast. As though to show the world that the church vigilant has no awe of rocks, the church of St. Antoine du Gros Morne sits triumphantly astride the cliff. Cap du Gros Morne is three hundred feet high but the hardy sea-dwellers make no complaint at such a climb to the altar of their faith.

The village lies in a fine little bay and the beach is crowded with gabled houses. The road rises on the eastern side and turns into hilly country a little distance from the sea shore and when we come down again it is to the village of Manche d'Épee. Sword Handle is a strange name for a fishing station, but it goes back to the day when the first inhabitants found a beautiful sword handle on a rocky ledge in the cove, mute testimony to the fate of some officer whose need for the sword was past. Three hundred people here depend on cod for a livelihood and till their tiny farms for what the sea itself will not give them.

Petite Madeleine, with its four hundred villagers, to distinguish it from Grande Madeleine which has seven hundred, stands on the old seigneurial lands which were granted to

Sieur Denis Riverin who settled part of it as long ago as 1689. The King of France was personally interested in the lord of the manor and his venture in the fisheries but it was not a success. Another interesting figure in the history of New France comes into its story when Michel Sarrasin became its seigneur in 1723. Sarrasin was a famous physician and scientist who came out to Canada and made it his home until his death. He was a correspondent of the French Academy of Science, a botanist of outstanding merit and a surgeon skilled in what little knowledge of surgery was available in the eighteenth century.

At Madeleine there is the inevitable church and lighthouse and a long covered bridge. These bridges which are found all around Gaspé are covered in so that the snow and ice of winters will not settle on them and overweight the structure. They belong to the days before good roads and road clearance. As the road climbs out of the cove the elevation gives a perch from which to glance back at a long view well worth remembering. There is a fertile plain in the valley of the Rivière Madeleine, closely cultivated, with threads of rail fences cutting it up into a checkerboard of fields. Against the luminous sky a slender, almost fragil, spire pricks the hills, accents their magnitude and becomes the symbol of their conquest. Below, the white lighthouse warns and beckons from the sea. The houses lie like pale beads strewn along the water's edge.

The seigneury of Grande Vallée des Monts has a long river running through it, at the foot of a valley so deeply cleft that it seems a veritable gorge. Even the little streams to be crossed on our highway are all deeply incised. The village of Grande Vallée is at the mouth of the Rivière de Grande Vallée.

The names along the shore oftentimes tell their own story of shipwreck and disaster. There is Pointe à la Frigate, Anse aux Cannons, where old guns are still to be seen in the sand, Anse à Breton, Anse du Tresor and so on. Cloridorme lies beautifully in country that has escaped for a little from the encroachment of the cliffs and the eye has more room to wander. Farther along are frequent and very primitive fishing stations, that seem to have so slight a hold upon terra firma that it is a miracle that they are not all washed out to sea with some high tide.

Grande Etang is so wild and rugged that it has not even been subdivided for settlement. There is a deep barachois and at its narrowest point the road crosses it. East of Grande Etang the road runs into the hills again, on the very edge of Grande Etang,—the Big Pond. Big pond indeed it is, a lake surrounded on all sides but this that opens to the sea, by great hills reflected in its still waters. It is an inviting spot more so perhaps because of its strangeness here along this rough coast. It has an air of secluded beauty.

St. Maurice of the Strand is the charming name of the village, literally translated, standing at L'Echourie. It is a pleasant place with a long, very shallow beach, where the tide retreats and leaves the little fishing boats stranded on the sand. There are many strange legends here and the traditions of treasures which no one ever discovers. One of its annual festivals is the picturesque blessing of the fishing boats. The custom came from Normandy or Brittany centuries ago and has accumulated touches that only the romantic French Canadian would contrive. All the neighbors come with their boats to share the blessing and all the best frocks and shoes and hats are brought out and touched up for the occasion. The fishermen themselves appear in unaccustomed finery. The clergy honor the ships with their richest vestments and the little choir boys all have clean white surplices for the occasion. The boats themselves are trigged out with flowers and ribbons and bunting enough to astonish every cod in the sea.

# 6

## *End of the Peninsula*

FEW who travel the Gaspé Road will hurry through this part of it. Petite Rivière aux Renards will reward a few hours spent here with some very pleasant memories. Here is a miniature fishing beach and village but behind it on the slopes of the hills is a quite charming settlement of farmers whose little houses and tiny fields have a character all their own. Quiet peace and contentment lie in this valley and it seems to take the stranger to its heart as long as he will linger in it.

Just above the little quay, almost among the flakes and drying nets of Little Fox River is a wooden cross, the constant reminder of the fisherman's dependence on his church.

This little community has been painted many times by many artists who find that it "composes" for them, and of course photographers also revel in its quaintness.

Rivière aux Renards is one of the most interesting larger settlements on the North Shore and a good place to break the journey. It is a most generously proportioned cove, for the rest of the North Shore lies in the foothills of the Shick-shocks and nature has made more room here for man and his enterprises. It is a town of mixed English and French speaking population. It owes its origins partly to a tragedy, for an immigrant ship from Ireland was wrecked nearby and those who escaped death drifted on rafts and wreckage until they grounded in the vicinity of Fox River. Having arrived in Canada unexpectedly and far from their destination and having lost what little they did possess, they accepted their fate and settled down on this strange shore to become fishermen.

The map shows that we have arrived at a place where the Peninsula of Gaspé comes to its conclusion. There is a short cut to Gaspé Basin from Fox River through the foothills to Ste. Marjorique, but by taking it the hurried traveller will miss some of the best of Gaspé.

Fox River is an excellent example of the barachois. The barachois is an alluvial deposit of sand and gravel which forms a lagoon. It may be an Indian word or it may be derived from the phrase "barre echoues" a grounding place or bar. The bar usually runs in the general direction with the coast, as here at Fox River, enclosing the mouth of the stream, but there are examples such as those at Paspebiac and Carle‧ ton where the sand bars form an angle from the shore. Paspebiac is a curious example of a barachois without a river. There is always a "tickle" or channel somewhere through the barachois, even when there is no river to seek an exit to the sea. On the bar the fishermen build their homes and their flakes and fish houses, only a few feet above the level of the water. Their boats sail through the tickle into the protected lagoon behind the barachois when bad weather threatens. In important fishing stations the stores and fishing houses of the great companies are also on the barachois. In many of these the federal government has built cribwork to reinforce the barachois and to create safe channels through the gravel with better anchorage within.

Every inch of the gravel beach at Fox River is occupied and the population long since outgrew the barachois and spread up the encircling slopes on both sides of the river, for now the town numbers more than two thousand people. The harbor is crowded and so queer and quaint are some of its houses and set at such a bewildering variety of angles to the road that here, too, both artist and photographer can find many points of vantage.

Here in the good old days of French Canadian life before the roads improved and the tourists invaded the country, the community life was very lively. Weddings lasted three weeks, when they were planned for the quiet seasons, and everyone joined in the revelry. The New Year's visiting, the Christmas mass, the ritual of first communion, all these were celebrated with festivities that lent color and romance to this little town.

As late as 1871 the traveller headed east of Fox River had to go by boat.

Fox River is celebrated as the scene of the only fishermen's strike. One of the son's of the town ventured off to the United States to seek his fortunes and was caught in the toils of industrial life. He learned about strikes. Eventually he came home, the travelled hero of the town, and told the fishermen they were fools to work so hard for so little. True, the fish merchants were omnipotent and the fishermen and their families felt the pinch of perpetual poverty. But the travelled one told them that all they had to do was to strike and the merchants, awed by the show of force, would give them all they demanded. Strike, he urged them, and leave the leadership to me. The poor, ignorant fishermen had never heard of unions or organized labor movements or strikes, but a strike seemed an excellent idea. Things were very bad. They were short of food and certainly action of some kind was imperative. Desperate men will listen to desperate and even foolish counsel. So all unprepared the fishermen struck for shorter hours and better returns. They plundered the stores and did a lot of property damage as angry and unorganized men will do. Presently two Canadian cruisers appeared off the mouth of the river and landed troops to take the situation in hand. Their mouthy leader had disappeared and twenty of the ringleaders were arrested, charged with rioting and all sorts of other grave things. All this was in 1909 just about the time the government awakened to some of the problems of the fishermen. The twenty arrested men were convicted and sentenced to jail terms, but after they had been properly impressed with the error of their ways, they were released and sent back to their fishing boats.

It was to be thirty years more before the fishermen of Gaspé reached the point of organizing co-operatively to protect their own interests. After the success of the co-operative movement in Cape Breton with its fine educational program, integrated with the economic and social projects of their co-operative efforts, Gaspé reached the point of venturing into fishing co-operatives. It was the year that the Second Great War broke out that the United Fishermen of Quebec were incorporated under the laws of Quebec. There are today thirty-seven local affiliates including those of the Magdalen Islands. They began with fifteen hundred fishermen as members, catching about five and a half million pounds of fish a year and selling it at less than two cents a pound. Now they have approximately three thousand members bringing in nearly fifty million pounds of fish selling at about five cents a pound. The co-operatives buy more than a million dollars worth of fish from the fishermen each year. At some of the principle fishing stations they have fine plants for handling all kinds of fish and fish products and stores for the sale of fishermen's supplies. They have their own journal, *Full Sails,* an educational program to raise the standard of living among the fishermen and their families and to enlighten them on social and political issues. Becoming aware, too, of the importance of research into problems affecting the fisheries, they encourage and support both national and provincial research projects. They are working, too, for the unification of all fishing co-operatives in Eastern Canada into a single council that can speak with authority for fishermen. One of their projects for the future is an annual Fisheries Exhibition to cover all the approaches to fishing, processing and marketing of the products of the sea. We shall see the buildings of the United Fishermen of Quebec in many fishing stations, as we go along the Gaspé Road and in them we shall see a new phase of Gaspé history in which fishermen are taking their social and economic security into their own hands and working co-operatively for the common good.

Now we leave Fox River and move on past Anse au Griffon, Anse Jersey and Anse à Louise. In some of these are some quite lovely old houses with architectural features worthy of notice. One of these is at Anse au Griffon, not far from the roadway.

As we reach Cap des Rosiers we come to the end of the St. Lawrence River. The cape is the official boundary between the river and the Gulf. Here the North Shore ends and we come to the eastern face of Gaspé Peninsula.

The Cape of the Wild Rosebushes owes its romantic name to Sieur de Champlain who did not guess what a history of disaster would gather around this menacing headland. It is not a great cliff like some of its neighbors but a low, stocky promontory, topped with a table land on which part of the village stands. On its very tip, where it is broken into jagged rocks, is the round tower of the lighthouse. Beyond the cape lies a treacherous reef which the St. Lawrence Pilot indicates as "abreast a conspicuous church". This church, like so many others along the Gaspé coast is as much a landmark to seafarers as the lighthouse itself, so long as visibility is good. When night blots out the margins of sea and land, the lighthouse sends its flashing yellow light across the mouth of the river, or in fog booms out great warnings of the dangers that lie in the Gaspé rocks.

Before the lighthouse and fog signal station were built here many a good ship went to its doom off Cap des Rosiers in blinding snow storms or thick, confusing fog. The most celebrated of the sea disasters off the cape was the wreck of the *Carricks*. She was carrying a long passenger list of poor Irish peasants who were forced out of Ireland in 1847 by famine and cholera. The ancient kingdom was depopulated, by death and exile, and to escape the horrors of that stricken land, these sad creatures fled to Canada. The *Carricks* was twenty-three days out from Ireland when one November day she ran into a blizzard in the Gulf. The driving winds forced her off her course, the white fury of the snow made it impossible for the captain to take his bearings. Like a doomed bird, with frozen sails heavy with ice and the shrouds festooned with snow, the *Carricks* plunged on until the snarling reef sank its fangs into her oaken hull and held her fast.

Tremendous seas washed over the poor ship and carried off those who were not caught and drowned in her hold.

Some of the survivors drifted about for hours until they were washed ashore in the cove. The ship broke up, and wreckage and bodies alike were tossed like flotsam and jetsam along the beach. The pitying fishermen took in the half-dead survivors and saved those that they could.

Today as you wander down to the beautiful encircling beach of Cap des Rosiers you have an eerie feeling of sadness, as though something of the piteous tragedy hangs over it yet. The day after the storm the snow lay in soft funeral wreaths upon the rocks and upon the evergreens. The black and sullen sea, its temper spent, rolled in long moaning waves upon the gravel, bearing with it the bodies of its victims. Why had they been pursued so relentlessly? Snatched from hunger and disease in Ireland, destiny would not let them land in the country to which they had turned in their despair. The shocked and silent fishermen set to work, some to dig long trenches for graves, some to hitch their oxen to their carts. All day long they worked from dawn till dark, gathering up the dead from the sea-wracked beach and laying them in their graves.

Yet out of all this sifting some few were saved to join their fortunes with the Gaspésians and their descendants are still living in this cove.

A curious relic of another wreck was discovered at Cap des Rosiers many years ago. Much more than a hundred years ago a fisherman picked up on the beach a medallion of Canadian white pine, apparently a part of the decoration of some old square-sterned ship. It was carved with the head of a bearded man and on the back were the initials J.C. and the date 1704. The fisherman set it in a little window that it fitted. Years later one of his descendants, making some alterations to this house, built a new wall over the old one, and so for many years the old portrait of Jacques Cartier, the discoverer of Gaspé, was hidden and forgotten. When the house was torn down, the medallion was re-discovered and roused the curiosity of historians who identified it as a portrait of Cartier probably off some Canadian-built vessel

55

sailing from Quebec. It had come to grief off wicked Cap des Rosiers.

Another of the known wrecks is that of the frigate *Louise* in the French regime. Her memory lingers in Anse à Louise nearby.

Cap des Rosiers must have been thrust up in some terrific upheaval of nature, for its sharp slates stand vertical to the sea. The great cove that lies between it and Cape Gaspé is one of the biggest in all Gaspé. The beach curves around the foot of Cap Bon Ami and down the length of the Forillon to Cape Gaspé. Along the way the sheer rocks descend vertically for hundreds of feet. It is worth while spending some time along this beach, to listen to the low dirge of the waves as they break in feathery loveliness and then draw back into the sea with a curious rattling motion among the pebbles. There is something mysterious about the place, something indefinable, only emphasized by a little house here and there with its brood of wide-eyed children. These ribbed and barren rocks, austere and yet somehow inspiring and reassuring, satisfy some inner need that sunny beauty does not reach.

This has been a terrible beach to fishermen who could find no shelter from storms here for their little boats. At Cap des Rosiers a huge new project is turning one end of the cove near the lighthouse into a harbor where the fishing boats will have shelter. But the rest of the beach and the mighty wall of the Forillon will remain what they are today, spectacles of nature that will draw many thousands of people from the inland towns and cities who will come in search of what Gaspé has to offer them.

Because of the nature of this point of the Peninsula the Quebec Government has wisely bought a park area just east of Cap des Rosiers and not far from Cap Bon Ami. The park is now behind wooden palisades that remind one of the Habitation at Port Royal in the first days of exploration in New France. To reach it the traveller drives past the new harbor, past the road that leads to Gaspé Basin, and follows the coast line on the road that mounts to the heights east of the village. About a mile along the road it dips into a bowl of woods and to the left is the gate to the park. This is to become a public park where the Gaspé visitor can see from the heights the cliffs of the Forillon. The keeper of the Park is a French Canadian with the name of Joseph Whelan. His great-grandfather was a passenger on the *Carricks*.

The Forillon, the very tip of Gaspé Peninsula, is a slender finger of stone, about four miles long. To cross the Forillon we turn back from the provincial park and take the road that runs southward from the harbor area. This bit of road is an ancient portage by which Indians and colonists alike avoided the long trip around the Forillon and made a short cut to Gaspé Basin. If you are in Gaspé in September or October it is here you will see another glory of Gaspé, the color of her hardwood forests. The incredible maples, burning with rose and crimson and scarlet, the birches all white and gold and all the other trees that turn to color after the first frost, make this inland journey a lovely bit for any who are sensitive to color.

As we reach the top of the Portage and begin to descend we will see the great Gaspé Basin, wide and placid, lying at our feet and will begin to realize the immensity of this stage on which so much of the early history of the country was played.

When we come down to the water's edge we will turn to the left on the road that leads to Cape Gaspé. There is nothing to compare with this curious bit of Gaspé. The south side of the Forillon, which is not so forbidding as the north side, was settled by Guernsey men who came here in the seventeen-nineties. As we drive along we will come to a charming little Protestant church. Around it is a churchyard in which these hardy eighteenth century colonists and fishermen are buried, with their wives and children. If the men who came here to live and work were men of courage, what shall we say of their womenfolk? Who can measure the loyalty and co-operativeness that filled those little homes in those lonely and hazardous days? Without these qualities there would be no homes on the Forillon today.

57

The beach was an excellent one, a few feet above sea level and about four miles in extent. The Guernseymen called it La Grande Grève,—the great beach. Unhappily it has become Anglicized into Grand Grave! Here the fishermen could build their flakes and spread their cod to dry. But to find places to build their homes they had to climb the sides of the Forillon. They became most ingenious farmers, for the farms of the Forillon may run up hill or down but they never come to a level plane. The roadway is a succession of crests and troughs, like a choppy sea, and extremely narrow. Along it you may pause to walk uphill to a little farm house or down hill to the beach as generations of these Gaspesians have done. There are many little coves and fishing stations down out of sight beyond the cultivated fields. Some of the larger coves like Anse St. Georges, and Anse Sauvage are good spots for the artist and photographer, who will find in the Forillon a new challenge to the interpreter.

The road to Cape Gaspé is a part of the Gaspé trip that the adventurous traveller will want to take, but it is not a trip that can be made by car. The fish trucks do make the trip daily, but for the present the road, though quite good, is so narrow and so spectacular that the visitor will not enjoy making it with his own car. The last part of the run is simply a mountain trail which can be negotiated well enough by those whose business takes them to the lighthouse but it is not intended for tourists. However, there is a way of getting there. At Hyman's store it is possible to make arrangements with some of the local people to drive on to the cape with a horse and buggy. It well repays the effort but visitors to Gaspé are warned that to attempt the road to the cape beyond Hyman's store on Grande Grève in their cars, is foolhardy. To make a turn along the road is almost impossible beyond Hyman's.

The trip as far as Hyman's is quite easy and comfortable to do, but beyond there it will try the nerve of the average driver. Some day doubtless the government of Quebec will widen the road and provide for tourist travel but as yet it is something for the adventurous, for the artist, and for those whose curiosity is whetted by the extraordinary character of the Forillon. The only road across the Forillon is a rough one that runs from the provincial park near Cap Bon Ami to Hyman's store. Of course for the people who enjoy long hikes, the walk from Hyman's store to the Cape is by no means excessive, perhaps about two miles.

The Forillon rises seven hundred feet at its highest point and varies between half a mile and a mile in width from its base to the Cape.

The Forillon can boast of the first mining venture in Canada. On his journey to Quebec that handsome genius, Indendant Talon, paused here to investigate rumors of a find of silver veins. Tramping up the slopes of the cliff to the site of the discovery, he was so pleased with what he saw that he sent home to France for engineers and miners and set them to work under the supervision of Captain Pierre Doublet. This was in the sixteen-sixties. Silver was much in demand at the time since Talon's king, Louis the Fourteenth, was busy furnishing his new Palace of Versailles. Among his fancies was one for chairs and tables of silver. New France might have won a good deal of favor in the king's eyes if it had proved to be a source of silver ore. However, they did not find enough to make the venture profitable and it was abandoned. Within recent times, traces of the working of these old miners has been located on the Forillon. Today Gaspé is being explored for its mineral wealth and for its oil, but not on the Forillon. The search goes on far in the interior. When you examine the map of Gaspé you will realize how very little of it we see as we skirt its shores, compared to the great mass of land it comprises. In the hills and valleys of the interior there is believed to be vast mineral wealth. Talon was merely the earliest of the hopeful prospectors of Gaspé.

The Forillon ends at Cape Gaspé, which once had two curious rock formations called The Old Man and The Old Woman. One of them is gone but the Old Woman can still be traced. The Cape, as the lighthouse keeper may tell you, is the farthest land towards the Atlantic and the next stop is Newfoundland. The Cape rises three hundred feet above the sea and is so sheer a cliff that it is difficult to get a vantage point to look downward towards the shore. Perhaps when you do peer over the edge down at the sea breaking ceaselessly into spray on the rocks, you may see seals playing in the frothy water off shore. The currents of Gulf and Gaspé Bay meet here and make intricate patterns of criss-crossing waves as you watch. It must be a terrible spot in stormy weather.

On the top of the Cape is an old light built above the lighthouse keeper's house. The light is three hundred and fifty-five feet above the sea, the highest light in Gaspé and indeed in all the St. Lawrence navigation. It is to be replaced by a modern light very soon. The limestone cliffs of the Forillon must always be well marked for this is a very busy sea route and one of the most important landmarks in North Atlantic navigation.

From Cape Gaspé we are now in the Gaspé Basin and its magnificence will be recognized as we turn back to drive by the farms towards Cap aux Os where we left the Portage. But along the way we will probably be more concerned with the fields and farm yards in their fantastic settings on either side of the road. The rare farmer who has a car must build a garage that is on stilts beside the road, because there is no room for one on solid ground. The drivers of this community must have nerves of steel. The farm animals, on the other hand, must have muscles of steel, for the cows that graze and the horses that work the land must have bred into them something of the mountain goat. There are bright little schools along the way and many of the children travel those narrow miles by bicycle.

After an afternoon well spent on the Forillon we return to the foot of the Portage and begin the long journey around Gaspé Basin.

# 7

## *The Pageant of Gaspé*

IT seems as though the Maker of Gaspé, after having shaped a North Shore destitute of harbors, relented when he came to the tip of the peninsula, that thrust itself so boldly into the sea, for here he carved a generous haven for sailors. Gaspé Basin is seven miles wide at its entrance and nearly seventeen miles long. It is a great roadstead, sheltered with hills. Between Sandy Beach and Peninsula there is entrance into an inner harbor that has delighted harrassed sea captains throughout recorded history.

Very few ships bound from Europe to Canada, in the days of canvas sails, passed Gaspé Basin without dropping anchor there. Sailors knew that it was a haven where they could rest, take on fresh water and fresh food, and set their ships in order after the stress and strain of the Atlantic. From sixty or seventy miles out at sea they saw good Mont Ste. Anne beckoning them from above Percé, and, steering by her rosy peak, they found their way to Gaspé Basin. Because of this most of the men and women who people the scenes of Canadian pioneer history, came and went in Gaspé, grateful to its kindly hills and quiet waters, carrying away remembrances of its glacier carved valleys, so that it became one of the best known spots on the Atlantic coast, to all the nations of Europe who were interested in the new world.

Long before the fleur de lys flew over Gaspé it was known to sea rovers from the north and a Danish archaeologist says that Gaspé was a Viking fishing station as long ago as the eleventh, twelfth and thirteenth centuries. So it is a sort of stage on which a shadowy pageant is always being played. It is haunted by the hulls of vessels long since gone to what-

61

ever heaven there is for good ships, and by a large and strangely assorted company of friends and enemies, speaking the tongues and wearing the costumes of many lands.

Three important rivers flow into it from the foothills of the Shickshocks and each forms a deep indentation in the Bay. The northern river is the Dartmouth with St. Marjorique at its mouth; the next southward is the York River with Gaspé town standing guard at its exit into the bay; the southern river is the St. John with the old Loyalist town of Douglastown overlooking its picturesque barachois. Each of these rivers has a wide, shallow estuary, broken up into tidal flats. To make the round of Gaspé Bay we have to detour far inland around these estuaries and come back each time to the little town that stands at the river mouth.

From the town of Gaspé there is a road leading into the interior. This is a secondary road to Lake Madeleine, 83 miles inland. The road follows the York River for three-quarters of the route. Unfortunately a large area has been burned over and much of the scenic value has been destroyed. There are at Lake Madeleine two camps where visitors can get lodging and can fish for brook trout. Travellers to Lake Madeleine are advised to spend the night at one of the mountain camps as the return trip cannot be made comfortably in one day.

As we ride we see up into these river valleys long views of wooded and fertile land, prosperous little farms and cosy homes, for this land is a friendlier place than anything along the embattled North Shore. Through St. Marjorique we pass up the Dartmouth River, which we cross on a very long trestle and a long covered bridge. There is a curious view from hereabouts of the great lagoon and its low lands.

The Bay between St. Marjorique and Gaspé is known as the North West Arm. Here sprawled on the low lands of the river banks is the old town of Gaspé. The surroundings are beautiful but Gaspé as a town is no longer prepossessing. It is a mill town and the railway runs into the heart of it. There have always been dreamers who believed that Gaspé

Basin would one day be a great port, and Gaspé a great industrial city, even a metropolis. All such dreams, fortunately for the natural beauty of the Peninsula, have come to nothing. Gaspé sleeps on unconcerned with "dreams of avarice" or merely blinks her sleepy eyes at the silver and blue of the tide sweeping in from the Atlantic or the flushed clouds hovering over her quiet hills at sunset. These are the things that are always with her. Her little booms come and go. Fretful promoters spent years of time and fortunes digging and drilling fifty wells for oil that lay too deep for the ingenuity of engineers of the time. Four hundred Norwegians came over three-quarters of a century ago to turn Gaspé into a mining country but the invincible hills held their peace and some of the miners settled down to farming. Gaspé retired to quiet and seclusion with a few more docks and a few more townships surveyed.

When the sea was the only approach to Gaspé, the town was a much more popular summer resort than it is now. When the railway came to Gaspé it opened up a great many more places to visitors and the Baie des Chaleurs towns began to rival old Gaspé. So although Gaspé was made the terminus of the railroad from the south, it did not contribute to its popularity. The railway station is under Fort Ramsay Bluff where, according to tradition, there lies buried the silver plate of a Governor of New France. The ship carrying it to Quebec was chased into the Basin by a pursuing English ship and the captain carried the Governor's treasure up the Bluff and buried it for safety. For some reason or other, they couldn't go back for it and no one else has been able to find it.

The first train that ran into Gaspé station was drawn by an old locomotive from the Manhattan elevated railway. What that old New York engine thought about Gaspé would have been worth recording as it came to a full stop amid the festivities of the villagers. Its old iron sides must nearly have burst with sighs of loneliness as it settled down to its old age in the cod country.

If indeed Gaspé became a winter port it would save a railway journey of some five hundred miles between Europe and Montreal but there are other considerations than mere mileage in the making of ports, and so Gaspé is hardly likely to renounce its old role and it will probably remain as it has been so long, a quaint and quiet village in spite of its magnificent harbor where a thousand ships could, literally, lie safely at anchor.

Within the sandbar that locks the inner harbor there is a generous six miles to manoeuvre in and forty-five feet of water that requires no dredging to keep it safe. Now the occasional passenger ship that goes into Gaspé, the freighters in search of timber cargoes, the graceful schooners and fishing ships, ride in lonely splendor in the great blue basin, for it is not nearly so busy as it used to be when whalers made it their headquarters and schooners on many errands fluttered their sails to rest in its quiet embrace.

When the Loyalists came to Gaspé one of their splendid dreams was of a great city on Gaspé Bay. Douglastown was laid out with high hopes. There were parks and squares and land laid aside for schools and churches and for the administration, on the maps of the town planners. Yet Douglastown never became anything more than a village. Today it is not even a Loyalist village. In a wave of Irish immigration, a century ago, when the people of starved and desolate Ireland poured into the new world, Douglastown of the Loyalists was swamped, and today the histories of Loyalists and Irish are merged into a Gaspésian loyalty. Douglastown lies above the great barachois at the mouth of the St. John River and faces the slopes of the Forillon whose toy houses and toy fields seem from here as though they were set up against the green velvet of its wooded crest.

This then is the stage of Gaspé Basin. If we can pretend to forget these patient little farms, these sturdy figures turning their whitening cod upon the sunny flakes, if we imagine there are no docks, no smoking mills, no church spires, and think of Gaspé with its forests uncut, its slopes untilled, then we shall see the spirit ships of old enterprises sailing up the silvery blue of the roadstead, to fight old battles and renew old adventures and play out the Pageant of Gaspé.

Who first discovered the "new world" no one knows; nor even if it was "discovered" or merely rediscovered long after it has been forgotten. When Europe pulled herself out of the Dark Ages and stretched her spirit in the reviving air of the Renaissance, she merely began to put into use knowledge neglected and unused for centuries. Some say the Phoenicians discovered America. They were a very practical people, and many of them were hard headed business men. Though they discovered a way to the tin mines of Britain they did not discuss their discovery in the market place. Indeed, there is a classic story of a Phoenician sea captain who found himself pursued by a Roman ship, very curious to know the significance of the Phoenicians' northward journeys. Rather than reveal the secret of the route he was to take to the British tin mining country, the Phoenician ran his ship aground and sacrificed his crew to his country's trade secrets. His deed was sung and commemorated in Tyre by a grateful people. The Phoenicians invented the alphabet for us, not in order to record their history or their literature, but in order to transact business. They were content to leave all the cultural glory to their neighbors while they traded and explored. They left their mark on trails across the Indian Ocean, Ceylon, Java, Sumatra, the Caroline Islands, Easter Island, Mexico and Peru. It would not be hard to imagine that they sailed into Gaspé Basin, too. Phoenician traders often sailed away for three years at a time and it was on these journeys that, according to tradition, they discovered America from the Pacific. So if men could forget how to make malleable glass, or copper hard as steel, or imperishable pigments, how easily they might forget a lonely continent known only to a few hardy sea rovers. Only legends of these forgotten sea routes survived through the centuries.

Perhaps it was these Phoenicians who implanted, in the mind of the Mediterranean people, the traditions of Atlantis, the lost continent. There were many who firmly believed in an unknown land that lay in the western seas. There was also the Irish tradition of St. Brendan's Isle, named for an Irish saint. It was a bewitched land, because no one ever was able to find it a second time. But was this strange in the days before compasses? There is the story of the Irish monk who, in the eighth century maintained that the earth was round. He horrified his brother monks who accused him of heresy. Brother Feargal told his judges that the Irish traded with a land on the other side of the world and proved it so conclusively that he was revered for his learning and finally was made a bishop. Indeed Irish tradition said that Irish Christians had settled in the new world to escape persecution.

Centuries before the Christian era the Greeks believed the world was round. When Europe turned to Greek thought and Greek wisdom for her awakening, the idea of the world as a sphere was revived. Dante grasped the idea and turned it to poetic ends in his *Divine Comedy* two centuries before Columbus put it to practical use. So it was that the light of learning burned on in the quiet of the cloisters and in the sanctuaries of the learned. In the Orient, of course, the idea of the spherical world never was overlaid by a picture of a world that looked like a plate. The nature of the universe, from atom to solar system, as spherical and planetary, was a fundamental factor in their philosophical and religious thought.

Perhaps the legend of Atlantis, that land of the fair and the wise, wiped out when its god-like ones stooped to conscious sins, frightened the mariners of the Mediterranean. In Egypt, Plato discovered in the temples the tradition, thousands of years old, concerning the lands in the western sea, yet nothing would tempt men out beyond the Pillars of Hercules to search for them, for the drowned lands were believed to be "an obstacle to those who sail here to reach the high seas". So while the Mediterranean mulled over the glories

Rivière au Renard

Going Up To Pasture

*Boats ashore—*
*October in Gaspé*

*Seawall at Pointe*
*à la Frégate*

*Fisherman's return*

*Harvest time in the Shickshocks*

*Little Fields at Petite Vallee*

*Grave of a Colonist*

*Valley in the Shickshocks near Mt. Albert*

*A Clearing in the Wilderness*

*Fisherman and
Farmer in Gaspé*

*Soapmaking at
Cloridorme*

*Mont St. Louis, once burned by Wolfe's men*

*Farming Between the Forest and the Sea*

"Making Fish". Cod
Drying on the Flakes

Typical Gaspé
Fishing Station

The First Gaspésians

The Rocks of Gaspé

*Lighthouse at Cap des Rosiers*

*Typical Beach at Grande Grève*

Drying nets on
Grande Grève

Weathered rocks at
Cap Bon Ami

*Guernsey Settlement
on the Forillon*

*Church and Graves
of Guernsey pioneers*

*One-Horsepower to Cape Gaspé Light*

*Farm and Fishing Beach at Grande Grève*

of the departed Atlanteans, farther north, in the misty seas, the Irish ventured forth.

Now it was not long after Brother Feargal had confounded his judges with his learning that Ireland was invaded by the fair-bearded Vikings in their carved ships. After they had plundered the Irish, they settled among them. In a century and a half they had imbibed a good deal of the culture and learning of their Irish neighbors. Among other things they heard about the exiles who had found the new lands far away from lovely Ireland. So in 860 the Vikings found and settled Iceland for themselves. By 981 they had discovered and settled in Greenland and by the year 1000 they landed in the new world far to the west.

Back of each adventure was a tale of passion and blood-shed and of human love and hate, of trusts betrayed and courage tested. The Viking tales were lost for eight hundred years but now from the fabulous fabric of the Sagas, sober scholars have disentangled the history of a most dramatic age. One of these stories belongs to Gaspé.

The Vikings who came out of the northlands and built such swift and beautiful ships for the conquest of their neighbors, were a race of barbarians, yet they had developed a poetic expression and handicrafts of woolweaving and gold and silver work of exceptional merit, and a rare knowledge of stars and of navigation. Their ships were wide and shallow with sharply designed prows and sterns, rigged with square sails and propelled by oars. Soldier-sailors they were, and when these fighting men travelled at sea they hung their painted shields along the outside of the gunwales of their ships, so that the vessels glowed with color and fantastic designs. Near the turn of the century a replica of one of these Viking ships crossed the Atlantic safely, to demonstrate the possibility of these long journeys recounted in the ancient sagas of the Norse people. Some of their ships were larger than Cartier's vessels, and could carry thirty or forty of a crew, with livestock and food supplies for several weeks. The golden age of the Vikings extended roughly from the beginning of the eighth century, when they invaded Ireland, to the middle of the eleventh. It was during this age that they found and explored the new world.

Eric the Red, exiled from Iceland for a deed of blood, settled in Greenland, and called it so to rouse the envy of those he had left behind. Leif the Lucky was a son of Eric the Red and his journeys to the new world are recorded in the Sagas. His sister, Freydis, an illegitimate daughter of Eric the Red, was one of the first white women known to have lived in Gaspé.

The story goes that about 1020 Thorfinn Karlsefni, a wealthy Icelandic merchant, famous as a navigator, set out on an expedition to Greenland. Eric the Red, who lived in a rude sort of luxury, invited him to spend the winter with him. Thorfinn stayed. The long dark days of winter were spent hilariously and never had there been such a Christmas season in the history of the settlement.

In Eric's great house there lived a beautiful widow, Gudrid, whose adventurous husband had frequently travelled to the new world in the west. In the smoky light by the broad hearth, Thorfinn and Gudrid found much to say to one another. She enthralled him with the stories she had learned from her dead husband, though Thorfinn would have listened to anything she chose to tell him of heaven or earth, so long as she sat near him with her long fair braids, bound in golden clasps, shimmering against the embroidery of her woolen gown. By spring Thorfinn had lost his interest in Iceland and Gudrid was a bride instead of a widow.

Now Thorfinn was all aglow for adventure in the new lands, so he organized an expedition. He had his own ship and he needed two others. One of these was commanded by Thorvard, the husband of Freydis, and the third by dour old Thorhall the Hunter, a mighty pagan. Many women as well as men joined the expedition and they set out one hundred and sixty strong, with Gudrid and Freydis as the great ladies of the adventure.

They sailed from Greenland and came at last down through

the Straits of Belle Isle. There on the coast they found the wreck of a Viking ship and so called the place Keelness, in commemoration of their unfortunate fellow countrymen. On they went past Anticosti and, sighting the mountainous coasts of Gaspé, they skirted the land, poking their curious prows into Gaspé Bay and pausing to wonder at the glories of Percé. At last they came to a pleasant, sheltered place we call Baie des Chaleurs. They called it Straumfjord.

They could travel only seventy-five miles a day at the best of times, so by the time they arrived here autumn was coming on. They landed their cattle, cut trees and built cabins in which they settled down for the winter.

It was an unfortunate winter. They found no Indians to help them, game was scarce and the cattle suffered from exposure and lack of food. They moved them to an Island, either Miscou or Bonaventure, but everything seemed to turn out badly. Thorhall the Hunter, impatient with their Christian prayers for help, went off by himself to work his own magic. They found him on top of a rock in the throes of intercession with his pagan Viking gods. Next day a whale was washed up on the shore and Thorhall exulted over the results of his pagan invocations. The Christian Vikings, hungry though they were, threw the meat back into the sea rather than accept the aid of his gods.

They survived, in spite of everything, till spring, when Thorfinn decided to search still farther south for the Land of Vines. Thorhall the Hunter snorted his disgust at people who wanted ease and plenty, and turned the prow of his ship westward into the St. Lawrence, never to be heard of again.

So Thorfinn and Thorvard went south and settled on the banks of the Hudson, trading with the Indians. But one day Thorfinn's great bull ran amuk among the Indians and caused a war between the red men and the white. Freydis was the heroine of this conflict, rallying the Norsemen to victory and saving the colony from extinction. It is the best thing that is recorded for us about this blood-thirsty golden-haired Viking.

The colonists decided to go back to Straumfjord, and so the third winter was spent on the shores of Baie des Chaleurs, while the men traded with the Indians, and fished and trapped in the country roundabout. However, there were too many quarrels over the women in the party for the success of the colony and to save them from exterminating themselves, Thorfinn decided to take them home to Greenland again.

That was the end of the first European colony in Gaspé, so far as song and story have yet revealed. They were a wild and valorous folk and it is a pity they did not settle and multiply in Gaspé, for they would have suited its dramatic moods and would have adorned every cove and headland with strange Norse legends.

Even after the failure of this venture in colonization, the Vikings continued to visit the new lands, for there is the Saga of Eric Gnupsson, Bishop of Greenland, who set out in 1121 to preach to the savages, or strangers, as they called them, in the land to the west. The last of the known voyages of the Norsemen to North America was in 1347. And as Gaspé lay along their route, and since its capes and mountains were the best of landmarks, doubtless as long as they ventured out so far in search of timber and furs and souls to save, Gaspé was familiar to them.

With the rise of Christianity in Europe the demand for fish increased. Fish and fishermen were inextricably associated with the Christian faith. Fish was the secret symbolism of the Christ; fish was the food of the fast days. When the original significance began to fade into dogmatic uses, fast days were made the instrument of "economic recovery" and the "new deal" for the fishermen of Europe. The church dedicated more and more days to the eating of fish, not so much for the good of the soul as for the aid of the population that depended on the sea fisheries for a livelihood. In fact, by the time nationalism had matured in Europe and nation struggled with nation for power and prestige, the navies leaned heavily on the fisher folk for recruits. So much de-pended on a great pool of sea-wise young men, that one of the great problems of the Reformation to the government of Britain was that of maintaining the fisheries. Since there were to be no more religious fast days, Britain had to institute political fast days, to ensure that the fisheries were maintained.

In search of a living for their loved ones, men will do strange and unreasonable things, and so even after the Vikings had quit Gaspé, the fishermen of Europe ventured farther and farther from home in their cockleshells of ships in search of cod. No one knows how many centuries European fisher-men have fished the waters of the Gulf. Lescarbot, the first historian of Canada, said, when he wrote more than three hundred years ago, that "for several centuries men of Dieppe and St. Malo and other sailors from Harve de Grace, from Honfleur and other places, have made voyages to these coun-tries to fish for cod". Being a Frenchman he said not a word about the English and Irish and Dutch and others who did the same thing. From the fantastic sea tales of these compass-less fishermen, the navigators and cartographers heard of the new land, tales told with a shrewd intention to outwit and mislead, for the men who found the silver hordes of cod were not any more anxious to disclose their routes than were the Phoenicians who had a monopoly of the tin trade.

But nothing can prevent the inevitable rolling back of the clouds of ignorance. All sorts of strange forces were at work, here and there in Europe, before which the fishermen and their secret fishing grounds could make no more effective resistance than King Canute before the creeping tide.

Up until a century before America was officially discovered, Europe had a nominal union under the Latin Christian church and in the use of the Latin tongue as a medium of statesmanship and culture. Europe, except for Russia, fell heir to the Latin tradition, while Russia and the East re-mained under the traditions of the Greek church and the Greek tongue.

71

Yet in spite of the cultural and religious unity of Europe, its little states had been gradually developing national consciousness and with it the use of the national tongues. The vernacular had been considered very rude and fit only for the common people, until the poets endowed the common speech with the spirit of living truth and human significance. The humanism of the Renaissance grew out of the new passion of the enlightened scholars and artists to share what they had with the working people of their nations. So Chaucer in England, Villon in France and Dante in Italy lovingly used the common speech of their fellow countrymen in their poetry so that all might share their ideas. Yet, when this was done, Europe was so steeped in ignorance that it had forgotten the old teachings of the world as a sphere and literally believed that any too venturesome ship might sail over the rim of the sea into outer space and oblivion. Suddenly Greek and Latin learning clashed and in the bewilderment that ensued men had to prove things for themselves or go on suffering the agonies of doubt. Driven by the lash of questions and ideas, men sailed hither and yon and found again the keys to knowledge and the skills for creating anew. They discovered that it was possible to sail all around Africa, and at last, all around the world.

The medieval world was suddenly vastly extended and turned out to be quite a different place to that which every intelligent European had always known it to be. The compass and the printing press had upset all those nice comfortable notions in which Europe had felt so secure in the twilight of knowledge,—the Dark Ages. It was a world revolution in thought. Three great streams of endeavor began to flow from the fountain head of the Renaissance. Discovery became the physical expression of the new emancipation; creative work in arts and letters became the intellectual expression of the new energy; and the Reformation was the spiritual result of the new freedom of thought.

Faraway Gaspé, shrouded in mystery, was to be drawn

into the written history of mankind as a direct result of all the turmoil out of which Europe received its new heritage.

Link by link the chain was forged. Marco Polo had written his bewildering adventures and was dead for twenty years before the Vikings made their last voyage to America. Columbus was born while Henry the Navigator was still directing explorations for Portugal; Cartier was born the year before Columbus discovered America; and before Cartier had ended his days, Henry of Navarre had begun his struggle for the French throne, from which he sent Champlain to found the colony of New France.

But by the time we come to Cartier, Spain was standing jealously over her rich discoveries to the south; England and France, slowly but surely were developing into rivals on the sea and had to divide what was left of the less hospitable northern shores between them.

# 8

## *The Mariner of St. Malo*

S T. MALO, on the rocky coast of France, had been, throughout its history, a stronghold of sea rovers, fishermen and swashbuckling buccaneers. In all its sons and daughters the love of the sea burned brightly. In its ancient inns many a strange tale was told by those who came back to St. Malo after adventuring far and wide on the newly explored sea routes of the world. Into this little town in the year before Christopher Columbus sailed on his famous journey to discover America, a child was born. His name was Jacques Cartier.

We know very little about his childhood and youth. Perhaps as a little boy his imagination was set afire by reports of the adventures of Columbus, as boys today are filled with dreams of aviation. Doubtless, as soon as he was big enough to do so, he haunted the stone quays and listened to the tall tales of the sailors. Perhaps in his early 'teens he sailed away on one of the ships that explored central and south America and gained some celebrity for it. There must have been a reason why, at the age of nineteen, he was invited to become a godfather. Throughout the rest of his life we find him acting the same role innumerable times and by deduction we can imagine that he was distinguished from youth and was a jovial man with a love of children, for he seemed to take pride in his role of perennial godfather. Another bit of evidence is the fact that at twenty-eight he married a lady of wealth who was considerably above him in social station. We find her in the role of godmother to an Indian girl known as Catherine of Brazil, perhaps a little maid brought home by Cartier from one of his journeys. He was

74

a man of more than ordinary intelligence and enterprise, for he came to be known as Sieur de Limoilou, by virtue of his estate near St. Malo. He was named King's Pilot and the High Admiral of France was his friend and patron.

Without a shadow of a doubt Cartier had heard from the fishermen of St. Malo of the lands across the sea where they fished for cod. Some contend that Cartier actually made the journey to the cod fisheries before the official project of discovery was set afoot. We can imagine Captain Cartier gossiping with his friend, the High Admiral of France, over a cobwebbed bottle of wine, toying with the idea of staking claims for the King of France in what remained unpledged in North America.

Great enterprises sometimes begin that way. An idle comment while Cartier cracked his walnuts; a thought that tickled the fancy of the High Admiral as he grew warm and mellow with his wine; by the third bottle, a full-fledged expedition for the glory of France.

It was not a plan to win favor in St. Malo. Probably the rich fish merchants of the town muttered into their beards and cursed these restless beggars who couldn't leave well enough alone. However, the business of exploration and discovery could not wait upon the pleasure of the merchants and in the spring of 1534, Cartier and his men set out to sea.

They passed south of Newfoundland and entered the Straits of Belle Isle. There they met a big trading and fishing ship from New Rochelle, in search of a port called Breste, on the north shore of the Gulf. If the crew knew it was the Gulf, they kept the matter to themselves and let Cartier sail off to make his own discoveries. The merchants had no desire to make the new world familiar to the old. Cartier sailed south and the first lands he officially "discovered" were the Magdalens and Prince Edward Island. As he went he logged the capes and headlands, the islands and the bays, giving them names and setting them down on his new maps. Turning westward he sailed past Mirimachi and the Island of Miscou and at last found himself in "a very fair country".

75

A headland here he named Cape Hope "for the hope we had of finding here a strait" leading to China. Into this "strait" they sailed and hugging the north shore "in order to find a harbor" they entered a small bay which promised to give good anchorage. "We named it St. Martin's Cove."

So here at last we find the Sieur de Limoilou in Gaspé, for he had cast anchor in Port Daniel and there he was to stay for eight days.

The day after his arrival he set sail in one of his ships up the shore and came to Paspebiac. Still off shore, he saw approaching him some forty or fifty canoes, skimming over the water to the rhyme of glistening paddles. Cartier was interested but suspicious. Apparently the Indians were accustomed to trading, for they landed on the gravel bar at Paspebiac and putting skins on the blades of their paddles, they waved them as a signal of their wish to barter. Cartier stroked his black beard and speculated. He decided not to land among them but he put off with some of his men in longboats and at this the savages leaped back into their canoes and went to meet him.

The Frenchmen were horrified as the lithe, painted, grinning Indians pressed around them on the water and Cartier, in a panic, ordered the firing of his two small brass canons. In dismay the Indians fled as fast as their canoes would carry them and drifted in a scattered circle well beyond his range, puzzled and outwitted. Theirs had been a friendly gesture and they could not understand the reception it had received.

Cartier retired to Port Daniel and next day the Indians followed him there and landed on a beach not far from his ships. By this time Cartier had thought the matter out and decided that under the protection of the guns of his ships he would venture among them. So, with sailors bearing baskets of goods, beads and combs, tin plates, bits of scarlet cloth, axes and knives and all other of cheap trinkets, he went ashore. The savages were overjoyed. They snapped up the French goods with childish pleasure and parted with everything they had save canoes and paddles. When the Frenchmen gathered up their bundles of furs, their souvenirs of bows and arrows, tomahawks and wampum, the naked Indians paddled off immensely pleased with themselves.

But to Cartier this was all byplay and what he wanted was to get through this "strait", so he pressed on up the shore. A few days later he was at Ristigouche, "where we were grieved and displeased". There was no passage to China.

On his way back, heavy of heart over his disappointment, Cartier traded again at Tracadigache. Here he paused to enjoy the abundance of red and white roses, the raspberries ripe on their bushes and the strawberries, scarlet underfoot. The whole land was sweet "with a strong pleasant odor". The days were warm, the winds vibrant with the songs of wild birds. Since there was no route to China, Cartier thought he might as well name this very disappointing landlocked bay. The most appropriate name seemed to be Baie des Chaleurs.

Cartier decided to hug the coast outward for awhile. One of the mysteries of this journey in his reference to Cap d'Espoir as Cap Pratto, as though it was already known by that name. There is, indeed, extant a reference which may apply to this cape, in a letter to Cardinal Wolsey from one Albert de Pratto, written seven years before Cartier rounded it on his way up to Gaspé.

It is curious that Cartier had so little to say about this remarkably beautiful coast. There may be two explanations. Perhaps some predecessor of his had already explored and described the strange features of this part of the peninsula; or it may be that he was so bitterly disappointed that he could see no beauty in this land. Certainly after finding so much in the bleak Magdalens to exclaim over, he might have found something in this sea-carved coast to rouse his languid pen to enthusiasm. But he did not.

On the night of July twelfth he dropped anchor between Bonaventure Island and Percé Rock. Although in the sunset of that summer day it must have been drenched in color and crowned with a halo of snowy wings, yet he had no heart for it. Next morning he wanted to set sail but the winds had risen so high that he could make no headway and so he returned to anchor at South Beach.

It was two days later before he succeeded in getting away. The wind had dropped but fog drifted in from the sea. By the time he got to Gaspé Bay he had no choice but to turn aside for safety sake and seek shelter. He nosed in until he came to the gravel bars that divide the outer from the inner harbors, and once inside he dropped anchor behind Sandy Beach and found "a good and safe harbor" which he proceeded to explore in his longboats.

So Gaspé Bay came to be the setting for that scene for which he and the High Admiral had plotted over their nuts and wine. The Frenchmen were at least eight days in the Basin and very busy days they were, divided between exploring the three rivers and in trading and exchanging ideas, as best they could, with the Indians they found there. These Indians were of another tribe. The Indians of the Baie des Chaleurs were Micmacs, but the two hundred or more found by Cartier in Gaspé Basin had come all the way from Quebec to fish for mackerel. They were such poor wild men that he thought them "the sorriest folk in the world". He gave them trinkets but they seemed to have nothing to trade, for they had only breech clouts and old worn skins on their shoulders. Their hair was shaved except for a tuft on the top which they braided and dressed with leather thongs so that it stood out as stiffly as a horse's tail.

Fish brought both red men and white to Gaspé, and so these savages who were accustomed to travel to the coast to catch mackerel and salmon were the first to come into contact with the white men. Probably these Indians had met the occasional party of rough fishermen for Cartier found that though the men were willing to meet him, they sent all their women, except for two or three, away into the woods for safety. Probably these were allowed to satisfy their curiosity because they could no longer charm the strangers. But Cartier was an astute sailor. He selected from among his trinkets some little brass bells which he gave to the women. They were overwhelmed with joy and played with them childishly. Now the Indian men were in a predicament. What would they say to the other women who would have nothing to show for their modesty when all the excitement was over? Discretion was all very well but here were these favored few with brass bells to flaunt before the others. They decided to throw discretion to the winds and so they sent a messenger into the woods where all the rest were hiding, bidding them come to the gift-giving.

So now they were all friendly and Cartier learned that they grew corn in Gaspé and that they dried plums and apples and gathered nuts to carry back with them along with the smoked mackerel and salmon, as supplies for the winter.

At last Cartier prepared for the final ceremony. His men cut down trees and hewed out of them great logs to make a cross thirty feet high. From the ship they brought a painted shield bearing the arms of the King of France and nailed it stoutly where the arms crossed. Beneath it "in Gothic letters" they set up the words "Long Live The King of France".

The Indians watched all these preparations with primitive curiosity. Cartier himself was imbued with a sense of the importance of the event. While his men worked he wandered about the pebbly beach and wondered what might some day come to pass on this great haven, greater than anything of its kind in France. He selected a spot, perhaps on Peninsula, perhaps on Sandy Beach or the site of Gaspé village, and ordered the perspiring sailors to hoist the cross into position.

Not a Frenchman in the expedition but must have felt a thrill of pride as he saw that symbol of church and state set up in Gaspé Basin. It was as though each one felt himself a part of the glory of France. From a distance, the Indians, now restless and uneasy, watched the French ceremony, the kneeling hatless men, the strange symbol towering so high above them, and heard the deep voice of the commander taking possession of the country for his king. Though they could understand not a word of it, the sense was plain enough.

They followed Cartier out to his ship, grown angry and resentful, and demanded with loud words and with gestures that he take his cross away, and showed by signs that the country belonged to them. Cartier smiled at them over the gunwales of his ship and told them by signs that it was to be a landmark by which he would find his way back again next year. Then he invited the chief aboard, with his brother and his two young sons. He gave the men axes, which put the uneasiness over the cross out of their minds, and then he dressed the boys in clothes like his own, to their vast amusement and delight. He invited the boys to return with him to France. The invitation, like a royal command, was not to be denied, and so he hustled the others off the ship and held the boys as hostages. Next day he hoisted his sails and as the savages drifted around him in their frail canoes, shouting farewells to the two half-frightened, half-elated boys, he set his prow towards Cape Gaspé and sailed away home. Beyond Cape Gaspé he saw in the north a dim headland. To the west was a misty mirage of hills. It is another bay, thought Cartier, ruefully, and so he sailed towards the headland, which was Anticosti, and took his course out into the open sea. He had missed the St. Lawrence.

By the fifth of September the Sieur de Limoilou was home again in his little stone chateau, telling his wife about his adventures and his disappointments, for which she praised and consoled him. Then off he went to Paris to tell the King what he had done and to show him the young Indians he had brought home to testify to his discoveries.

That winter Cartier must have kept the boys, Taignoagny and Domagaya, in his home for he learned to speak their tongue in some fashion and they learned to speak French. From them Cartier learned the mistake he had made in crossing the mouth of the great river and turning into Baie des Chaleurs instead. The boys told him tall tales of the Kingdom of the Saguenay, of its jewel hordes and of the people who lived far up the river. The stories might have been derived from the ancient tales of the Vikings, retold by the camp fires by the old men of the tribe.

The next May, Cartier was ready to set sail again. There is a plate in the Cathedral of St. Malo to mark the spot where he stood to be blessed for his second venture and doubtless his two young Gaspésians stood nearby watching the ritual.

On this journey he coasted along the Gaspé shore under the "marvellously high mountains". He reached Quebec and wintered there and it was in 1536 before he sailed back again past Gaspé with the poor remnants of his crew, after the terrors of that scurvy-ridden winter on the banks of the St. Charles.

Cartier wrote the story of his journeys, but it was sixty-fours years before the journal of his first voyage got into print in French. The second journey had been regarded as more important than the first. The English and the Italians both published the journal of 1534 within half a century after it was written, but it was 1598 before France took the trouble to publish his tale of the Gaspé adventures and then it was a translation from the Italian. By that time the journal was lost.

Curiously enough it was in the year of Confederation, 1867, that the discovery was made in the Bibliothèque Nationale in Paris of the original manuscript of the journal of 1534. Little did the tough old mariner of St. Malo imagine the nation that would grow out of the lands he discovered or that its territory would be a Dominion stretching from sea to sea. Nor did he dream that four hundred years after he raised the tall cross in Gaspè that his deed would be commemorated by ceremonies at the same spot. The North West Passage did not lie in the Baie des Chaleurs but the nation whose forerunner he was, now has Europe for a neighbor on the east and China a neighbor across the Pacific to the west and her people can fly from one to the other in less time than it took him to sail from the Baie des Chaleurs to Anticosti.

Cartier had no one to carry on his traditions, nor were circumstances such that he was able to make any use of his discoveries. He lived the rest of his life quietly in his sturdy and comfortable home, set as a sailor would like it to be, on a hillside overlooking the sea. Like many another sailor he became something of a farmer, too. His home was built on two sides of a great courtyard and on the other sides were shelters for his goats and his chickens, and workshops for his servants. Probably in Chateau Limoilou he pondered on the follies of the long wars that prevented France from establishing herself in that "fair land" beyond the seas.

Strangely enough Cartier's first journey in 1534 synchronized with two other events that were characteristic of the age. As he was setting out for Gaspé, Calvin left Paris to found a new church in Geneva; and Loyola, a Spaniard, left Paris with the first recruits for his new Order of Jesuits. Thereafter France was convulsed with religious wars for three-quarters of a century. The spirit of reform that gave birth to the Protestant churches permeated the old church as well and by the time Henry of Navarre had won his way to the throne of France and was ready to lend his aid to the founding of New France, the Church of Rome was purged and renewed, and a missionary zeal was the blossom of its new spirit. At the same time the reformed religion had grown so in power that France then sheltered two great religious elements of almost equal strength.

So, long after the Sieur de Limoilou had been laid to rest, the three currents that had set out from Paris in the year 1534 again intermingled. New France was colonized. To the Huguenots it owed the wealth and enterprise of the merchants who founded its fur trade and to the Jesuits it owed the fierce devotion of its missionaries who went wherever the

Indians could be found. So, although the old mariner may have been impatient with the endless struggle that gave France no time to think of the lands he had discovered, yet Huguenot and Catholic alike were making themselves strong by struggle and adversity for the task that lay so far ahead in the then uncharted future.

# 9

## Gentlemen Adventurers

THE next act in the Pageant of Gaspé is set nearly a century after Cartier has departed. The religious wars are over. Champlain has been governor of a trading post at Quebec for twenty years and there Huguenot merchants are bartering for furs.

Yet even in the peace that followed the wars, the bitterness of religious animosity poisons the enterprises of such visionaries as Sieur de Champlain. Jealousies at court and personal frictions have thwarted most of his hopes and after all these years of colonization he has only a handful of settlers to show for his work on the St. Lawrence. The great Cardinal Richelieu who holds the king in the hollow of his hand, resents the enterprises of the heretics in New France, while the heretics refuse to encourage the missionaries of the ancient church. So between them both, Champlain sees New France in peril.

In the meantime some historically amusing things are taking place in Europe. While Catholic and Huguenot struggled in France, Catholic and Protestant battled for position and prestige in England. The age of Elizabeth had passed and on her splendid throne sat the son of her dearest enemy, Mary, Queen of Scots. King James brought to his court many Scottish gentlemen, among them the poet and dreamer, Sir William Alexander. Now King James and Sir William looked across the seas and saw a New France and a New England, but no New Scotland and their Scottish pride was affronted. Like good Scots, they made up their minds to do something about it. What they concocted was a grandiose scheme with a feudal flavor that looked very pretty on paper. The colony, to impress the world with Scottish scholarship, was to be called Nova Scotia. It was to consist of a number of baronies, the holders of which were to be ennobled by the King in elaborate feudal ceremonies. Since such ceremonies according to tradition must take place on the feudal lands in question, a bit of land on the esplanade leading up to the gates of Edinburgh Castle was marked off and declared to be part of Nova Scotia. And so it remains to this day. Here it was the Barons of Nova Scotia were granted their titles and lands by King James and there they pledged their swords and services to him. Sir William was overlord of all Nova Scotia and each of his barons had to swear to settle so many Scottish families on their lands within so many years.

Now that the land he ceded to Sir William belonged to the King of France did not seem to bother King James one whit. It comprised not only Nova Scotia as we know it today, but also New Brunswick and Gaspé and what France called Acadia. All Sir William had to do, to take possession, was to oust whatever Frenchmen happened to be settled already in his dominions.

Sir William, the poet, did not accomplish very much in the years of his overlordship and eventually the scheme failed, but he did leave us a name for a province, a flag and a whole host of romantic traditions. There is at least one barony of Nova Scotia still extant in the British peerage.

By the year 1627 King James was dead and his handsome young son Charles was on the throne. Charles had married Henrietta, a sister of the King of France. King Louis, thinking it might be useful to have a stick to beat his gay young brother-in-law with, in case of need, had paid only half of Henrietta's dowry. So the stage is set, with one royal young rake with empty pockets and another royal young scamp in a huff because Acadia was being called Nova Scotia. Poor, patient Champlain found himself in Quebec with empty storehouses and hungry colonists, all that he had to show for twenty years of effort.

That very year Richelieu decided to put a stop to a lot of humbug from the heretic Huguenots. He formed a fur trading business called the Company of One Hundred Associates. He ennobled a dozen of them to lend a little glamor to his enterprise and handed over to the company the government of New France with a monopoly of the fur trade. In return the Company was to settle sixteen thousand colonists on the St. Lawrence within fifteen years. News of the project brought overwhelming joy to Sieur de Champlain in his shabby fort at Quebec, not because he was antagonistic to the Huguenots, for his wife was a Huguenot, but because he believed that help was forthcoming. In imagination he could see villages along the river shores, ships in harbor and trade and agriculture flourishing as they ought to do in the rich new land.

But meantime the Huguenots who had been ousted so unceremoniously from the fur trade of New France were not taking the situation meekly. They needed the beaver skins of New France for their hat manufacturing business, and they were determined to have them. While the Charter of the Company of One Hundred Associates was being ratified in France, in England a counter-enterprise was on foot.

Gervase Kirke was a rich London merchant who had come up from the country in the days of Queen Elizabeth, a boy bent on making his fortune. His people had been landowners for two and a half centuries but he was a younger son and to him London in the days of Elizabeth was a place of golden opportunity. Having founded his fortune, he found a wife in Dieppe, the daughter of a Huguenot. They had a large family of sons and at this time, the eldest, David, was thirty years of age. Through friends and relatives in Dieppe, Gervase Kirke and his sons knew all about the Hundred Associates and the charter for the monopoly of the fur trade. They heard, moreover, about a rich fleet of provision ships that were to set sail in the spring of 1628 for Quebec. So Sir William Alexander and Gervase Kirke put their heads together and formed another company. The Scottish and

English Trading Company. The young King, nothing loath to turn a trick against his shabby brother-in-law, gave the three eldest Kirke brothers letters of marque to "explore" the St. Lawrence, and any other part of "Nova Scotia" that piqued their fancy.

Richelieu must have been caught napping, for in the spring he fitted out a fine fleet, loaded to the gunwales with goods of trade, supplies for the colony, and settlers and their families. He sent out a hundred and fifty guns to defend Champlain's fort at Quebec, but they were all stowed away below decks. He did not even think it necessary to send a convoy of warships with the ships, so confident was he that there was none to molest it. In command of the expedition was Admiral de Roquemont.

While de Roquemont was sailing his fleet across the Atlantic, three good ships under the command of three good looking young English brothers, were slipping secretly down the Thames, with every inch of sail spread and long pennants floating in the spring breezes, fast in pursuit.

The Kirke ships, being faster and lighter than the supply ships, reached the St. Lawrence first and sailed straight away up to Tadoussac. There they found Basque fishermen and one of these they despatched up to Quebec with a very courteous note asking Champlain to kindly hand over the fort to them. Captain David Kirke signed himself "your affectionate servant". Champlain gave them a stout answer though his cupboards were bare and his people hungry.

David, Lewis and Thomas Kirke did very well at Tadoussac and seemed to think Quebec could wait for another time, so they turned back down the Gulf to wait for the French ships. They rounded the long finger of the Forillon and swept into Gaspé Bay. No doubt they chuckled as they sailed right up to the gravelly barachois to the inner harbor. For there, like plump pigeons, lay seventeen French ships!

What a scene for the pageant! Even on that vast stage the masts of seventeen ships made quite a little forest with their shrouds and sails and fluttering flags. The bay was blazing blue and silver under a hot summer sun. The hills around the luminous horizon were dark with forest growth and wheeling along the shores, screaming in bewilderment like eerie voices in a Greek tragedy, were the sea birds, setting all the sky in motion.

Admiral de Roquemont put up a feeble defence but his instinct to fight was tempered by his responsibility for the helpless colonists under his protection. His ships were too heavy to manoeuvre and all his guns were in storage. A frigate or two would have turned the tables on the Englishmen but Richelieu thought he could get away without the expense of them. So there was nothing to do but surrender. Richelieu would have gnashed his teeth in fury had he been there to see the blue flag of France lowered and his Admiral rowed from his flagship to the *Abigail* as prisoner of war.

Then Gaspé saw one of its strangest sights. The Englishmen investigated their prizes, set aside those they chose to take back to England, loaded them with prisoners and the pick of the goods. Ten of the ships they put to the torch.

So of the twenty ships that sailed into Gaspé Bay only ten sailed out again, with the proud *Abigail* leading the way home to England.

You may imagine the excitement in London as the fleet of prizes sailed up the Thames and news spread about them. London loves a bit of romance and three London men with seven prize ships deserved all the flags and bells the city could muster for a welcome. The proudest merchant in London was Gervase Kirke when his boys handed over their logs and told him what they had done. And King Charles enjoyed it, too.

Paris saw another side of the story. David, Lewis and Thomas were declared public enemies of France and their effigies were burned by royal command in the Place de Grève.

The Kirkes sold their loot and ransomed their prisoners and fitted out another fleet. By next mid-June they were back in Gaspé. All they found there this time was a little sailing boat from Quebec with a handful of starving colonists who had been sent there in search of fish to sustain Champlain's people. So they knew he had neither food nor munitions. Quebec fell to them that summer without any difficulty and when the *Abigail* returned to Gaspé in the autumn, Sieur de Champlain was aboard as a prisoner of war, with most of his colonists. Lewis Kirke was governor in his stead at Quebec.

Champlain was more of an honored guest than a prisoner in the hands of the courteous David. It was three years before Quebec was restored to him. Henrietta's dowry was still owing and King Louis of France offered to pay up those four hundred thousand crowns if King Charles would restore New France to the Hundred Associates. King Charles' pockets yawned. The King got his gold and the young Kirkes and Sir William Alexander had to pocket their dreams. Acadia went back to the French and for the sake of a queen's dowry the French and the English were to struggle through another century and a quarter of conflict and many thousands of good men were to die on both sides of the lines of battle.

# 10

## *A Little Private War*

THE colonies in America, the children of Europe, carried the animosities of their mother countries in their hearts for the hundred and fifty years in which France and England were neighbors along the Atlantic. The ill-defined boundaries did not help to smooth out their difficulties and if there was nothing else to quarrel about there was always somebody or other trespassing on fur trading lands and fishing grounds. Ancient hates flashed and burned, fed by the irresponsibilities of privateer and buccaneer. And the coasts of Gaspé felt the heat of the feud.

Half a century after the Kirkes had made bonfires of the French ships in Gaspé Bay, the coast was once more disturbed by these distant quarrels. This time Boston was the disturber. Both French and English had built up a good fur trade by this time and each was using Indian tribes as catspaws in the endless border wars. For the most part the French seemed to get the better of it and consequently New England was terribly incensed at the losses they were suffering. They could not foment a war between the kings of France and England, so this time Boston decided to wage a little private war of its own. Her merchants were delighted to invest in an expedition which would demolish Quebec and drive the irritating Frenchmen off the continent. The man to whom they entrusted the enterprise was Sir William Phipps, one of the most romantic figures in New England history. Phipps was not quite forty but in those four decades of life he had packed a lifetime of adventure. He was one of the sons of a gunsmith who had twenty-six children. Only five of them were daughters. Young William was first of all a shepherd. At eighteen he left the hillsides and apprenticed himself to a ship's carpenter. After years of ill-paid or unpaid services to his master he found himself a skilled craftsman but an unlettered one. So he put himself to learning to read and write. When that was done he considered himself ready for adventure.

His next step was to build himself a ship. In spite of all his self-discipline and sober planning, William Phipps had a good deal of the boy about him yet. He wanted his ship in order to go treasure hunting in the Spanish Main!

His first venture was a failure but his second one won the interest of the Duke of Abermarle. With his help and patronage he fitted out a new expedition and went to the Bahamas. And there he found his Spanish galleon. Out of her rotting hull he raised box after box and bale after bale, of treasure trove. There was gold and silver plate, quantities of heavy doubloons, jewels and altar vessels. Phipps was an honest man and although he sold his cargo for three hundred thousand pounds, by the time he had paid off his patron and his crew he had only sixteen thousand pounds for himself. However that was a tidy fortune for the times, and the gunsmith's son was a man marked for distinction.

So when the Boston merchants got together over this magnificent project to take Quebec by private enterprise, Sir William was just the man to suit their purpose. They decided to do the thing handsomely and though at heart they were after the monopoly of the fur trade, it was an excellent opportunity to say they were doing it as punishment for the raids of the Indians and the coureurs des bois made "at the instigation of the fiery Jesuits". In that cause twenty-five hundred men enlisted and thirty-two ships rendezvoused in Boston harbor. There lay such ships as *Six Friends, Beginning, Delight, Friendship* and so on.

The flotilla set out and made its way by easy stages along the coast until on the twenty-fifth of August, "we made sail and found that this land lieth in the Bay of Heat" and so Sir William had arrived at Gaspé. The flotilla sailed along the Gaspé coast, pausing to take on fresh water and to fish. "Here we caught much cod."

Apparently they did not turn aside at Percé because Phipps' first act of war was to burn the French houses and barns and fish sheds at Barachois and the little settlement at Gaspé, before he mustered his fleet to round the Forillon into the Gulf.

The Gulf gave no welcome to this maurauding Englishman for the winds roared down out of the north and west and beat back his square-rigged ships. After several days he found he was making no headway at all. So up went the pennants and all the ships read the sign to turn and run for the shelter of Gaspé Bay.

It was only after this that Phipps took a look at Percé and found there only "the ruins of a small town, lately burned". Desolation was everywhere. The untended cod were spoiling on the flakes, the cattle lowing forlornly in the neglected fields. Men landed on Bonaventure to run up the British flag and to carry off all the dry white cod they could find.

While they lingered, waiting for a change in the weather a small barque came down from Quebec for fish. In spite of the fact that it was faced by a hostile fleet, the little ship gave battle. Phipps was amazed, but the end was inevitable. A few days later came another little ship out of the storm and it too showed the same plucky spirit, but it was made prisoner.

At last the strong north west winds fell and the spuming sea subsided into rollers that broke resoundingly along the rocks. Once more Phipps and his ships ventured out of Gaspé Bay.

Phipps reached Quebec and sent in to Count de Frontenac a demand for his surrender. Frontenac told him he was a pirate, and that his king and queen, William and Mary, were usurpers. After a picturesque battle in the lovely Basin of Quebec, Phipps ruefully withdrew, rounded up his battered ships and went back to Gaspé to lick his wounds.

He lost nine ships before he got back to Boston, but he got a title for his trouble and two years later he was made Governor of Massachusetts. And a very good Governor he was. New England remembers him because he put an end to the baiting of witches.

# 11

## *"Armies of Shadow"*

A HUNDRED and fifty years of rivalry between the French and English colonies could end only in one way,—in a war to settle the supremacy on the American continent. Back of the colonial disputes and jealousies was the heritage of centuries of political and religious quarrels between the mother countries. So when England arrived at those decades of expansion and conquest in which her soldiers and sailors placed new kingdoms at the foot of the throne, the American question had to be settled.

James Wolfe, a lanky young man with red hair and a curious profile that lent itself to caricature, was one of the most significant figures of those times. Hopelessly at the mercy of a managing mother, Wolfe seemed to find consolation and outlet in his military studies. He was not content to be merely a professional soldier, but deep in his forlorn young heart he carried an ugent vision of reforming army life. He had a huge distaste for the things that were petty or squalid in preparing for war or in prosecuting it. He was conscious first of all of his own shortcomings and took himself very seriously in hand, almost monkish in his sober pursuit of all the accomplishments and proficiency that would make him worthy of the arts of war, as he regarded them. At odds with himself as a man, he hoped to make himself content with the soldier.

When Wolfe first sailed into Gaspé Bay in the late summer of 1758 he had distinguished himself as a truly great soldier. With the rank of colonel he had been despatched with his regiment in the spring of that year with the expedition to lay siege to the fortress of Louisbourg in Cape Breton.

The siege had been an epic one and there Wolfe had brought to bear his skill, his genius for strategy and his personal qualities as a leader.

The siege was over. The fleur de lys was down and the union jack was up over the great gray fortifications. The defence had been heroic and by the time the French had capitulated it was too late in the year for the fleet to sail up the St. Lawrence to hammer at the walls of Quebec.

Despatches were sent off posthaste to Halifax and to London with the news. Halifax brought out all its silver plate and wax candles and dined itself royally. They boasted that Haligonians drank sixty thousand gallons of rum to celebrate the Louisbourg victory. In London there was a royal procession and the depositing of the captured colors in St. Paul's, to say nothing of bonfires and fireworks to pronounce the nation's exuberant joy.

Wolfe was now a brigadier-general but he had to miss all the excitement of the victory for he was despatched with troops and ships to carry the torch of war into the fishing coves of Gaspé. Wolfe's soldierly heart despised the sorry task.

"Sir Charles Hardy and I," he wrote sarcastically in a letter home, "are preparing to rob the fishermen of their nets and burn their huts. When that great exploit is at an end I return to Louisbourg and then to England."

Sir Charles Hardy was in command of the seven ships and Wolfe of the three regiments sent to Gaspé. They arrived at the entrance to Gaspé Bay on the fourth of September and made their way down those miles of superb water until they dropped anchor just outside Sandy Beach and Peninsule.

Peninsule was the sand bar that formed the northern half of the dividing wall between outer and inner harbor. Sometimes it is still called by the name the Basques gave it, Penouil, for from the earliest days of the fisheries, this sand spit was a favorite spot with white men. By the end of the French régime it had become a settlement of no little importance and Gaspé Bay was the headquarters of the French customs. As

Wolfe sailed up to the bar he saw there a very comfortable little colony. The home of the Intendant was the chief thing in the place, a two storey, high-gabled stone house with wings and great chimneys. It was a dwelling of very considerable dignity. Around it lay a garden full of bright autumn flowers. Scattered around were the cabins of workmen and dependents and a few settlers.

The gun boats were signalled off to anchor across the Bay behind Sandy Beach and the transports lay off Peninsule. When all was ready Wolfe and an escort rowed ashore to investigate. The spit lay like something under a spell. Not a soul was to be seen or heard. The cabin doors stood open, half finished tasks lay about, abandoned in sudden fear. The saw was in the log, the milk settling in the churn, the half-culled peas lay in a basket. Wolfe wandered up to the stone house, in his scarlet coat and cocked hat, his hand on his rapier hilt. The bees droned lazily over the flower bed, the white-washed stones were intense in their whiteness along the path. He pushed open the great door. There was an air of disorder, an eerie sense of turmoil and distress. For here, three days before, Intendant Revolte, lord of the manor of Gaspé, died, "with the hearty curses of the whole place". Revolte was one of Bigot's men, battening on the misfortunes of New France, one of those who hurried along the events that led to her downfall. Had Wolfe come one day sooner he would have found the dead Intendant lying in state in the stone house.

Those who hated him so had him safely buried before they saw, out on the blue rim of the horizon, seven stately British ships. The widow, Madame Revolte, who perhaps was not among those who hated and feared the Intendant, fled to the woods with all her maids and neighbors. Some three hundred French, men, women and children, were in hiding in the hills around. No doubt some of the venturous ones were stationed where they could spy out the doings of the invaders and went back to report that the bay was swarming with red coats. Certainly they must have guessed that this meant the fall of Louisbourg and it was with hearts filled with misgivings that they lay hid in the autumn forests. September had come and the winter was not far away. What might fate have in store for them at the hands of these exultant enemies?

Wolfe guessed what had happened to the inhabitants and next day he sent parties of soldiers into the woods to search for them. Flight was impossible. The hills were as dangerous to the women and children as the enemy. Sadly they stood their ground until the red coats had overtaken them. But their fate was happier than they could have hoped. "Everywhere he went with his troops," wrote one of his company, of Brigadier-General Wolfe, "desolation followed, but he would not suffer the least barbarity to be committed upon any one of the persons of the wretched inhabitants." Wolfe found that kindness need not be incompatible with duty and manliness. So the widow French lady and her motley attendants were brought back from the woods and offered food and protection and transportation to France.

Wolfe liked the great Bay of Gaspé. It was a lovely time to linger in it. Clean cut against the cold blue September sky the hills were molded in monumental forms. The hardwoods had turned, and here and there, in patches on the slopes around were effects of color that must have delighted him. From the vantage point of the decks of his ship the great valleys of Gaspé opened up to view, with the rivers winding their way through the meadows. The woods were full of game, the waters of fish. After the reek of crowded transports, the wretched business of destruction at Louisbourg, the smoke of battle and the spilling of blood, Wolfe found in the peace of Gaspé a cleansing quality that appealed to him. There were fifteen hundred men under his command and a host of officers, so after he had delegated the unwelcome duty of destruction to them, he moved ashore, took up his residence in the Intendant's stone house and set out to enjoy a month of hunting and fishing and an outdoor holiday.

It was a happy interlude in his tragic life. Let us hope his days were full of quiet happiness and contentment for there was to be but one more chapter to his life. Out there in the Bay, at anchor near Sandy Beach, lay his funeral ship,— the *Royal William*. In a year's time she would be bearing past Gaspé again, with the young general, wrapped in his military cape, lying dead between her decks, with the conquest of Quebec to crown his memory with renown.

One by one the destroying ships came back to Gaspé to report to the young general in the Intendant's house. Mount Louis had been burned. The Intendant there offered a hundred and fifty thousand livres as a bribe to have it spared. Pabos with "twenty-seven good houses and seventeen indifferent ones" had been put to the torch along with forty boats. Grande Rivière is an ash heap. Sixty houses and eight fishing boats have been destroyed. Colonel James Murray went farther afield to Mirimachi. He was a mere youngster of fifty-four at this time. Years later he married, had his first son at seventy-eight and lived to be ninety. When Wolfe, his friend and commanding officer, died on the Plains of Abraham, Murray took command and became the first British Governor of Quebec.

At last even the leisurely robbing of fishermen of their nets and burning of little homes was done. The fifteen hundred soldiers were back aboard their transports. Wolfe had taken reluctant leave of his Gaspé home. The prisoners were all stowed away for their journey to France. But Peninsule could not be spared. Cabins and barns, fish shed and mansion, all were put to the torch. When the fleet set sail slowly all was indeed desolation in Gaspé.

To this day there are relics of the French where the little settlement of Peninsule once stood. There are the blackened stones to tell of the English bonfires, a smokeless chimney to recall the tragedy of war.

Trivial though this work of destruction seemed, it had more significance than appeared on the surface. The loss of the Gulf fisheries was a great blow at French power and prestige. They were the breeding places of seamen and the reserve on which the French navy depended for reinforcement. To utterly destroy the fishing villages was a taunt to France that her power was waning and to cut off her supply of fish for fish days was to bring home to every Frenchman the implications of the war. So Wolfe's stay at Peninsule was not without its importance in international affairs. If he made a holiday of it, he deserved it and the shelter of Monsieur Revolte's stone manor house was a last kindly gesture of the gods of war, for he hated ships and sea voyages, even though all his fame was to arise out of expeditions that carried him across the seas to glory and to death.

Wolfe got home to London at last to receive his share of praise and reward. Pitt and the King made General Wolfe the commander of the land forces of a great new expedition against Quebec. A magnificent fleet was rounded up and put under the command of Sir Charles Saunders. Saunders had two hundred vessels, ranging in size from the greatest warships of the day down to whaling boats. His flagship, the *Neptune,* carried ninety guns. In all there were forty-nine fighting ships with nearly two thousand guns between them. Of ships crews and fighting men there were eighteen thousand in all. Under Wolfe was an army of nine thousand of the finest fighting men in Britain,—including the Highland regiments. Wolfe himself had helped to subdue Prince Charlie's followers and now he was proud to command the fighting Highlanders in their fearful kilts and tartans.

The first rendezvous was Louisbourg. The second was Gaspé Bay. Never had the old French harbor seen such a sight. By the first week of June they had all assembled and were ready to start for Quebec. Doubtless there were spies in the hills above the Basin to see the fleet dividing into three squadrons, under red, white and blue pennants. From Louisbourg to Quebec was a thousand-mile journey and Saunders intended it should take on something of the pageantry of a naval conquest. Never before had any admiral had such an armada to command.

99

It took the ships two days to weigh anchor and form the sea procession. Some hurried on ahead to chart the route, some to bar the river to the French ships which might be on their way up the St. Lawrence.

It was difficult navigation all the way. There were no charts, no pilots, no lighthouses, no bouys. Their way lay by St. Paul's Island, Bird Rocks, Cape Gaspé, Anticosti, Point de Monts, Bic and Tadoussac.

They sailed on a fair June day. Much depended on the weather, for contrary winds and stormy days would disperse the fleet and make havoc of the navigation plans. If such a thing happened all the ships had orders to reassemble in Gaspé Bay. Anxiously Wolfe and Saunders scanned the skies but nothing could have been better or luckier. For three perfect days they sailed on with practically every ship within sight of Saunders' flagship. That must have been one of the proudest journeys in the annals of British seadogs. As far as he could spy with his long glass sailed the ships of his command, every sail bent to the breeze, flags flying, guns bristling.

When all was well under way off Cape Gaspé the *Hunter* was ordered to put back into the Bay to look about for any ships that might have had to drop out or were in difficulties of any kind. She found the Bay empty. The gulls circled screaming over the silent beaches and the ruins of Peninsule. The *Hunter* ran back along the length of the Forillon and signalled that all was well. From the Cape the ships took fresh bearings and veered into the Gulf. The times were "big with the fate of nations" but for the time being it seemed like a pleasant jaunt. Wolfe took the opportunity while the *Neptune* rounded the Cape to write his will. On the table beside him lay the miniature of the lovely woman who loved him but would never be his wife. Lovingly he bequeathed, out of his meagre fortune, enough to set the miniature in a jewelled frame in which it was to be returned to her after his death. He sensed the fate that lay ahead of him. There would be no pleasant aftermath to the siege of Quebec. Let us hope that she had loved him with more than a common love and that this last year of his life was warmed with the tenderest affection a woman has to give. When the miniature was returned to her she could not bear to see her own painted face among the jewels but she wore the talisman, stitched into a bit of black velvet, until she died.

The gulf winds were hospitable and the great fleet swept up the river to the drama of Quebec. Broodingly Wolfe watched the shores and their villages, under the purple Laurentian hills, and as he paced the decks he dreamed his own dreams. If only he might be spared when the work of conquest was done, how pleasant it would be to come back, with Katherine Lowther as his bride, to rule the newly won colony. Instead of burning fishermen's huts, to help build them new ones. But the angular, ill-fated young Englishman never saw the hills of Gaspé again. Conscious of his destiny, he was torn between gratitude for the greatness of his opportunity as a soldier and deep-rooted doubts that sprang from his knowledge of the folly of men and the mystery of life.

And so they sailed past Gaspé, a water pageant forty miles or more in length, to grapple with the enemy for the possession of a green and pleasant land.

# 12

## *The Indians of Gaspé*

THE Micmacs who claimed Gaspé as part of their hunting grounds were a small but decidedly interesting tribe of Algonquin-Huron stock. They are today the only Indians in America who are as numerous as they were when they first came in contact with the white man. They have very definite characteristics. For one thing they have been a long-lived people. One of the Indians who met Cartier when he was a boy in Baie des Chaleurs was still alive,—very much alive,—and the chief of his tribe when the French settled Port Royal. He told Champlain and his companions that he remembered the coming of the French ship three-quarters of a century earlier. Nicholas Denys, when he came to Acadia, discovered Micmacs who went hunting at the age of one hundred and twenty to a hundred and forty. The oldest man he knew was a hundred and sixty, according to his own account. Cortereal and Cabot each took home with them Indians who were probably Micmacs as evidence of their discovery of a new land.

The Micmacs lived in birchbark tepees, sewed with roots of black spruce, when the French came to Gaspé, just as they still do when they are hunting and fishing. They made beautiful dyes from vegetable matter, red, violet, blue, flame and many others and with these they painted themselves and decorated their possessions. They loved to adorn themselves for war and for ceremonial dances.

According to Indian custom, a man might have two or three wives if he chose and if he could support them. The first of them to present him with a son was mistress of the household. They were a very simple and democratic people and their religion was based on a faith in the sun as the basis of all life. They had a very beautiful ceremony in which newly-born children were presented to the sun. On such an occasion the mother took the child up into a high place with an unobstructed view of the horizon, such as Mont Ste. Anne at Percé. Here above the wooded slopes where the sea spread to the distance, she stripped him of his swaddling clothes and laid him on a skin. Then lifting him in her outstretched arms she offered him to the great spirit in the sun, praying that he would make her child strong and fearless and happy.

At other times the whole tribe would resort to such places as the altar-like dome of Ste. Anne's for the tribal ceremonies of dedication and supplication. Then the chief himself would throw aside all his garments and, naked and with outstretched arms, he would face the sun, imploring its beneficent care for his people.

The Micmas studied the heavens and had a crude knowledge of astronomy and the points of the compass. They had names for many of the stars. Like most Indians they had a great gift for oratory and their tongue is a very flexible and expressive one. Rand, who was a student of the Micmac tongue, said that its declension of nouns and conjugation of verbs "are as regular as the Greek and twenty times as copious.".

Like all people who live close to nature, their imagination peopled the world with all sorts of gods and spirits. In thunder storms they always built a fire out in the open and tossed into it gifts of tobacco to assuage the anger of the Thunder God. They persuaded him in that way not to throw balls of lightning at them. Never, they said, was an Indian struck by lightning. They had a wealth of legends, among them one relating to the flood, like the Montagnais. Their chief god, Glooscap, was a kindly being, always helpful and happy, a most cheerful sort of deity.

One of the occupations of the Micmacs was the making of wampum. This was one of the most precious of all things in the possessions of the Indians of all tribes. It consisted of a kind of bead, usually white or purple, made from shells by rubbing them down until only a ring with a hole in the center remained. Wampum was very rare and very valuable. Girls collected it as gifts from lovers as European women collected jewels. Its chief use was in the making of strings or belts which were exchanged in the making of treaties. When it was woven into a design each form was significant of the terms of the treaty. The Keeper of the Wampum in any tribe was the equivalent to the keeper of the royal archives. For generations Indians could repeat the terms of treaties as they were recalled by the designs on their collection of wampum belts. The Micmacs traded wampum with the tribes farther west.

The Micmacs from the beginning of the white man's regime were friendly to the French and hostile to the English. Indeed their devotion to the French cause prevented English settlements in their tribal lands and although they were officially at peace with the English at the close of the war in 1760, it was not until after the War of the American Revolution that they became entirely reconciled to the English cause. When the French Canadians made their frequent raids on the New England colonies, raids that so incensed the English colonists that they sent Sir William Phipps' expedition against Quebec in retaliation, usually Micmacs followed the raiders and lent them help in the work of fire and slaughter.

The Micmacs have a wealth of legends but it is difficult now to extract those that belong to the Indians themselves and are not colored by their association with the white races. But among them is one which foretold the coming of Europeans.

The legend goes that once upon a time a young Indian girl had a strange dream which troubled her for many days. She went to the wise men of her tribe and asked its meaning. She said that in her dream she had seen, a small island drifting towards the coast. On it were tall trees and living beings like men, dressed in rabbit skins. Among them was a tall

104

man in a white robe. The wise men sent her away scornfully, saying they could make nothing of her silly dream.

A few days later the girl who had been wandering on the beach, ran back to her people around the fire and told them she had seen an island, such as she had dreamed of, coming slowly towards the shore. They went back with her to the beach and saw for themselves that certainly some strange thing was taking place. At last the island reached a point near them and they could see strange creatures moving around under the tall trees. With them was a man in a white robe. They all landed and presently it was the man in the white robe who learned to speak their tongue and then taught them mark-writing. The wise men were very much displeased with the whole affair, for one thing because this dream had come to a mere girl, and for another because they had not been quick enough to catch its meaning and foretell the new religion which the man taught them with his mark-writing. Thereafter the wise men opposed the white priest because they had missed the chance to prove that they had previous knowledge of what was to come and therefore could not turn the situation to their own benefit.

As a matter of actual fact the Micmacs were among the first of the Indian tribes to contact the white fishermen. Each year as they came down to Gaspé for mackerel they met the Basque and Norman and English fishermen searching for cod. At last the Indians became so accustomed to the return of the white men that they met them every year at appointed places. At the sight of the first ships far out at sea they lit fires on the headlands which made pillars of smoke by day and bright beacons at night by which the white men's ships came safely to anchor. So when Cartier came the Micmacs were quite accustomed to the rites of trade and barter. The fishermen were a rough lot and the philosophical Indian must have been puzzled from time to time at their crudities and rapacity but there is no record of bloodshed between them.

Membertou was the most famous of the Micmacs. When Sieur de Monts planted his little trading colony at Port Royal, Membertou and his tribe hung around the post, greatly intrigued with the white men's ways. He was a frequent guest at their table and was invariably friendly and helpful to them. The Recollects found in Membertou their first convert to Christianity. Following the chief's example his sons and grandsons and many of his people professed the new faith and were duly christened in great state in 1610. There is a little church at Annapolis Royal to commemorate the event. Membertou would not accept the ways of the Christians unquestioningly. He balked at the Lord's Prayer. "I will not ask for daily bread because I may get no fish," he said sturdily.

At another time a missionary fell ill while he was visiting Membertou's tribe. Membertou was very uneasy, so he visited the father and urged him to write a letter to the French post saying that he had died of disease and that Membertou did not kill him. The priest declined. "I may write the letter and then you will kill me," he pointed out. "Then pray Jesus that you may'st not die so that we will not be accused of killing thee," suggested the old man.

After Membertou's spectacular tribal conversion, the Micmacs were not so easily induced to accept Christianity. One missionary worked among them for two years and had at the end of that time christened only one small child.

The Indians had a great deal of scorn for the white man's way. One of their chiefs, Silmoodwa, once went to France on a visit. The king asked him to show the court how the Indians killed their game and dressed their meats. A space was enclosed in the forest and a deer driven in. Full of scorn, the Indian amused the ladies and gentlemen of the court by showing how he killed with an arrow, skinned, dressed, smoked and dried the meat. He made no effort throughout to conceal his contempt for those who were amused by the performance.

LeClerq, the missionary, relates an incident which discloses the inherent Indian contempt for the white newcomers. He says one day a Frenchman asked his help as interpreter with the Indians and urged LeClerq to ask them why they did not adopt European ways. The French traders were anxious to see the Micmacs dependent on their manufactured goods. First of all they wanted to see them living in houses like the white men, so that they would give up their nomadic lives. The Micmacs listened to the questions and then replied with the oratory dear to the Indian heart.

"I am greatly astonished," began the chief, "that the French have so little cleverness as they seem to exhibit in the matter of which thou hast just told us on their behalf, in the effort to persuade us to convert our poles, our bark, our wigwams into those houses of stone and wood which are tall and lofty, according to their accounts, as these trees. Very well. But what do men five or six feet in height need with houses which are sixty to eighty? For, in fact, as thou knowest very well thyself, Patriarch, do we not find in our own all the conveniences that you have with yours such as reposing, drinking, sleeping, eating and amusing ourselves with our friends when we wish? This is not all, my brother, hast thou as much ingenuity and cleverness as the Indians who carry their houses and their wigwams with them so that they lodge wherever they please?"

He went on quite reasonably to point out that the French called the Indians' country a little hell, and France a terrestial paradise, but the Indians, from observation, considered themselves much happier and "content with the little we have" whereas the French were very anxious to leave their terrestial paradise every year and risk the seas and all their dangers to come to this poor country of Gaspé. If France is a country of every luxury why do you come here to enrich yourselves? he asked. "You must be incomparably poorer . . . you glory in our old rags and miserable suits of beaver." In miserable Gaspé these superior French engaged in fishing cod which was "the wherewithal to comfort your misery and the poverty that oppresses you". The Indians, he pointed out, had no need to go in search of comforts. All they needed lay close at hand. "We feel compassion for you in the sweetness of our repose and we wonder at the anxiety and cares you give yourselves night and day in order to load your ships." He pointed to their rude living . . . cod, cod, cod, for dinner, supper and breakfast. "You get all your morsels at our expense." Which, therefore, he asked calmly, is the wisest and happiest? And as a final thrust he informed the Frenchmen that there was no Indian who did not consider himself infinitely more happy and powerful than any Frenchman.

Such then were the people who hunted and fished in Gaspé at the coming of the white men. The Micmacs then numbered between three and four thousand people. They are now about four thousand. Those who actually lived in the Gaspé Peninsula were called Gaspésians and many of these are now on the reserve at Cross Point. They have retained their speech and many of their characteristics and are intensely proud of their traditions.

# 13

## The Cod in Politics

CONVULSIVE events in human history, such as the Reformation in Europe, have many curious and far-reaching effects. The tenor of life was disturbed in every direction and the fisheries certainly did not escape the re-alignment of society.

A great part of life in the days before the Reformation circled around the monasteries. There in the quiet, solid centers of religious life flourished the arts and all the deeper learning. There the books and manuscripts were collected and the monks, free from the frets of the medieval world, studied in peace and copied the precious manuscripts for those who demanded them in other schools and libraries, since there was no printing. From time to time they produced new manuscripts of their own. There, too, philanthropy was fostered. The poor, the sick and the sad turned to the monks and nuns for succor. Under the conditions in which they existed the monastic orders did what they could for those in need. It was unfortunate that the monastic tradition divided the religious and the scholarly from the common folk and created an abyss between the contemplative life of the few and the working life of the many. And in spite of their attempts to aid the people who suffered under the feudalism of the middle ages, the monasteries amassed great wealth and the religious orders exercised considerable power.

The Reformation was a revolt within the decadent church led by priests who found the worldliness of the priesthood too far out of alignment with the teachings of Christ and of the early church. The result was a movement of protest, but ultimately a Protestant Church; and moreover a great reform movement within the Roman Catholic Church as well which proved to be very important to its history. In the turmoil of adjustments while these things were taking place many of the wealthy monastic institutions were dispersed and their lands and wealth appropriated by the state. With this transfer of wealth went also a transfer of responsibility; when the Reformation disturbed the balance in the old medieval society, the state assumed the duties of the orders it had dispersed. The king and his aristocrats had to busy themselves with books and scholarship and encouraging education, and also with caring for the poor and the sick.

Among the most curious problems of the Reformation was that of the fast days. The Roman Catholic church had specified a great many fast days in every year and on these days the people could not eat meat but they could eat fish. So great was the demand for fish in the Catholic countries that a large part of the population depended on the fisheries for a living. France continued to be a Catholic country after the Reformation,—a fish-eating nation. Thousands of its fishing boats were afloat on the North Atlantic from the Bay of Biscay all the way round the North Sea to Iceland and Greenland, Newfoundland and Gaspé. From these seafaring people France recruited her navy.

The Tudors of England were a shrewd and far-seeing family. They realized that Protestant England would suffer the most appalling consequences if her fisheries became depleted. England depended on her navy, her wooden walls, and the men who manned her ships. Unless England ate quite as much fish as she always had done, she would not have the fisheries to support her navy. So, they decided, England must eat fish, not for the good of her soul, but for the good of her fleet. English fish-eating became a sort of "political lent". The Tudor fast days supported the fisheries and the fisheries supported the navy, and presently Queen Elizabeth, great Tudor that she was, brought England to a new age of sea power. So it was that in the century and a half that followed, Frenchmen and Englishmen contended bitterly over their rival claims to fishing grounds.

So here really lies the secret of the British taste for fish and the ubiquitous fish and chips. British sea power still depends on the men who go down into the sea in ships to search for food.

However, even this is changing, for now that ships are machines even landlubbers from the prairies often become good seamen, but in the days of sail only men bred to the sea could be counted on for naval recruitment. And what scorn these old sailors still feel as they contrast the old skills of the sail with what they call pushbutton navigation!

The greatest fisheries in the world are in the North Atlantic. The Catholic countries depend upon them for their fish. Spain, Portugal, Italy, Argentine, Brazil and Uruguay and some others, import vast quantities of North Atlantic dried and pickled fish. Gaspé does a big export of certain types of dried cod to the Italian communities in the United States. The North Atlantic fishing grounds are divided among several countries, but Canada has the most extensive fisheries of any country,—deep sea, offshore and fresh water fisheries. Now that Newfoundland has decided on joining the Canadian federation as the tenth province, she will bring additional fisheries of immense value into the Canadian scene.

The dried cod of Gaspé is considered the finest procurable because the cod fishing is off-shore; that is, the fishermen secure their fish a few miles off the coast and return each day with their catch. In a few hours after the cod is taken from the water it is in brine and the curing process has begun. Deep sea cod fishers who prepare the cod on their ships cannot give it the same systematic attention that it gets in the fishing stations on shore. So Gaspé cod is granted to be the best on the market.

The fishing banks of the North Atlantic teem with innumerable millions of cod. "It is a kind of inexhaustible manna," as Nicholas Denys so aptly put it three centuries ago. For at least five hundred years systematic cod fishing

111

has been carried on in these waters and as many are now being taken out as ever in their history. A cod produces four and a half millions of eggs, so nature provided amply far in advance of man's religious and political needs and set here in the cold northern waters titanic stores of food.

Fishermen knew this part of the world long before explorers became curious or kings covetous. It is an old tradition in Jersey that on their way to Iceland some Jerseymen were once blown off their course and found themselves on the Newfoundland Banks where the waters were literally alive with cod. They say in Jersey, too, that it was Jerseymen who went to Bristol talking about Newfoundland who gave Cabot news of land in the west.

After Cabot had made his first trip of exploration and named Newfoundland he went back to tell that Tudor king, Henry the Seventh, what he had seen. He said that when they reached the cod banks and looked down at the fish in the sea they seemed like a floor of silver. Cabot told the king that he had lowered a basket over the side and then drew it up full of fish.

As surely as nationalism developed in Europe, so surely did the interests of the fishermen clash. Some of the nations quarrelled among themselves and while they did so other nations preyed upon them all and pirates took toll of the hardworking fishermen homeward bound with cargoes of cod. The Turks were among the fiercest of these buccaneers. In 1612 alone, more than a thousand British seamen were carried off prisoners by the Turks and scores of ships were destroyed. The Moors made it their business, too, to get their share of ships and cargoes. In one disastrous season Plymouth reported twenty-seven ships and two hundred men taken in one day.

The pirate "racket" was brought to its peak, however, by an enterprising Englishman who organized piracy on a business basis. He was named Peter Easton, and he had a fleet of ten sails. He marked out a sea area which was recognized as completely under his control. Instead of taking and destroying the fishing ships, he merely taxed them. Those who paid the tax cheerfully got safely home to market. Those who refused took the consequences.

From the proportions of the pirate enterprises which flourished on the fishing trade we can arrive at some idea of the importance and magnitude of the trade itself. Fishing was one of the adventurous traffics of the centuries in which the new world was discovered and explored and colonized.

# 14

## *"La Grande Barbe"*

WHILE King Louis of France was hedging over his sister's dowry, the Scots in Acadia and the Kirkes in Quebec were reaping what profits they could out of their temporary possession, hoping and praying it would be made permanent. But, as we know, the bulging bags of gold louis were more alluring to King Charles than that vast wilderness on the other side of the Atlantic where a handful of adventurers were trying to plant his colonies. Acadia and New France went back to King Louis.

So after a delay of a few years the Company of a Hundred Associates got down to work in earnest. One of its first jobs was the ousting of the Scots from Port Royal. The gentleman they selected to take over Acadia from the Barons of Nova Scotia was an officer named Isaac de Razilly. In 1632 he arrived, elegant in gold lace and armed with parchments and seals, to take over his duties as Governor of Acadia.

Monsieur de Razilly was one of the Hundred Associates and so had cause to be ardent in his duties in settling and developing Acadia. For one thing he should always be held in remembrance, and that is that he planted the colonies of Acadians who did so much to give character and romance to the lands they tilled and harvested. They had a long and troublous history but they were a people of strong character and strong attachments. Even today an Acadian remains first of all an Acadian, no matter where you find him.

Monsieur de Razilly brought with him two devoted lieutenants. One was his cousin, Charles de Menou, Sieur d'Aulnay Charnisay, usually known simply as Charnisay. The other was Nicholas Denys, the hero of Gaspé, the valiant, unfortunate, seigneur of the land of cod.

From the beginning Charnisay was employed in matters which took him far afield, while for the first few years Denys was closely associated with Monsieur de Razilly. Denys was a matter-of-fact man, with the qualities of a merchant and trader and colonizer and so he was employed in founding fishing and lumbering stations, while Charnisay, wielding the sword as well as the controversial quill pen, got himself embroiled in the disastrous affairs of the Bay of Fundy.

Three years after his arrival Monsieur de Razilly died. It was the same year that Governor de Champlain died at Quebec, and so confusion fell upon the two colonies at the same time.

Charnisay by reason of his relationship and his influence at court, was appointed to succeed the good Razilly. But Charnisay was the stormy petrel in the affairs of Acadia, and the feuds that set the colony by the ears for many years to come impinged on every life in the settlements along the whole coast. .

Razilly was buried in his settlement at La Havre and Charnisay immediately transferred his little capital to Port Royal. There he felt like a king rather than a king's deputy and he set out to rule with an iron rod and to wipe out whatever rivalry he might find.

Meantime over at the mouth of the St. John River, on the other side of Fundy, Charles de la Tour had built himself a fort and was conducting a very profitable fur trade with the Indians. He and his agents travelled up the water routes and portages to the St. Lawrence or to the Baie des Chaleurs where they met the Indians with their reeking bales of skins. Surveying Acadia from his perch at Port Royal, Charnisay saw in Charles de la Tour the greatest threat to his own supremacy. He sharpened his talons and fumed impatiently. The next ten years are a record of the furious feud between the two men.

Things got to be so bad in Acadia that by 1638 the King decided to divide the territory into three parts, to see if that could satisfy these fiery midgets fighting on so vast a stage. All that lay south and west of the Gut of Canso went to Charnisay and La Tour and everything north and west he put into the hands of Nicholas Denys.

But there was no peace. The eternal jealousy of Charnisay, obsessed with his own importance, would permit no peace. He drove La Tour into exile and ousted the hard working Denys and so made himself master of the whole of Acadia again. But it was not for long. In a few years he had thwarted the King and thrust his greedy fingers into the possessions of others. Then one night in May of 1650 Charnisay was crossing the Basin of Port Royal in a canoe, when he was upset in the darkness and was too far from shore to make himself heard. Chilled and exhausted at last he lost his grip on the canoe, perhaps realizing in those last hours that to-morrow all that would be his of the vast kingdom he had taken by guile and force would be six feet of grave. So died Charnisay unshriven and unmourned.

The death of Charnisay was the signal for the return to Acadia of his two rivals, La Tour and Denys. They seem to have been friends for their interests did not clash. La Tour's heart was in the fur trade, Denys' in the fisheries. La Tour wanted the St. John River and the travelways of the interior. Denys wanted the wild coast and the pebbly beaches for his cod flakes. They might have worked things out amicably but a third man arrived on the scene at Port Royal,—Charnisay's creditor, the business man, La Borgne, out for mortgages and profits. Whether Madame Charnisay was catspaw for La Borgne, or whether that colorless woman for once undertook to play the Amazon, does not appear very clearly, but once at least she managed to make Nicholas Denys her astonished prisoner. Yet, when La Borgne drove Charnisay's children out of their father's home, it was to the big-hearted and big-bearded Denys that they turned for shelter. He kept them at his palisaded post at St. Peter's throughout one winter.

116

La Tour, safe in his stronghold on the St. John, laughed La Borgne to scorn, made a trip home to Paris and came back with a bulky parchment dangling with red seals, that made him overlord of Acadia in Charnisay's place. Denys, slower witted than his neighbour, followed him to Paris, bought from the Hundred Associates all the land that once had been granted to him and gained the title of Lieutenant Governor and Lieutenant General, although all he had to rule over comprised his own fishing establishments. In the same year, by way of making a final settlement of the Acadian tangle, La Tour married the widow of his old rival, Madame Charnisay. For all we know they lived happily ever after.

But things never stayed settled for long in Acadia. Just as La Tour felt he had things in hand and Denys was settling down to his fishing in earnest, England pounced upon Acadia and my Lord Cromwell began carving it up among his friends. For some curious reason they left Denys unmolested and like a philosophical fisherman, he stuck to his nets and his flakes and let those rule and quarrel who had a taste for such things.

Denys was the first great Gaspésian, in the sense that he had a great love for Gaspé and was devoted to her interests. Like many another fine and simple character, he seemed to have failed in all he undertook and yet his dreams eventually came true and the future he foretold for Gaspé was even greater than he hoped. Up and down these picturesque shores he sailed in his little ships, his great beard blowing about his ears, his heavy brows shading his piercing eyes, all the while planning and contriving for his beloved fisheries.

His first settlement was at St. Peter's in Cape Breton but as he became more and more interested in Gaspé he moved up to the Baie des Chaleurs. First on Miscou Island and later at what is now called Ferguson's Point near Bathurst, on the New Brunswick side of the bay, he developed his fish stations. Much of his time was taken up with fighting encroaches on his grants. It was a far flung seigneury and those who chose to poach on his beaches and his woodlands very often did so quite deliberately in the hope either that he would overlook them or that he would not have the power to put them off. When he did succeed in ousting them he made bitter enemies for himself. Sometimes his ships were seized on various pretexts and if he recovered them it was always at the cost of fine or bribes or both. Once when he was congratulating himself on having recouped some losses by fur trading with a new tribe of Indians who had found their way to his post and had stowed their bales of skin safely away out of sight, he went to bed chuckling. But during the night he was called out by shouts of "Fire!" and he had to stand by helplessly while store houses, goods and even his own house were consumed by the flames. The fire was never explained but apparently Denys was convinced that it was the work of one of his enemies. Everything was gone, "flour, wine and arms". It was after that that he turned his back for good upon his old estate and moved to Baie des Chaleurs.

His personal life is only faintly sketched in as the background of his years of devotion to the fisheries. He was born of one of the most celebrated of old French families, that of de Fronsac. About the time that Denys came out to Acadia with Monsieur de Razilly, the great Cardinal Richelieu adopted the title of Duc de Fronsac. Denys himself never made use of that part of his name, but he named the Gut of Canso, the Strait de Fronsac. By 1677, when he was twenty years of age, Denys' son, Richard, was known as Richard Denys de Fronsac.

Nicholas himself was not in any sense a courtier. He was made of simpler and sturdier stuff. Bluff and hearty, unskilled in the use of insinuating ways, he had many of the qualities that made Jacques Cartier a great discoverer. His heart was always with the sea and with the men who lived by it. Apparently Denys did not find time to marry until he was past middle age. His son, Richard, the apple of his eye, was not born until he was fifty-nine years of age. Of Madame Denys we hear not a word, though the woman he would choose to rule over his rude mansion must have had a shrewd, homely wit and a capacity for meeting pioneering emergencies. Doubtless he chose a woman of good birth but who was satiated with the routine of life in France and ready to share an adventure overseas. The home he took her to in Baie des Chaleurs was a log chateau with four bastions and a palisade of sharpened cedar logs. Six cannons poked their black noses through apertures in the walls as a precaution against enemies, though his white ones were more to be feared than his red ones. Round about his house was an orchard of pear and apple trees which he grew from seed and a great garden in which he grew all sorts of vegetables and small fruits. Beyond spread his wheat fields within the encircling forests.

The government now owns the site of Denys' old fortified chateau. The site of the house is awash at high tide, for the sea had eaten away part of his garden. Nearby under an ancient willow are the graves of some missionaries and "a French Admiral" as the old timers say. The French Admiral is none other than that stout old Nicholas Denys, "La Grande Barbe" of Gaspé. For like Razilly, La Tour and Charnisay, he sleeps in the Acadia of his hopes and dreams.

Denys established the first sedentary fisheries in Acadia. Before that fishermen had come only for the fishing season and returned to France as soon as their catch was done. Denys pinned his faith on fishing settlements where the fishermen would not only settle on the seabeaches, but they would bring their wives and children there as well. To his dismay, even the fishing began to fall off. Here were vast untapped resources in cod, salmon, mackerel, herring, sardines, sea cows and seals, but instead of the fleets of ships from France increasing in number, they grew less and less. Here "where we have been from time immemorial", he pleads, let us build up a fishery colony second to none in the world.

He saw shrewdly enough that it was internal jealousy, intrigue and greed that were ruining the French colonies. "Exposed to the encroachment of the strongest" the colonists had too much to contend with. When he grew lyrical about

Gaspé he added sadly: "One can live there with as much satisfaction as in France provided the envy of the French one against the other does not ruin the best intentioned plans."

He boasted of the fertility of the country. He said it produced the finest wheat in the world and the finest apple trees. He said his seigneury was "the principle part of New France" and that it could produce coal equal to that of Scotland, and he sent home some to France to prove it to the King. He maintained that the climate of Gaspé was the same as that of France since it lay in the same latitude and "it is easier to people than any of the lands of America where we have colonies because the voyage is so short". But Gaspé remained as beautiful and as tenantless as ever.

When Denys was seventy-four years of age, after he had lost half a dozen fortunes and been buffeted by many adverse winds, he still had the heart to settle down to writing a book about his beloved fisheries. He may not have had "the symmetry of words", as he deplored, but he had a burning love of the land and a life time of experience at his command. His book is the classic of the cod fishing world and in it the fierce old Viking speaks out of every page of his own long devotion to the sea. Perhaps he never saw the translation of his book into Dutch for it appeared the year of his death and it is not likely that it reached him in his log chateau in time to gladden his old heart.

Apparently he followed up the appearance of his book in print by a visit to France. What a sight it must have been to see this weather-beaten old man in his archaic finery, making his way up to the King in the shimmering splendor of Versailles. There all the lavish luxury that the seventeenth century could provide was heaped in profusion about the magnificent King. Painted walls and gilded frames, acres of mirrors, silver furniture, sparkling fountains and hundreds of marble figures set among the trees, all these to testify to the grandeur of the King and the splendor of his court. Among the courtiers moves old Nicholas Denys, bowed with the years, with his ancient velvet coat hanging loosely on his

120

wasting bones, his old fashioned peruke framing a face as hard and brown as an Indian's. One hand grasps his stick and the other rests on the arm of the handsome young man who walks beside him, Richard Denys de Fronsac. There is a name to make the court pause, even if his great, springing figure, his easy, natural grace, had not already intrigued the interest of the ladies. But Nicholas is close to ninety. He has lived for half a century among cod fishermen and Indians. His voice has lost its polished accents, his speech is pithy but hardly courtly. And he is confused by all this magnificence, by the bored King and the simpering all around him. His audience is anything but satisfactory. Richard leads him away again and off they go on their way to Gaspé. All the way the old man recalls things he meant to say to the King. Back home again he wrote a letter to the King. He begged pathetically for another audience. It would be worth going all the way back across the sea again to say those things he had forgotten to say, for the sake of Gaspé. He could not believe there was no place at court for a man without youth or influence.

"The lustre of your majesty when I came before you to present your majesty with a fox, make me forget what I had proposed to lay before your majesty concerning the expenses you have been at for Quebec and also what your majesty might do for New France, that is, that part of your dominion from the mouth of the St. Lawrence to the English possessions." He had not the skill in writing, he protested, to explain himself but he pointed out to the King that "by bestowing on this country only one quarter of the expense you have bestowed on Quebec it would produce in one year more than Quebec can do in forty". France, he pointed out, was too dependent on English and Dutch fishermen while indeed Gaspé could supply the market and bring in a royal revenue "and besides would be a nursery of able seamen to serve in your majesty's fleet".

What might have happened if royal Louis had listened to the petitions of his loyal old pioneer writing from his lair on the Baie des Chaleurs? What if Louis had fortified and colonized Gaspé? If Frenchmen had settled the rich valleys of New Brunswick? Perhaps the British might never have taken Louisbourg or rendezvoused in Gaspé Bay for the siege of Quebec nor Wolfe have died on the plains of Abraham.

"It is too large a subject for my dull pen," writes old Nicholas.

Three years later, at the age of ninety, the staunch heart failed him and he was laid away under the willow tree. The following year the seigneury that had been his for thirty-eight years was revoked because he had not settled eighty families on the land as he had promised to do. The land he loved was lost to his name and family. Five years later Richard, his son and dearly beloved, was lost at sea at the age of thirty-six. The only descendants of Nicholas Denys are those through his daughter, Marie, who married Sieur de la Valliere of Quebec.

Perhaps from somewhere, where the complexities of life here in this world are simplified, Nicholas Denys knows that the Gaspé of his dreams had been realized, that the sedentary fisheries are among the best in the world; that the book he wrote is read more frequently today and with deeper appreciation, than ever before; that in spite of his awkward phrases and stilted words, the readers love the bluff old author who had a tale to tell, and told it well. If he had "every possible literary fault" he had also a great many virtues, of which honesty and steadfastness in his purpose were not the least. He was as big and dramatic and simple as the country of which he wrote. If he failed it was because, in a day when duplicity and silkiness of words were keys to success, he was content to be an honest man.

# 15

## 'Tis an Honest Trade

COD fishing has not changed in any of its essentials since Basque and Norman and Channel Islanders first spread their catches to dry on Newfoundland and Gaspé. The fishing stations of today are permanent villages but all the operations of curing and drying are exactly the same as they were in the days of Nicholas Denys. Throughout Gaspé, in every little cove, the fishing boats with their dark sails, land the limp silver bodies of the cod on the gravel beaches, and instantly the work of heading, cleaning, splitting and salting begins. In the great stations, the "fishing rooms" carry out the same processes on a larger scale, but "making fish" is the same wherever it is done.

Nowhere has the process of fishing and curing been described more graphically or accurately than in the book that Nicholas Denys wrote in the hope of rousing the interest of France in the fisheries of Acadia. In Denys' day as many as five hundred ships crossed from France to the cod fisheries. Each ship had its beach in what is now Nova Scotia, New Brunswick, Baie des Chaleurs, the Gaspé coast or Newfoundland. For hundreds of miles the coasts were studded with little summer settlements preparing food for Europe.

Each fishing ship carried provisions for six months and a cargo of salt for the curing. The crews were engaged on a sort of partnership basis and paid in proportion to the season's catch. The proceeds were divided into three hundred parts, usually two hundred parts for the owners of the ship and one hundred parts to be divided among the crew. Every last man of them, from captain to cabin boy had his allotted share. Each ship, in addition to its crew, had thirty to fifty men for the fishing.

The trip across in the spring was pushed with the utmost speed. Once arrived at their destination the whole company set to work with a will to prepare for the fishing. The fishing boats were usually brought over on the ships in parts, each part numbered and ready to be assembled. Each man was assigned his duty and those who went to work under the ship's carpenter hammered and caulked and tarred from dawn till dark to get the boats ready. Oftentimes boats were hidden away in some inland pond or up a stream, and if there were any of these they had to be found, transported and renovated for the season's work.

Others were put to work building huts for the fishermen. They consisted of sides made of stakes driven into the ground and woven with branches of fir into walls. Over them the ship's sails were tied for roofs.

One of the chief parts of the fishing station was the stage, built on stakes at the water's edge. It was placed so that at the end of each day's fishing, the fishermen could sail in to the end of it and toss his cod off onto the platform. If the tide was low he sometimes had to toss the cod over his head.

Then there was the cookhouse where the steward was installed for the summer. A house was built, also, for the captain, who kept up a show of no little dignity. Incidentally, he kept the stores in one half of his house, safely under lock and key.

Meantime the beachmaster had his boys at work on the "grève" or pebbly beach which had to be kept thoroughly clean and free from grass and seaweed. Refuse had to be raked off and, if necessary, gravel had to be carried from other parts of the shore to make it all fit and proper.

Last but not least were the great flakes on which the cod were spread to dry. They were made much as they are today, except that instead of wire netting, branches of trees, stripped of their foliage, held the fish and let the air circulate from below while the sun beat down on them from above. The

Acadians still use the old French name for these, which was vigneaux.

At last everything was ready for the fishing to begin. The ship lay at anchor, stripped of all sails and shrouds, as though it was laid up for the winter. Eight or ten boats, depending on the capacity of the mother ship, lay moored in the cove. A long cable, attached to a great stake on shore, was anchored tautly into the water. From this cable the boats all swung at safe distances from each other. The stage was finished, tables and barrels stood waiting the uncaught cod, the acres of flakes lay waiting. The captain bustled about from beach to cabin, casting his eagle eye over everything, to make sure all would be well when the rush began. On the last day of preparation, the men dropped off to sleep with the knowledge that there would be a minimum of sleep or relaxation for the next few weeks.

On the first day of fishing everything was in a whirl. Nets were set for bait, of which the cod required vast quantities. Herring was best, for its silvery flash under water caught the greedy eye of the cod. Before dawn the little boats started out for the fishing grounds. Some were rowed, some used sails. Each had a favorite spot, selected on a pet theory of the fishing crew. The cod were caught on lines. If the fishing was good the men were busy all day, baiting hooks, hauling up the lines, tossing the fish aboard, baiting the empty hooks and dropping them back again for more fish. Towards sunset, their day's work was done. Weary and hungry, they set out for the beach, timing themselves so that only one boat approached the stage at a time.

Their food all that long day consisted solely of sea biscuits, of which each boat carried a box. Of these the men might have as many as they wished; for drink they carried a keg of wine and water, "which does not intoxicate" says Denys naively, "for from one barrel of wine there are made four, or sometimes, five without any other miracle than some water".

As a boat arrived at the stage, the fishermen tossed the fish up on long hooked sticks. Up on the stage boys stood

125

waiting to help if the fish were too heavy for one man to heave up.

For every three fishermen in a boat there were two men ashore to maintain the station, for there was a great deal to be done once the fish were landed. Up on the stage the cod were washed in great tubs and tossed onto the splitting table. The splitters and cleaners were highly skilled men and all their work was done in rhythmic movements learned only after years of training and generations of aptitude.

On the splitting table one man siezed a cod, slit it round the gills and from throat to tail, then pushed it on to his neighbor, who, with a deft movement, almost a single motion, removed the colorful entrails. Then, twisting the cod, he broke its neck and tossed its head away. Another swift movement pushed the cod towards a barrow and another separated the liver and roes from the entrails and deposited each in its separate receptacle.

The most important single operation was done by the slitter whose sharp knife and strong wrist performed a remarkable act of skill, repeated hundreds of times every day. The cleaned and headless cod came to this slitter on its side. Pressing it against a little ridge of raised board, he inserted the knife beside the spine at the neck. One incredibly swift slash down to the tail laid the cod open flat. On the unerring skill of the slitter depended the grade of the dried cod, for much store was set on fish neatly spread and evenly balanced.

As fast as the cod passed through his hands it was pushed on to a boy who removed all clots of blood and bits of loose skin and then tossed it off into a barrow. Weighing was the last operation before the cod reached the barrel of brine.

Tails to the center, they were neatly arranged and covered, with just the right sprinkling of coarse salt. Usually, in those days, the big cod were pickled in great casks and the smaller cod, after a certain number of days in brine, were carried out for their first exposure to the sun and air.

It required about a month of sunlight to cure the cod on the flakes. White fish was the term used to describe a properly dried cod, for the drier it became, the whiter the flesh. Day after day they were turned by the tireless station workers, for curing depended on constant care and a sharp lookout. When the cod became slightly dry they were piled up at night in stacks of eight or ten or twelve under little cabin-shaped wooden covers. When they were stowed away so they were said to be "en mouton". It kept them free from the dampness of the night and preserved the warmth they had absorbed during the day. The dryer they got, the bigger the stacks became at night, until as many as twenty-five of them lay under each little wooden hood. If rain threatened they had to be carried into the fish houses and when the flakes were dry again, they all had to be carried out and spread once more.

The final drying of the cod was done on the beaches. A foundation of rocks was laid in a circle. The hard, dry fish were piled up, skin side down, the necks laid precisely on the circumference and the tails to the center. The pile might be anywhere from six to twelve feet in diameter, and when complete, and the biggest cod laid on top, piled to a peak in the center, sheets of spruce bark would be laid over the whole to keep off rain. When it was complete it looked something like a windmill without arms.

Seventeenth and eighteenth century fishermen were queer, unwieldly figures. Each man wore a coat of sheepskin and loose, long-legged boots that came up just below his knees. Over these he wore an apron of sheepskin with the fur turned in and the oiled side out. This, tied around his waist, kept the coat close about him and then hung over the top of his boots so that the water, whether sea water or rain water, slid harmlessly off and left him warm and dry. Over all this he had another long apron from neck to thighs, and on his head a great woolly hood. Three such grotesque figures shared a boat.

Sometimes the cod moved on to some spot at a distance from the main fishing station and then the fishermen "made a dégrat" or moved after them and set up a temporary station to take advantage of the occasion. At times the fish would come in more than ordinary numbers to the fishing grounds and the small boats would be overwhelmed with the wealth of the catch. When these days came the work at the beach increased beyond the capacity of the shore staff and so, after the day's fishing, the fishermen had to turn in and help on land. They would be allotted to speed up the cleaning and salting operations and it was sometimes twelve or one or two in the morning before they finished. Only then did they get their supper and often they fell asleep over the food, too weary to taste it, and were roused again at sunrise to get out to their boats for the day's work.

All week long the men lived on their sea biscuits, and cod and mackerel and herring. Their drink was the watered wine, "this economical magnification" as Denys once called it, but there was good reason for that. The men grew very thirsty at their work and if they had been allowed anything stronger the results would have been disastrous. On Sundays they rested and had pure wine and pork to celebrate the day. The captain fared a little better for he planted a garden and had his salads, and he brought with him from France enough poultry to provide him with eggs and roast fowl.

There was often a good deal of ingenuity shown in the contrivances used to promote the fishermen's work. For instance, when they had to work far into the night the station was wierdly lighted. Here and there tripods were set up, made of slender tree trunks. On them were set blocks of wood. Suspended over the blocks were bowls of oil, each with a tiny hole in the middle of it. The blocks were set afire and the drops of oil fed them and threw up tremulous yellow flames. How strange the beaches must have looked with the tongues of fire throwing their dancing, flickering light over the wet tables, the gleaming knives and the silvery bodies of the cod, while grotesque figures, all in rhythmic motion, sang the ancient chanties by which from time immemorial fishermen had speeded up their work.

Even so long ago they had discovered the way to make cod liver oil. They used great casks, just as they do now, with two plugs in the side of each and a network of twigs and branches inside. The livers were thrown in on top and left open to the sun until the oil seeped out of the putrified and reeking mass. Blood and water settled on the bottom of the cask and the oil floated just below the twigs. One plug was removed to draw off the oil and the other the waste fluid at the bottom.

When at last the season was over, the ship was rigged again and the boats hidden away from the eyes of envious neighbors. The hull was filled with rock ballast and the rocks covered with fir branches. The walls of the ship were lined with fir, the storerooms were emptied of whatever remained. Then the loading began. For every quintal of fish that went aboard a stone was dropped in a hat as a counter. The choicest fish went into the dry storerooms for safety, for much of the fish was spoiled on every voyage, as much as a third having to be allowed for waste. The rest went in as bulk cargo and was battened down as tightly and dryly as possible. Then they set off for home, with their little cannon planted on deck to ward off, if possible, the pirates lying in wait to take toll of the honest work of the fishermen.

Such was the fishing industry when Nicholas Denys was striving so hopefully to establish sedentary fisheries. The phrase originated with him. He saw in a policy of permanent fishing stations great good for the glory of France and the advancement of Acadia. Several others tried it, as well as Denys himself. One was an Englishman named Tiveden, who started at Cape Sable; another was Denys' encroaching rival, Sieur de la Giraudiere, who cost him so many losses. Another was Captain Pierre Doublet, who had come out with the silver miners to the Forillon. Denys regarded him with too much contempt to admit him as a serious rival. "He thought himself wise by hearsay," he said scornfully. Doublet came to Percé to announce that he had a grant of the Magdalens and though Denys pointed out that the Magdalens

129

belonged to him, it troubled Captain Doublet not a bit. Neither did it worry Denys. Old Nicholas chewed his beard and dropped an eyelid over one eye. He told Doublet to go ahead. "We shall not have much trouble to chase you away." Denys was right. In two years Doublet's losses were so great that he packed up and went away never to come again.

Denys experimented with trawls and nets to catch cod. Since machines were making stockings, ribbons and silks, and had "multiplied the industry of men without their number," he planned to do the same things for the fish trade, since he thought that profit was "the first incentive of all conditions of men". Even in faraway Gaspé, in the seventeenth century, the machine age had begun to impinge upon her pioneers. But machines have rumbled away for centuries and Gaspé has felt their steel clutch least of all. Gaspésians still catch their cod with hooks.

# 16

## *Percé*

A CONTEMPORARY philosopher, in the midst of a profound book on mathematics and the evolution of human consciousness, pauses to say that "a thing may acquire its own individual and unique soul and in that case it exists quite independently of our receptivity . . . many things possess such souls, especially old things".

Even without scientific authority to justify that thought, few who come to Percé will deny that Percé has a soul of its own. True, it is the most dramatic spot on the Atlantic coast. But many places are beautiful, or even fantastic and many more are romantic. But Percé is all these things and something more.

Percé Rock, painted and photographed times without number, from all the wrong angles, and detached from its surroundings, may seem banal to those who have never been to Percé. In these representations it is a big wall of rock with a hole in it, and a means of publicizing an over-advertised spot.

This rock with a hole in it has about as much relationship to beauty as a seal with a ball on its nose to natural history. Percé Rock is a part of Percé as a whole, and that Percé is not just a geographical spot, it is a mood and a story, a place-spirit, something that reserves itself from the hasty and impatient, the superficial and unimaginative, but for the traveller with open eyes and an open heart, Percé is generous.

It is a curious destiny that awaited Percé, and indeed, all Gaspé, this role of pouring into tense and tired visitors the resources of the peninsula in natural beauty, human friendliness and the intangibles of serenity, at some times, of stormy energy at others, and yet always the healing and recreating power which natural beauty exerts over the human spirit. Among the invisible exports of this country are uncountable memories and experiences carried away by men and women from all over the world, who come to see Gaspé. The more leisurely they are, the more they see of the land on foot and at varying hours of the day, the more they learn of the life and labors of Gaspésians, the greater the enrichment they carry away with them, back to the offices and classrooms, the factories and salesrooms of the cities in which they spend all but their holidays.

More human folly is due to loneliness than to almost any other emotion, and many of the tense, anxious, successful citizens of big modern cities are basically lonely people, chiefly because they no longer take the time off to cultivate the deep human relationships which could obliterate that loneliness. We have more intellectuals in the world today than we have people who are capable of undemanding, understanding love, and so perhaps much of the rushing around that sophisticated modern people are doing is unconsciously a search for those rare human situations which satisfy the human spirit. And here in Gaspé, unsophisticated, often very poor, homes are overflowing with the emotions that come from shared responsibilities, collective work at home and in the fields, and the loyalty of fishing crews, facing daily danger together. There is a native wit and a native grace about the Gaspésians that the traveller will flavor if he takes the time to visit with them, over the nets or over the fences. For if there were not these human graces, if these homes lacked affection and loyalty, co-operativeness and ingenuity, life on these broken acres and these gravel beaches would be bleak and unlovely indeed. Gaspé is prosperous today but that is something recent and new, and the spirit that enlivens life among the Gaspésians is something that has been wrought out in generations of poverty, oppression and isolation. They take their prosperity gaily because they never became dour or embittered in times of hardship. Gaspé homes are overflowing with young Gaspésians who, along with the religion and the skills of their parents, also learn the little graces of life that prompt them to wish all who pass their way "happy journey" and to say to them "you will be welcome if you come again".

These are some of the things the intelligent visitor must know before lovely Percé reveals herself generously to him. The search for beauty is an attitude to life and for those who acquire that attitude, Percé is an unforgettable experience.

From far across Malbaie, as the road rounded from St. Peter's to Barachois, we could see Percé,—a far away miniature Percé, but unmistakable,—on the other side of the Bay. But when we approached Percé wrapped herself in swathing veils of thick white mist. From Barachois we could see the fog lying like clouds along the tops of the mountains that lay between us and Percé. The road runs through a little settlement called The Corner of the Beach,—Coin du Banc,—and presently turns into the pass over the hills. We moved up in such great curving sweeps of road climbing up the hillsides, with woods on one side and gorges on the other, that presently we found ourselves in the fog. Up and up and up we went in one persistent climb, as the fog grew whiter and thicker and closed in upon us.

At last we reached the summit and on a little table land a few dark trees emerged, eerie ghosts, motionless and lonely. Then the road plunged down before us, almost lost in the woolly intangible mists. It was an awe-inspiring descent, but as we neared sea level we had a sense of bafflement. Below, somewhere was the loveliest spot in Gaspé, as everybody said. For us there was nothing but the implacable fog. Perhaps that was our penance for an indifference to Percé due to those banal photographs and bad paintings we had so often seen.

As last we slipped from under it. The road had reached the sea. As though under a half-raised curtain, the stage of Percé, between the sea and the ceiling of fog, revealed itself as lying in a great bowl of broken hills, with fishing boats and white cottages all around.

Later the fog lifted but the sun came and went fitfully, playing queer tricks, flashing silvery swords across the water, ripping the veils of cloud to show light on the ribbed majestic rocks. Even hushed by fog, and half-concealed, Percé was beautiful; it haunted us with some unexpected and unnamable quality.

And then clouds and mists suddenly disappeared as though the spell was lifted. Percé Rock was not merely a stone wall with a hole in it. It was part of a beautifully proportioned whole, related in form and color to the sheer bluffs of the mainland, to the sharply scalloped Murailles, to the rosy brow of Mont Ste. Anne and to the distant Island of Bonaventure.

Percé Rock is the axis around which the extraordinary charm of the place revolves. For a rock, there is nothing less static to be found anywhere. It is as many faceted as a great jewel. Its form, color and significance changed with every step we took. From the heights above the village, the Rock looked like a great ship nosing into port. From a dozen points the Rock looms over the village, over the beaches, over the roads, in compositions so lovely and so deeply moving that the creative artist's or photographer's problem is to make a selection of its points of vantage. We went about taking a little here and a little there, like pilgrims with begging bowls.

We climbed Mont Ste. Anne by the ancient Indian trail and from the red rocks of her sheer, naked brow, we looked down on a sight that cannot be excelled in all America. On that sunny afternoon we stood twelve hundred feet above the sea, with the woods behind us and the horizan unbroken on every side. As far as the eye could see along the coast, the shore lands were broken up into patches of fields and meadows. From the height the whole thing looked like an architect's model countryside. There was the Roman Catholic church, the clustering houses set squarely along the village streets, the white roads running out into the surrounding country, the fields ploughed into brown homespun, or shaved into the greenest of green velvet, between the straight fences. Each separate tree with its separate shadow, seemed set out by a careful hand. Each tiny house, picked out by the slanting sun, was dazzling white and the roofs a bewitching black. The little English church on the hillside, surrounded by its graveyard, looked exactly like a toy. The twin beaches, north and south of the Rock itself, were sickles of sand and the tiny fishing boats were black specks bobbing around on the very blue sea. Everywhere the sea glinted and scintillated great silver coins of light, flung lavishly about like a royal bounty. And there, at the heart of it all, riding proudly, lovely, alight and colorful, was Percé Rock.

When we climbed the undulating road that once led round the coast to Malbaie, we passed the point called romantically by the fishermen, Pic d'Aurore,—The Peak of Dawn,—and again we saw the village from another angle. When we walked to Surprise Hill and then to Cap Blanc, we saw new facets of its charms. At other times we walked over the rocks at the water's edge and watched it closely, and sometimes we crossed at low tide to search for fossils in its stoney sides.

Percé Rock was in a generous mood and withheld nothing from us. After showing us so much of beauty from pale golden dawns to the silver mysteries of moonlight, there was still another picture to carry away with us. It was the last day of our stay. We had been over in the shadow of the Rock on an afternoon of intense color and great ragged clouds. The light came and went moodily. We had turned our backs on the Rock after the ritual of our farewells and were homeward bound. Some one turned back and cried, "Look!" There, revealed in that last lovely gesture of farewell was the soul of Percé. The clouds had parted somewhere over the hills and we could see "the light distilling water of gold as the sun dropped". The great rock seemed some insubstantial, vibrant thing, as though the golden scarf of light was trying to veil the sentient soul that the rock concealed. Every rib and angle of the stone was deeply etched with light and shadow, its sides dripped rose and amethyst and green behind the shimmer of gold. It seemed to have neither weight nor matter, but only the spirit "that things possess . . . especially old things". Born of sea and storm, of frost and fire, and the terrible tumult of the elements, old and wise in the ways of wandering men who from age to age have sought shelter in its shadow, Percé Rock has "acquired its own individual and unique soul". The revelation of it came in that fleeting moment between shadows, like a scene from a mystery in a temple.

So "from a hundred visions, I make one" and in that last glimpse of Percé and her Rock was born an imperishable memory.

Percé Rock and Mont Ste. Anne have been landmarks for travellers ever since Europeans first came to Gaspé. The story of how Mont Ste. Anne got its name tells how a Frenchman, probably a fisherman, was lost in a fog as he neared Gaspé. His young son was with him and the frightened child begged his father to make a vow and pray for safety. To please the child the father vowed that, if the fog lifted in time to save the ship he would burn a candle as high as the mast of the ship to good Ste. Anne. No sooner had he made the vow than the fog lifted and he saw ahead the sheer red rocks of a mountain. As soon as he saw that he was safe he regretted his rash vow. A candle as high as the mast of the ship! But there was a way around that. He named the mountain for Ste. Anne, as an honor of more duration than even his long candle would have been.

Percé Rock is 288 feet high at the "prow" and 215 feet at the sea end, and about a third of a mile long. "I have seen it when it had only one opening," wrote Nicholas Denys. Since then other openings have worn through the rock and the arches over them have broken, so that today again there is only one. One is opening in the detached column of rock at the outer end, once a part of the Rock itself, now isolated by the fall of the bridge over an opening, in 1845. It lies several hundred feet off Mont Joli and can be reached dry shod at low tide. The Rock is an immense treasure house of fossils and they can be found in the broken stone at its base. The rock in and about Percé is very colorful, some of it red conglomerate and sandstone, some uptilted beds of limestone, green and grey. The picturesque Murailles, with their peaks known as the Three Sisters, with Mont Joli, Cap Cannon, the Rock itself, are all the result of what is known as "modern wave work" for the changes in and about here are so swift, geologically speaking, that they are measurable. Percé Rock is breaking down at a rate that dares geologists to set a limit to its life, but as it is thousands of years away, it is too early to "view with alarm" its ultimate fate. Some fishermen can remember changes in the beach, emergence and subsidence.

The entire Gulf coast is a treasure hunting ground for geologists. Frequently museums and universities send groups of men to work along the shores gathering specimens so that, word by word, they can work out the puzzles of our world that have waited so long to be solved.

When the Percé beaches were first used as a fishing station no one knows. Fifty years after Cartier mapped the coast of Gaspé, a hundred and fifty French ships went to the Gulf every year to fish. Some of them undoubtedly came here. With Nicholas Denys it first comes into recorded history and he tells us that in his day there were five hundred fishing boats about Percé and as many as eleven ships anchored in the vicinity of the Rock.

When Laval came to New France in 1659, the first landing place of this first Canadian bishop was at Percé. He arrived in May and transferring to a small boat, perhaps a fishing boat, he spent a month on his way to Quebec, visiting all the scattered remote settlements along the St. Lawrence, baptising and confirming as he went and by the time he reached Quebec he had consecrated a hundred and forty people into the church.

In 1665, Jean Talon, the Great Intendant, landed here also and in 1689 the most dramatic figure in the history of New France, Comte de Frontenac, came to Percé, bringing back with him the survivors of the Iroquois who had been taken prisoner by French treachery at Cataraque and sent to France as galley slaves. Frontenac was returning to the vice-regal kingdom that he loved and served so well and from which he had been ousted by jealous and foolish rivals.

In 1672, the year that old Nicholas Denys published his remarkable book on the merits and delights of Acadia, including Gaspé, by the irony of a royal whim, Percé was carved out of his great seigneury and granted to his nephew, Pierre Denys, Sieur de la Ronde. Pierre's seigneury stretched from Cap Blanc to Malbaie and half a league up Gaspé Bay, to say nothing of the miles it reached into the hills of the interior. He set seriously to work to develop the fishing rights he had acquired. He had two partners, Charles Bazire, of Quebec, and Charles Aubert de la Chesnaye. The Aubert family added the name de Gaspé to their titles and perhaps this was the origin of it. Years later, Phillippe Aubert de Gaspé, an old man imprisoned for debt, nursing in his heart the traditions of the old regime (which had passed when he was a boy and the English came to New France), spent the evening years of his life in writing a book that has been a classic in Canadian literature, in its original French and in its English translations, "Les Anciens Canadiens".

Pierre Denys had his fishing station at Gaspé but he built his manor house at Barachois in Malbaie, by the Little River that flowed through the gravel bar. Behind the bar his boats found winter harborage, safe from the pounding seas. It was indeed a manor house of fine proportions, with plenty of room in it for the fifteen people that comprised his household. There was a large courtyard, with various storehouses and workshops around it in the old French fashion. There was an acre of garden, cribbed in a white fence, twenty cattle in his stables, and thirty acres of cleared and cultivated lands.

In summer Denys took up his residence at Percé to be on hand to superintend the drying of his cod. At Percé, too, he built a chapel and a mission house.

Up until 1663 all Gaspe had been part of the Jesuit mission, but they abandoned the field and when Pierre Denys undertook a mission to Gaspé, his young son, Joseph Denys, a twenty-three-year-old Recollet, and his friend, Didace Pelletier, of his own age, undertook the work of spreading their faith not only among the Micmac Indians, but among the riotous fishermen as well.

Young Father Pelletier had a gift for architecture and although the mission church must of necessity have been a simple enough affair, he took the construction of it very seriously. Probably he realized that in such a setting as few church builders had ever had at their disposal, he must build something worthy of the scene, something that would not spell out to the Indians the insignificance of the French and the grandeur of their own natural world. In 1683 Father Pelletier chose a spot that is believed to have been on Mont Joli, not far from the spot where the white cross stands today, so that the snowy walls and the pointed spire of the church of St. Peter of Percé might be seen by the fishermen far at sea and prompt them to think of Him who had sought his own first followers from among fishing folk. In the spire was a bell that sounded its appeal along the shores and into the forests, calling red men and white alike to the sacraments of the church. Not conent with a chapel at Percé, Father Pelletier built another one, the chapel of St. Clare, on Bonaventure Island.

Alas, the life of the little Mission of Percé was to be short. Its fate is told in a bulky book of adventures written in the seventeenth century by Father LeClercq, the best known of all the Gaspé missionaries, because his work has been best recorded and that by his own impetuous pen.

It was in 1675 that Father LeClercq, the Recollet, set off from Quebec. He landed at Percé in the midst of the fishing season. He spent the following winter at the home of Sieur de la Ronde at Barachois. His Superior at Quebec had provided him with the books and papers necessary to study the Indian language and he spent months diligently at work. When spring came and he tried out his newly acquired learning, he discovered to his dismay, that he had been supplied with the wrong language! He had to set to work and begin all over again on the Micmac tongue. That summer he lived in a wigwam with the Indians on Gaspé Bay and the next winter moved on to Ristigouche and then Nipisguit, where old Nicholas Denys lived.

Two years later Father LeClercq had devised a Micmac alphabet or set of hieroglyphics, to be used as baits for the memories of his wandering flock. He realized that they had no mind for abstract ideas and their wits wandered when they were supposed to be saying their prayers. The symbolism he invented attached ideas to words and so they got along famously.

However, although the Indians were childishly interested in all his strange activities, they were painfully unimpressed with Christianity and in 1679 he gave up the Gaspé mission altogether. It was seven years later before he left Canada and we leave him at last as the superior of a quiet monastery at Lens in France.

It was there, in the cloistered peace to which he had retreated, that he heard of the fate of the Percé Mission. It was in a letter from Father Jumeau who, on his way to Percé, had been wrecked off Cap des Rosiers. He was rescued and later on went to Percé to see the scenes of desolation and desecration there. Nor were his troubles over. When he set off after seeing the depredations of the American invaders of Gaspé, in the hope of reaching France on a fishing vessel, he fell prisoner to privateers from Flushing who boarded and seized the French ships.

The story Father Jumeau told related how two privateers from the English colonies had sailed into Percé under French colors so that the French were unprepared for the disaster that came upon them. There were five ships at anchor near Percé Rock. The crews and the settlers, of whom there were then eight or ten families, fled to the woods. The privateers put prize crews on the ships, burned eighty fishing boats and then landed to spend eight riotous days,—among the earliest holiday makers at Percé!

They were English and Protestants, so the mission house and the chapel were merely symbols of the hated papacy. Drunk with the success of their enterprise, the English poked about from cabin to cabin and storehouse to storehouse, in search of loot and mischief. The church they turned into a guardhouse where they amused themselves by taking shots at the images of the saints and the paintings of St. Peter and the Virgin.

The commander of the Englishmen devised a final ceremony to desecrate the altar of these fishemen and Indian converts. Taking the crown from the battered image of the Virgin, the privateers tied it securely on the head of a captured sheep. The poor, bleeting woolly beast struggled until they tied her feet together. Then in solemn mockery, probably wearing the vestments of the priests, they carried the sheep to the altar and there slew it, in derision of the mass, which they abominated. After that they set fire to the four corners of the church.

When they had sailed away with their prize ships and their loot, and left the entire settlement devastated, the refugees came back from the woods to mourn over the fate of Percé. Father Jumeau, poking about in the ashes of his little white church, found the charred carcass of the sheep, with the twisted crown rakishly upon its head.

## 17

## *Traditions of Percé*

WHEN Father Jumeau found the sacrificed sheep and the desecrated crown, he had only one consoling thought. Out of the desolation of Percé, one thing was inviolate and that was the cross that stood serenely on the top of Mont Ste. Anne.

Long before the white man came to Percé there was a trail from the sea to the summit of the mountain. The Indians, time out of mind, had climbed Mont Ste. Anne to make their ritual of gratitude to the Great Spirit that lived in the sun. There the Indian mothers had carried their new-born babes to offer them to the Great Spirit for his blessing and protection.

Realizing the significance of this mountain top to the Gaspesians, Father Jumeau had conceived the idea of translating the spiritual meaning from pagan rites to those of the Christian church. He had won both Indians and Frenchmen over to the idea of carrying to the mountain top a symbol of his church, the cross. They worked together to make a huge cross that would be seen very far away at sea and when it was ready they went together in procession to the top of the mountain for the ceremonial program so dear to the hearts of seventeenth century Frenchmen, and so impressive to the Indians. This was the cross that stood on Mont Ste. Anne when the raiders pounced on Percé. The enthusiasm of the American privateers for desecration did not mount to the point of climbing the trail to the distant cross on the sheer red rocks. So they let it stand. Ste. Anne was "two musket shots from the shore" as the Frenchmen put it and to reach the cross would have been no mean climb.

Today the old Indian trail has been cut into a road and
the trip to the top is one no visitor should omit. The only
way to get there other than by walking, as the Indians did,
is by jeep. But a less appropriate approach to the crest of
Mont Ste. Anne would be difficult to imagine! It is worth
the time and effort required to walk the path which is not
too difficult, since every year the whole parish makes the
religious pilgrimage to the top, the very young and the very
old all joining together in this traditional community act of
devotion. The road begins by passing the Roman Catholic
church and rises into the hills, through pleasant woods, and
finally crawls along the edge of a deep gorge.

Many years ago, in order to fulfil a vow made in an entreaty
to Ste. Anne, a Gaspésian engaged a young artist in France,
named Cotté, to create a giant figure of Ste. Anne with Mary
as a child. The great wooden figure the artist sent to Percé
was to be covered with leaden plates. At the cost of great
effort and ingenuity, the figure was transported to the top
of the mountain. There she replaced the gilded cross that had
long since rotted away. For many years Ste. Anne stood on
the heights but Gaspé weather was more than Ste. Anne
could withstand indefinitely, and at last the figure toppled
to the rocks. Rather than let it lay there so forlornly, the
people of the parish brought the pieces down and stored them
away in a lumber room of the church. And there they lay
for many years. At last, however, some of those who remembered Ste. Anne's vigil on the mountain top decided that
something must be done to restore her to her rightful place.
Percé had little money to spare in those days but in a cause
like this perhaps the good Ste. Anne herself took a hand. Certainly the money was forthcoming and presently Ste. Anne
was restored and whole. With the same devotion shown by
the parishoners of Father Jumeau, the people of Percé followed Ste. Anne up the mountain side to her old place at
the top. There one summer day they said mass on the spot
made sacred by the invocations of pagan and Christian alike.

So when you have finished your climb you will see Ste. Anne, a serene Ste. Anne wise in her maturity, the long simple lines of her figure and draperies expressing the artist's feeling for the beneficence of this woman saint so beloved by sailors. On her arm, peering up into her face, is the little figure of the child, Mary, searching perhaps, the artist would have us believe, for the secret of that strength of which she would stand so much in need in the years ahead.

At the foot of the road to Mont Ste. Anne stands the church erected to succeed to the little white church of St. Peter on Mont Joli. Behind the church is a sad little cemetery very strangely placed on a queer gravel hill that the people of Percé long ago chose for the burial of their dead. It has only a few feet of elevation and it is alone in the middle of the fields that were first cleared by the fishermen cutting fir branches for the fishing flakes. On the top of the hill is a tall black cross and the figures of the Calvary. Without any plan or order the graves cluster as closely to the cross as they can. To carry a coffin to a grave in this bewildering little acre of God must be difficult. The dead of Percé crowd together like sheep about their shepherd. Sad little crosses mark the graves, some crudely carved by unaccustomed hands, some painted white, and some, in lieu of paint, are wrapped in black cloth or white cloth. Some are only inscribed in lead pencil. Here and there a slate stone or a bit of marble marks more enduringly some single grave. Here lies a little stone in a wooden crate, weathered by the passing years. It has never been unpacked, perhaps because the grave was forgotten by the time some absent one saved enough to send this stone that was intended to keep some memory green. Yet over it all hangs something of that dignity that death always bestows. Purple Indian tea and golden rod, blue bells and Queen Anne's lace spread a splendid pall over the hill and its dead, except where some faithful hands have cleared little spaces about some graves and marked them out with colorful stones from the beach. It is in keeping with the spirit

of the people of Percé that at last they become one again
with the very stones of their birthplace.

Percé is one of the important stations of Robin, Jones and
Whitman, the successors to the eighteenth century enterprises
of Charles Robin. Their flakes border the main road in Percé
and their fish and store houses stand near the water. Facing
the road on one of them is an old ship's head. Around their
property are the little old boundary stones with the initials
C.R.C.,—Charles Robin and Company.

They do not turn curious visitors away from beach or fish
house, so here you may see all the processes which Nicholas
Denys described so graphically in his seventeenth century
book about Gaspé. Here the fishermen come about sunset
with the day's catch and toss it ashore up onto the beaches
into the hands of those who take off the head, slit and clean
the cod, separate the livers from the entrails, with exactly
the same motions that Denys' men used when he owned Percé
as part of his vast seigneury. You may follow the patient
horses as they drag the barrows into the fish house. There
the fish are weighed and put down to the credit of the fishermen. A quintal is a hundred and twelve pounds, a draft is
two hundred and twenty-four pounds. The fisherman always
had to allow fourteen pounds to the quintal for wastage, but
when a boat and two or three men could bring in as many
as thirty-six drafts in a day, that was not too important. But
there are times when fishermen have brought in as little as
thirty-three pounds of cod for a day's work. Years of poor
fishing alternate with years of good fishing, and the lean
years bring heartbreak to the fishermen's families.

Watching the work in the fish house can be fascinating.
When the fish are brought in from the beach they are washed
and tossed to the slitters. The dextrous movements of the
slitter's hands are too swift to follow with the eye, for with
trained hands and muscles he lays the great fish flat and
boneless in an incredibly short time. When that is done the
cod is ready for its immersion in the brine. The man who
stows them away in the great casks uses his salt shovel with

145

a nicety so that the salt is evenly distributed and the casks are built up to the brim evenly and precisely. The fish houses are remarkably clean and sweet smelling, considering the possibilities. When the salted fish are ready for the sun, the process of drying begins and in favorable weather it takes a month to "make" fish.

Just north of the fishing station is a rocky little hill fenced off and set apart as a park in memory of Sir William Logan. There is a medallion on the rock to commemorate him as the founder of the geological survey of Canada. It is most appropriately placed since Logan's first work in Canada was a tour of the Gaspé coast in 1843. What has been published of his diary is well worth reading. He came to Gaspé from Halifax and engaged the services of an Indian guide who paddled and cooked for him in his long and adventurous journey. There were "few roads of which to avail myself," wrote Logan. He explored a hundred miles of coast from Cap des Rosiers to Paspebiac. "It is the grandest scenery I have ever known," wrote Logan, as stiff and weary with his struggles with heavy rocks and specimens, he faithfully took the time every night to make an account of his day's work and impressions. The Indian, oddly enough, was called John Basque and probably carried in his veins the blood of some adventuresome Basque fisherman who came to Gaspé in the early days of its fisheries.

Logan was entranced with birch bark and its uses. Not only was it used to make a quick fire, but it made a roof for his head, shoes for his feet in an emergency, dishes and baskets and boxes; even, when the necessity arose, writing paper. Logan was a great scientist and a great character, and the memorial at Percé does honor where honor is due.

The little cape at Percé which juts out from the shore and divides the South Beach from the North Beach is two-pronged. It is called Mont Joli. On its tip is a white cross. From the road this white cross has for its background the high prow of Percé Rock, rich in color. It was on this Mont Joli that the first church in Percé is believed to have stood. There

*Percé Rock from behind the town*

*The Rock from the northeast*

*View from Captain Duval's house*

*Quiet Harbor*

*Atop Duval Cliffs on Bonaventure Island*

*Percé Rock is part of the Bird Sanctuary*

*Farming on the heights above Percé*

*Young gannets*

*Ceremonial gift of seaweed*

*Happy Landing*

*Fragment detached
from Percé Rock*

*Fleet at anchor,
North Beach, Percé*

*At the foot of the cliffs, Bonaventure Island*

*At anchor in the lee of Bonaventure Island*

*Ex-serviceman Duval,
scion of the privateer*

*Young gannet
learning to fly*

*Mending nets at
Grande Rivière*

*Fishing fleet in
Baie des Chaleurs*

*Repairing the lines,*
*Baie des Chaleurs*

*Preparing for*
*another day's work*

*Family Differences*

*Gaspé Village*

Little Miss Gaspé

Historic well at
Cross Pointe

are now several buildings on it. One of them is a charming little cottage with steep, sharp gables. On the southern side is a round window. The cottage has a history. It was known as The Captain's House and is very old. It is the last surviving dwelling of the captain of a fishing fleet. He came here with his ship and proceeded, just as Nicholas Denys described, to set his fishermen to work, to build cabins and stages and flakes, stripped his ship as if it was laid up for the winter, and settled himself in this little cottage, season after season. It has been moved from its original site and now has a new lease of life.

On the southern prong which is called Cap Cannon is a large house with a history. Way back in the 'eighties an American artist named Frederick James brought his bride to Percé on their wedding trip. They both fell rapturously in love with the place and both felt that here they could "live happily ever after". However, they had to go back to Philadelphia, but they kept on thinking about Percé and its wild loveliness of hill and cliff and sea. Presently they bought a piece of land on the edge of this Cap Cannon and lived in a little old French house on their holidays here. They liked it so much that they planned to build a real home. The artist made a model of the house he wanted, complete in every detail inside and out. This he presented to the local carpenters and woodworkers and asked them to build the house for him. The old French house was to form one part of it, the studio. The new part of the house was to be built around it. And there, just as the local workmen made it off the pattern of that little model, it stands today. It is a curious house, a "mélange" as the French call it, of many times and fashions, neither old nor new, just a house that grew of itself, but inside it is charming, with wide sunny rooms and generous windows that let in the marvellous views and lights of Percé. The old French house has a great fireplace on one side and a great north window on the other.

Here, decade after decade, Frederick James painted his fisher folk. Here he brought the villagers to hilarious parties when the place was festooned with greens and long tables were laid, acting the role of seigneur in a manor house. If they had thought about it, they might have planted a may-pole for him beside the door on a spring morning just as their kinfolk once did on the St. Lawrence.

Frederick James died. The woman he brought to Percé as a young bride, was a woman of years. Still the dream of Percé persisted and she would not leave the home they had built and loved in common. Sometimes she slipped away to the world of art and fashion on both sides of the water, but always she came back again to the peace and quietude and the memories of Percé. Year after year went by and she continued to play Lady Bountiful to the village, keeping up the old customs that had grown up around their lives together. But she grew old and feeble and eccentric. Her dogs were famous for their number and variety. She was served by the French women who knew her ways and her wishes. Long and lonely years went by and age depleted her strength. Always she was the charming lady, the lover of lovely things. Old and frail as she was, none could persuade her to leave the house against which the cold sea winds blew all winter long. She was eighty-four years of age before her friends took her back to the city from which she had come as a young girl, and there at last she died.

Not far from the path which leads up to the top of the twin bluffs is the old burying ground of the English in Percé. A few slabs of stone, half hidden in the grass, mark its site. Unmarked is the grave of the most celebrated of those whose ashes rest here. You will read there of Peter John Duval and of his "short but painful illness" and the regrets of his "afflicted survivor" but you will read nothing about his father, the hot-blooded old Captain Duval, who lies beside him. Though his grave is unmarked he is still a brave old ghost of Percé and we shall meet him presently across at Bonaventure Island.

There are all sorts of queer ghosts about Percé, not least of them is the big black pig that walks the Irish Town Road on nights of revelry. Percé Rock itself is said to have eerie visitors on occasion. One of the treasure stories of Percé concerns a sea captain who induced one of his sailors to help him up to the top of the Rock to bury some treasure in a strongbox. The sailor, suspecting no harm, agreed. But when the treasure was hidden, the captain killed the sailor so that he should tell no tales. The sailor is said to haunt the Rock but in justice it should be the captain who is earth-bound, condemned to hover over a treasure he could never use.

There is another story about a sailor from a frigate that dropped anchor here. He fell in love with a Percé maid and couldn't tear himself away from her when his ship was ready to sail. So, as the best place to hide away from his irate officers, he betook himself to the top of the Rock. Although they fired a few shots at him, they could waste neither time nor ammunition on him, and so after the ship had sailed far enough away, he crawled down from his hiding place and for all we know lived happily ever after.

There is level land and grass on the top of the Rock and when the cleared lands of Percé were very limited it was the custom of the farmers to climb the Rock every year and cut the hay that grew there. In 1837 a farmer by the name of Pierre l'Egle, being too exuberant to be prudent, danced a jig on a projecting rock. The rock fell and took him with it. Thereafter climbing Percé Rock was prohibited. The angles of the Rock have changed so much that in any case it is now probably impossible.

# 18

## *The Island of Birds*

IT WAS Sieur de Champlain who named Bonaventure Island when he came up the Gaspé coast exploring in 1603. It lies a mile and a half or two miles off Percé and is the largest island in the Gaspé region. This Bonaventure is not only a famous little place but it is an unforgettable island to those who take the time to girdle it from the sea and walk its quiet woods and fields. Its high cliffs, that face seaward, are a sanctuary for birds, but landward it slopes gently towards the water's edge and is tree clad except where a few farms have been cleared. Here, too, are the landing places where fishermen for centuries past, have dried their cod.

Bonaventure Island, drowsy and gentle as it seems to summer visitors today, has known far more exciting days. In 1690 Sir William Phipps set up the British flag here for a little while, and a century later the Janvrins, privateers from the Channel Islands, outfitted their ships in the lee of the island, and sent them to prey upon the French in the long strife between England and France.

There is a piratical strain in human nature and perhaps that is why tales of pirates enthrall so many of us, but fortunately as time goes on we do seem to be developing a counterbalancing collective sense of conservation which appears in many of our national and international efforts to preserve life and to protect what is beautiful. If it was not for this sense there would be no seabirds today on Bonaventure Island.

Long ago when the fishermen or the explorers came to this side of the ocean in their little ships, one of their chief problems was to secure supplies of fresh food. They fished and hunted for game, but they were also in need of eggs. They found that the eggs of gulls and gannets and other sea birds would be good food if they were fresh. The gannets, for instance lay their eggs in May and the young are hatched in July. So when the fishermen arrived late in May or June they went to the breeding ledges, broke all the eggs, and waited for the distressed birds to begin all over again by laying new eggs. These fresh eggs the men collected for their own use. Consequently even when the birds laid again and again in order to reproduce themselves, the hatching of the young came so late in the year that the winter was upon them before they were mature enough to look after themselves. No one will ever know how great a part of the bird population was destroyed in this way.

But later on when the fishermen no longer needed to depend on sea birds' eggs, an equally disastrous age fell upon the birds. There was a fashion for feathers and to supply the market modern pirates slaughtered tens of thousands of birds for the sake of long quills, wings and tail feathers for the millinery trade.

There was a time when a hundred thousand sea birds nested on Bonaventure Island but in the 'nineties not more than twenty-five hundred came there to breed.

It was not until 1917 that the Migratory Birds International Convention Act was passed. In conformity with the spirit of the act the Dominion Government in 1918 chose Bonaventure Island as a bird sanctuary. It was an ideal spot, for the dozen families who inhabited the island were on the landward side, and a large wooded area separated them from the bird cliffs which rise perpendicularly nearly three hundred feet on the seaward side. Today there are at least sixty thousand birds who make their homes in the sanctuary, half of them gannets, and the numbers are increasing yearly.

There are excursion boats to take the visitor around the island but the wise traveller will take a day off to make the acquaintance of the island and the birds, by arranging with a fisherman to make the trip slowly in an open boat. When the encircling trip is over, the fisherman will land the traveller in some little cove so picturesque that the joy of island exploration begins as soon as foot is set upon the clean gravel beach.

So with a cheerful and friendly fisherman we set out from the beach at Percé in crystal clear and windy weather and head for the northern end of Bonaventure. Then we come under its gaunt stone cliffs and close enough to see the strange formations of the rock and the modelling done by the sea when the winter storms lash at the cliffs. As we go on there is an eerie sound growing upon us, the strange harsh, penetrating music of the birds. There are a few of them here, whirling and swooping above the water, but as we go on their numbers increase, until at a turn in the shore line we can see the crowded ledges towering far above our heads, and tens of thousands of the birds. This is an experience a sensitive traveller will never forget, as strange and beautiful and haunting a memory as he will carry away from Gaspé.

How can anyone communicate in words this world of sound and motion and color, of fantastic designs in the cliffs, of beauty of form and movement?

The fisherman will shut off his engines and the fishing boat will rest in the movement of the waves while we gaze and listen, entranced and astonished. The birds on their nests or standing at rest on the ledges, are wing to wing so that they seem like snow drifts on this sunny summer day. How they can make their nests secure on those narrow ledges is one of nature's secrets but there they build them about eighteen inches apart, and there they mate and build and jointly care for their nests and eggs and fledglings. Each pair of gannets lays one egg, three to four inches long, and the summer and autumn are spent in caring for the young bird, teaching it to fly and swim and fish, and then as winter approaches, the migration south begins.

About one-twelfth of the world's gannets come to Bonaventure. The gannet is a large white bird with a wing spread of slightly over six feet. It weighs about eight pounds and eats its own weight in food daily, depending on the herrings chiefly and timing its coming and going to synchronize with the migrations of the herrings. Their nests are crude and made largely of seaweed. They must carry many tons of seaweed up to the cliff ledges every year. The birds are hatched usually in July and are shapeless little creatures at first, but presently their eyes open and they produce a white down which clings to many of them until late in the autumn. Even in October many of the young gulls are covered with a fluffy white coat over their demure grey feathers but these are the late ones and are probably a source of anxiety to their parents. Usually in September most of them are mature enough to set out across the Atlantic to begin a four-year journey before they return as fully mature birds, to nest on the cliffs of their ancestors at Banoventure.

The gannet parents know how to co-operate. Each takes turns in incubating the egg by holding it in their webbed feet. Perhaps nature is very wise in keeping the young gannet blind in its early infancy until it gets used to its rocky, windy home and becomes accustomed to its parents and their habits. What a view of its world the young gannet must have when its eyes first admit the light, the gleam of sun on the sea and the unbroken horizon.

This is the world into which the fisherman has brought us. The very air vibrates with the shrill chatter of this community so intent on teaching its young how to live. Tens of thousands of them fill the air with raucous sounds or with a drifting whiteness and silvery forms that would challenge even an ecstatic poet to the limit of his imaginative wit. Here they hang, motionless against the burning blue of the sky, "a drift of pinions" and then with a swift turn, put their powerful wing muscles in action, mounting upwards only to turn again and dive towards the surface of the sea after their prey. Gorged with a herring in its gullet, the gannet will rest, on the sea or on a ledge for perhaps half an hour to digest its meal. But flying or floating or restlessly moving about on a ledge, the sea birds are always beautiful, always providing us with food for imagination and memories, giving us those intangibles which we can carry away with us and cherish as long as we live. The authorities set aside the island for the sake of the birds, and probably none realized when it was done how the by-products of that act would be an unending stream of memories to enrich countless thousands of men and women who in the future set off on their holidays to seek for beauty.

There are two distinct bird cliffs on Bonaventure Island, divided by a smooth face of rock without so much as a shelf to house a gull. It is said that the birds of one cliff never trespass on the neighboring cliff, nor do any of them exchange visits with the birds of Percé Rock. If they dared to venture on their neighbors' territory, they would be met by shrill defiance and sharp talons.

The birds are safe now in their eyry for no one can approach them up the face of the rock and they seem to know it. They challenge the intruder mildly, swooping down over our heads in curiosity as we invade their black and silver kingdom. We have no compunction about disturbing them for even this little intrusion merely agitates them enough to enhance their loveliness in motion. Faster and faster they circle above us, beaks outstretched, yellow feet trailing. But on the ledges are others who have neither fear nor curiosity but who regard us with serenity and indifference and go on crooning to themselves and their young, a low monotonous sound below the strident cries of those on the wing.

But all good things come to an end and presently we have rounded the island, wondering what happens to all our birds when gales blow in from the sea. Presently we come to the sloping lands where for generations a few families have farmed and fished, and then we are brought ashore in a cove that would be a perfect setting for a pirate crew. No one who set foot on that gravel beach and climbed the curious, spindley contraption that serves as a stairway to the top could ever be persuaded that there is not pirate treasure buried somewhere on Bonaventure Island.

The romance of Bonaventure is centered around the life of Captain Jean Duval, as rollicking a privateer as ever drew sword or boarded a captive ship. Captain Duval, the story goes, was a good Norman who was unjustly jailed and punished by the King of France. The injustice rankled in his heart, and in his imprisonment he vowed that when he was free he would have his revenge. So when his chance came he became a privateer, and under letters of marque from the English King he made war on his own account upon the ships of France. It was a risky business for if he was caught he would have been strung up for a traitor. However, he was impelled by a passion stronger than his fear, so he did not count the cost and his luck was with him. Indeed, so great became his reputation in France that the citizens of Bayonne formed a stock company to outfit a brig of a hundred and eighty tons which was to set out for the express purpose of finding and destroying Captain Jean Duval.

The ship mounted sixteen guns and it was disguised as a merchantman. She set out on her first voyage acting the part of a leisurely cargo ship and put herself in the way of luring the privateer into attacking her.

Now Captain Duval had a little ship called the *Vulture*, armed with four guns. She was a hundred ton ship and carried a crew of twenty-seven. By the tilt of her prow and the spread of her sails, she seemed to show that she knew she was the terror of the coast of France from St. Malo to the Pyranees.

Captain Jean Duval carried the great parchment, with the seal and signature of King George the Third, setting out very plainly, in a clear round hand, that he had the right to prey upon the King's enemies. He wore a sword that the King had given him to carry out the terms of his letters of marque.

So this was the ship that cut through the rollers of the Bay of Biscay one day and sighted on the horizon a slowly moving merchantman. The crew was all agog and the captain set his course in her quarter. The men stood ready with their grappling irons and cutlasses ready to board their victim, when the ship suddenly threw off her disguise, poked the black noses of her sixteen guns through the ports and opened fire on the privateer. The men of Bayonne, aboard the big ship, laughed because they thought Captain Duval had sailed right into their trap.

It was certainly a poser for Captain Jean Duval. The Bayonne ship was a big one, nearly twice as big as the *Vulture*. Her guns were high. And then suddenly it was Captain Duval's turn to laugh. He ordered the *Vulture* close in under her gunwales and from short range he raked his enemy from stem to stern with his vicious little guns. Dusk was falling. Duval knew that his enemy was crippled and helpless. He hauled off, poured grapeshot into her rigging and watched her as she limped away. In the darkness probably one was as glad as the other to escape without pressing the issue any farther. Duval got off scot free and the stock company at Bayonne watched the return of their brave new ship, rent and torn.

Probably Captain Duval thought it best not to push his good fortune too far, for shortly after this he came to Gaspé and bought part of Bonaventure Island. There he built a fine home and, judging by the bits of his old silver that survived on the island until a few years ago, he brought an air of good living into his new home. There was good red mahogany and fine furnishings and roomy wine cellars. Then he went into trade but he was a better privateer than he was a business man and he seemed to lose more than he ever made. One of his sons became a British officer. Having a son in the army, in those days, was an expensive business and Peter John's debts ruined his father.

The Island was quite a nice settlement in Captain Duval's time, with at least twenty-five houses, with barns and storehouses on its lovely slopes. Today the descendants of Captain Duval still live on the Island but they have never regained the fortune lost a century ago.

In the 1860's a ship bearing the young Prince of Wales, Albert Edward, son and heir of Queen Victoria, ran aground on Sandy Beach in Gaspé Bay. But as his ship passed Percé and Bonaventure Island the guns at the fishing station boomed a salute and the village bells rang cheerfully. On the Island, the great-grandson of Captain Duval came into the world about the same time, so, of course, they named him Albert Edward.

In his last years he was a quaint old philosopher with something about him that called up the image of the old privateer. He was proud of his great-grandfather and nothing loath to talk about him, if you could waylay him somewhere along the Island roads where he could sit on a rock and cudgel his long memory at his leisure. He was proud, too, of being of Norman blood and would tell you that the Normans conquered England. But he would never admit that Captain Duval's son, his grandfather, was born in the Channel Islands. For Jerseymen he had a profound and inextinguishable dislike. So he wouldn't have his grandfather a Jerseyman. He could recall the days of his youth when he worked in the Jersey rooms as a fisherman, before legislation and humanitarianism stepped in to break the feudal ways that held Gaspé in the thrall of the big companies.

Albert Edward's son is the head of the family today, a fine looking elderly man who is the official keeper of the bird sanctuary. Here is a strange evolution of a family from privateer to guardian of the rights of birds. The bird cliffs have been named Duval Cliffs in honor of Willie Duval, and the eighteenth century privateer now basks in the reflected glory of his great-great-grandson who will be remembered for generations to come for his bird-wisdom.

There is another generation of Duvals to carry on the name. Willie's ex-soldier son, gay and good-looking, plies a little ferry from mainland to Island. All that remains of the heritage of the first Duval of Bonaventure to his great-great-great-grandson would have been the great parchment signed by the English sovereign, George the Third. But unhappily, a few years ago some visitor induced old Albert Edward to give her the letters of marque under which Captain Duval became a privateer. They have disappeared, but members of the family and historians of Gaspé are trying to trace the visitor and find the document.

When we start out for the bird cliffs we shall probably wander across the fields and pastures of the Duvals and make our way into the woods over the little trail that the keeper of the birds has made on visits to his charges. It is a long walk and can be made comfortably only in waterproof shoes or rubber boots, but after half an hour or more of walking the trail comes out on the open land where a few sheep may be grazing. On the other side we find the birds and settle down quietly to watch and listen. They have no fear of the visitor and give no sign of antagonism, which is a very good thing, because a hostile seagull could be a dangerous foe. But because they are friendly we can sit down eight or ten feet from the top ledges. They grow accustomed to the new-comers and perhaps a little curious too, but they will pay no attention to us except that a few will fly overhead circling nearer and nearer until they seem to be almost within arm's reach. It is unlawful to frighten them or disturb them in any way, but no one who would take the trouble to visit them on the top of the cliffs would have any desire to interfere with their life. Here we can sit for hours watching their little community affairs, their quarrels and gossiping, their flights and returns, the stretching of their lovely wings, the wagging of their shapely heads from side to side as they move sedately about the very narrow ledge. Three hundred feet below we can see them diving and floating and watch their swift descents and ascents, all the time listening to the perpetual chatter and screaming that constitutes their form of communication.

There is one sound the visitor who sits here will probably never forget, a sound so soft and gentle that we would miss it altogether if we were not sitting quietly at rest. It is a rustling sound, like the frou-frou of taffeta petticoats, made by a woman's light, swift steps. But it comes from the birds as they fly near to peer at the strange creatures who sit so close to their stoney dwelling places. Of the many sounds so characteristic of Bonaventure Island, this is the one that will haunt us in days to come when we recall those magic hours when we escaped from the anxieties and tensions of our modern world and steeped ourselves in the beauty of sky and sea and rocks and birds.

Sometimes the birds utter strange sounds that could be mistaken for human cries for help or moans of suffering men. So perhaps before you leave, someone will tell you one of the legends of the Island, the story of Gou-Gou, a giant ogress who made her home here. She was so tall that the masts of sailing ships came only to her waist and she could wade from the Island to the mainland without getting her knees wet. For bed time snacks she enjoyed unlucky Indians and so she gathered them up by the dozen and carried them off to her cave where she nibbled at them at her leisure. To prove her existence, the Islanders can point out the black and red stains made on the rocks where she laid out her great cloak to dry.

And so we climb carefully down the shaky piratical gangway that leads to the beach and the landing place of our little boat. Out of the rocks above our heads drips the clear cold water of a spring that runs somewhere back within the ancient rocks. It falls with a tinkling sound, flashing in the sunset light with all the colors of the crystal. So we cup our hands and catch the sweet cold water just as sailors and fishermen have done for centuries past, and quench our thirst before we go down to the edge of the beach and embark for the mainland with young Duval. He sits in the stern with his hand on the tiller, and a beret on the back of his head, but by the gleam in his eye we know that the venturesome spirit of the old privateer will never die while there are men bearing the name of Duval on Bonaventure Island.

159

# 19

## Coasts of Storm

LEAVING lovely Percé reluctantly, even in imagination, the white road leads us up and out of the village into Anse à Beaufils. The summit at Cap Blanc, the first headland we come upon, is properly called Surprise Hill, for if you should be travelling from the Baie des Chaleurs towards Percé, it is here you have your first glimpse of Percé Rock in a great bowl-shaped amphitheater, with the village and its dramatic headlands set out like a spectacle on a stage.

The land hereabouts is raised above the sea some considerable height. Cap Blanc juts out like a tableland, shaved completely clean of trees and cut into well-cultivated fields. Its rock walls are light in color as the name suggests. The tip of the cape has been entirely washed away so it ends in a blunt, slightly indented cliff. The sea has formed a little beach where the tide licks at the slowly disintegrating rocks. Over the edge creeps a fringe of green from the fields above. Squarely in the center, at the end of the cape, is a red and white lighthouse.

Cap Blanc and Percé Rock are two arms that encircle the South Beach and form, with Bonaventure Island, the safe harbor of Percé for storm-bound ships.

The highway crosses the base of Cap Blanc but there is a roadway down across the fields for those who want to visit the lighthouse.

Anse à Beaufils is a fine sickle-shaped cove and there is a small settlement of that name. It has a good harbor with a safe inner haven where a big fishing fleet can shelter in all kinds of weather and it is one of the important fishing stations of the South Shore. It puzzles even the oldest in-

160

habitant to say why it has been called the Cove of the Stepson but there is a legend of "the stepson of a man close to the King of France" and himself of noble birth, exiled here for some obscure reason. No one knows the story behind the exile but the thing that impressed the Gaspésians was that he was somebody's stepson.

There is a shallow indentation in the shore line from Cap Blanc to Cap d'Espoir. It is kinder to think of this great headland by its original French name than by the derivation it got from the twist of the English tongue,—Cape Despair. When the sea rages, the shores between these capes is a fierce and terrible place, so it is little wonder that Englishmen thought of it as a place of despair, or that Frenchmen sometimes called Cap Blanc by an alternative name of Cap Enragé. The coast has bitter memories in the annals of the sea. Anse à Beaufils is the only habitable place between the two and its musical-comedy harbor had to be built up of stout cribwork to resist the waves. Its fishing boats huddle inside and hang their black and brown nets to dry in weird draperies festooned on masts and spars, for there is too little beach to provide for the ordinary fishermen's needs. For the fishing boat that misses the narrow entrance to the harbor, or for the ship that fights a losing battle against the terrors of Cap d'Espoir, this is a fatal shore.

The first village of any size along this shore is Grande Rivière, not particularly interesting or distinguished today but once a very important fishing station and granted in seigneurial tenure as long ago as the seventeenth century. The most celebrated of its seigneurs was Charles Robin, the Jersey merchant, although he did not think much of its red and white rocks, and its good rich soil as the setting for a colony of thrifty farmers. He saw there only a good trading center and fishing station.

During the first of the eighteenth century, Grande Rivière proceeded slowly from obscurity to a very nice sort of prosperity under the lord of the manor, who combined his claims to nobility with a shrewd trading instinct. When the Seven

Year's War began, its seigneur was Francois Lefebvre de Bellefeuille, the royal commandant in Gaspé. He lived in a manor house built on a little island in the harbor, with his wife and family. It was a mansion of no little dignity and space for it had eight rooms on the ground floor. Madame de Bellefeuille ruled it thriftily and her maids were busy at spinning wheel and loom and in the herb garden. Sage and onions hung in pungent rows to dry. There were bins of peas dried in the sun, casks of pork in brine. Seigneur de Bellefeuille did a trade in fish and all the necessities of the fishermen and colonists. So the war was a very unwelcome diversion in the affairs of Grande Rivière and everyone went about their accustomed business in the hope that its red tides would ebb and leave the little seigneury in safety.

Indeed, they were quite unconcerned. One bright day in the autumn of 1758 they were going about their affairs as usual. The great copper pots stood on their tall tripod legs before the fire. The spit turned slowly with a roast giving off pleasant little sibilant sounds. The table was set with white linen and briskly polished silver. Suddenly a cry of warning went up that an enemy ship had rounded Cap d'Espoir with scarlet flags flying and red coats lining her gunwales.

With a single thought for safety the French colonists fled to the woods, the cook in her cap and the maids in their aprons, the servants from the farmyard and the fishermen from their flakes. The copper pots went on simmering, the salad dripped on its white towel but not a soul was left in all the village of Grande Rivière. The ship dropped anchor, the long boats rowed towards the shore and out stepped the Tommies unopposed.

Cautiously they explored the empty barns and houses. They found the seigneur's silver and linen and family keepsakes packed away in boxes ready for transport to Quebec. Now if the French had stayed to meet the English their fate might have been an easier one. Wolfe's instructions had been specific,—to meet and confer with the French and win their confidence, then offer them either the opportunity to go to Quebec or passage to France. But the *Kennington* was the ship told off for the invasion of Grande Rivière and her commander was a choleric captain who had small liking for the rocky coasts of Gaspé. He told the soldiers they must do their work with all speed and that he would not lie long in the vicinity of the village. Indeed, scarcely were they landed than he began signalling for them to return. The troops did not want to be stranded in hostile country and as they could see that the only way to get in touch with the French was by pursuing them to the woods, they were torn between Wolfe's explicit instructions and the *Kennington's* impatient signals. The captain of the *Kennington* had the more immediate influence and so the soldiers set the torch to everything in Grande Rivière. The manor house went up in smoke, along with barns and stores, flakes, stages and fish houses. Sixty cottages and cabins added to the size of the bonfire, two hundred chests of warm clothing among the goods of trade, sixty casks of molasses, great stores of wines and brandies and rum and eight thousand quintals of cod and the eighty fishing boats that had caught the cod, all went up in smoke.

When the *Kennington* returned to Gaspé with the story of its achievements, General Wolfe was thoroughly indignant. Such off-hand destruction and callous disregard for the safety of the colonists was far from his policy. To remedy what he could of the disastrous affair he despatched a fishing boat with a crew of French fishermen back to Grande Rivière to carry his apologies to Seigneur de Bellefeuille and his dependents and to offer them transport to France. If they did not choose to accept it the fishermen were at liberty to remain with them and make their way as best they could to safety elsewhere. The boat did not return. They all preferred to risk hardship and danger to safety with the enemy.

So these distressed French folk hid in the hills and looked down upon the smoking ruins of the village built up with such pioneer courage in fifty years of effort. The hopes of three generations made a mighty spectacle upon that dramatic shore line wantonly demolished by the British raiders. It was the funeral pyre of French power in America.

Grande Rivière is one of the settlements in the shallow arc between Cap d'Espoir and Pointe Macquereau. It is a shore line of fifteen miles with three rivers running into the sea, Grande Rivière, Petite Rivière and Rivière Grande Pabos. The sea off this coast is a rich cod fishing ground but the waterfront is destitute of those good harbors for ships so necessary for fishing stations. The mouth of Grande Rivière was particularly dangerous of approach for like all Gaspé rivers it was enclosed with a sandbar. When the sea was rolling high the sand and gravel would be washed in, in such quantities that the entrance to the river was entirely closed up. When the storm abated the river had to force a new exit wherever the barricade was weakest, so after every storm ther was a new tickle and the sailor returning to Grande Rivière could never be sure where the channel would be. A careless sailor, or an unfortunate one, might run his vessel aground.

Grande Rivière was a favorite place of shelter for the Norman fishermen whose ships anchored at Percé. They went out in their fishing boats to Orphans Bank, as the area off this shore was called, and if a sudden squall blew up they were a long way from safe anchorage behind Bonaventure Island and usually made for the barachois here. Consequently as they sheltered in the river from bad weather they had time to spare for making friends with the Indians. As a natural consequence many Norman fishermen married Indian girls and settled down to live along this exposed and treacherous shore. You must know full-blooded Indian girls in their native settings to realize how attractive they can be with their eyes burning like embers beneath the dusky pupils, with their lithe grace and rich vitality. To stormbound men, weary of the eternal masculinity of the fishing stations, these happy girls working around the camp fires and sharing their baked meats with the strangers, were very desirable. At the time of the Cession there were seventeen families of Norman Indians living near Grande Rivière.

At Grand Pabos the harbor was not quite so uncertain and it was regarded as one of the most important settlements in this vicinity. The Grand Pabos was a river of two great arms that stretched back among the foothills, each arm with many tributaries. Petit Pabos was less important, though it forms a most picturesque barachois before it reaches the sea. We cross Petit Pabos near the water's edge and have a curious view of it, with the sea on our left and the great mud flats and low shores of the barachois far inland.

No one seems certain whether or not Pabos is derived from an Indian word meaning "stretch of water with very little movement" which is an excellent description, or from a Basque word meaning "shallow waters". When we drive into the Pabos country now it seems un-Gaspésian and might just as well be somewhere in northern Quebec or Ontario, for the lumberman has been here with his axe and the country is stripped of its forests. Hardwoods and pines and cedars once made the seigneury of Pabos very valuable. Immediately after the Cession of Canada, Governor Haldimand invested his money in the purchase of this seigneury with an eye to eventually settling it with farmers and millers but he never achieved his object. He sold it to Felix O'Hara, another soldier-seigneur who had been with Wolfe at Quebec. Seventy-five years later it passed into the hands of a company who proceeded to "develop" Pabos and first of all stripped it of its trees. Eventually the government had to step in to prevent the total deforestation of the land, and then it was opened for settlement. Much of it is still scrub lands and we see in the town of Chandler, on the site of the old fishing station of Pabos, what industrialization would do to this lovely land of Gaspé.

The farmers in this vicinity are most enterprising and successful. Gaspé peas are a late summer delicacy, especially on the Montreal market, and tremendous quantities of them are raised hereabouts. Butter is also an important export, as the herds of sleek cattle indicate along the way. The farmers near Cap d'Espoir boast of wheat that grows six feet high.

In addition to the cod fisheries, lobster trapping is a very important occupation off Cap d'Espoir. The two largest lobster canning plants in Gaspé stand at St. Joseph's to cope with the two thousand pounds of nightmarish sea creatures that the fishermen turn out on their docks every day when the season is good. St. Adelaide de Pabos also cans lobster and in addition to what goes into tins, quantities of fresh lobster are shipped out to big cities.

Fresh cooked lobster is one of the delicacies of the Gaspé tour. Even out of season it can be seen upon the menus for the hotelkeepers buy lobsters in season and keep them alive in seapools or use deep freeze methods.

There is a legend associated with this shore which is said to have some historical association. Fishermen will tell you that some times at twilight on a summer's day, when the sea is quiet and the winds are low, when the clouds are melting into colored fragments over the horizon, burning with the last reflected glories of the sun, that the waters become agitated with memories of a storm long since passed. Huge waves suddenly roll in from nowhere. Combers break on the beaches with hissing roars and wash in foam over the rocks. Then in the distance there comes an old warship with all sails set and steering a course that brings her swiftly head-on to the cliffs. On her decks are soldiers and sailors in costumes of long ago. On the bridge is a commanding figure, evidently the captain, and by his side is a woman in luminously white garments. The winds howl, the sea roars and the phantom ship flies to her doom. Paralyzed with fear, panting in terror, the fishermen watch helplessly. There is a horrible crash, a thin heart-rending cry from the woman, screams of anguish from the men. It is the climax. As suddenly as it came, the storm is gone. Tradition persists in saying that this was one of the ships of Walker's expedition of 1711 that was blown far out of its course and wrecked at Cap d'Espoir.

It was in that year that little Queen Anne of England sent out an expedition to take Quebec, an enterprise which seemed to occur frequently to English men and women. It was a combined military and naval affair. Admiral Sir Hovendon Walker was in command of the ships. He was a middle-aged man at the time and was knighted shortly before he sailed. General Jack Hill was in command of the seven thousand troops. Now Jack Hill was a brother of Abigail Hill, or Mrs. Masham as she was at this time. They were poor relations of the Duchess of Marlborough. She said Jack Hill was "a tall ragged boy that I took and clothed and the Duke of Marlborough made a colonel of, although he was of no use as a soldier". He was then made a page to Queen Anne when she was Princess Anne, presently he became a captain in the Coldstream Guards and then promoted to brigadier-general for the expedition to Quebec. Meantime the Duchess of Marlborough had gained tremendous influence over the Queen and was virtual ruler of English policy for a while. The Duke, the idol of the English for his great victories, worked hand in hand with his ambitious wife. The result was inevitable and all sorts of intrigues were launched against the too-powerful Marlboroughs. The expedition against Quebec, which was a secret one, was part of a conspiracy to discredit the Duke and his wife. Mrs. Masham had replaced the Duchess in the Queen's favor and so her brother, Jack Hill, as incompetent a general as the Queen could have named, was put in command of the campaign on the St. Lawrence. There were at least ten fighting ships and thirty transports in the fleet.

The expedition crossed the Atlantic safely but sheer bad navigation and lack of intelligent direction landed the fleet on Eggs Island in the Gulf. Eight large ships were tossed like toys on the rocks and nine hundred men, many of them veterans of Marlborough's campaigns, went to their death. The first that New France learned of this venture to subdue it to Queen Anne's fluttering sceptre, came weeks later when a French vessel sailing down the Gulf saw hundreds of dead, in the brave and gaudy uniforms of famous British regiments, strewing the rocks, and hulks of broken ships awash on the shore. The rest of the fleet turned and sailed home. Whether the ship wrecked on Cap d'Espoir had lost its way and took the Baie des Chaleurs for the mouth of the river, or whether it was one of the fleeing ships returning home and seeking supplies of fresh water, no one knows. Its identity as part of Walker's fleet rests on the tales of the fishermen and their descriptions of those whose ghostly wreck plays itself out on the waters of the Gulf.

Gaspé has changed since we left Percé. All the southern shore is more tractable in the hands of Nature and it has been rubbed and worn into something more easily put to the service of colonists. The tiny coves and dearly won acres have been replaced with great farms and cultivated fields and rich harvests. Once we have passed Pointe Macquereau we are, even geographically speaking, in a different part of the country, for it is the point that marks the end of the Gulf of St. Lawrence and the beginning of Baie des Chaleurs. The road shows the difference in the character of the country. We are leaving the seashore to run through an agricultural country that lies on the fringes of a sportsman's paradise. Never very far from the barnyard is the home of the moose, and the farmer can also vary his home grown diet with trout and salmon. The road returns from time to time to the seashore but hereafter we shall climb slowly along the slopes that characterize the lands of the Baie des Chaleurs.

Across the Bay lies New Brunswick, a shore that is not nearly so high as that on the Gaspé side. This sheltered Bay is the largest in the Gulf of St. Lawrence. Here Cartier landed on the mainland of Canada for the first time. Here came the Acadians, fleeing from the invaders who were bent on their expulsion and exile; here was fought the last naval battle in the Seven Year's War; here the royalist exiles from the New American Republic found a home.

Geologically the Baie des Chaleurs is a treasure hunting ground. Scientists from all over the world have worked on its shores in search of scientific secrets. Anthony Piourde, who started out as a simple French farmer, with a natural curiosity about rocks, spent more than forty years of his life collecting specimens for the great universities and museums of the world. Famous geologists became his friends and this intelligent Gaspésian learned to toss off his tongue long scientific names with a French-Canadian flavor to them. He developed an extraordinary technical knowledge of the rocks of his native land.

Jaspar and cornelians are found all over the Bay and are known as Gaspé stones.

Within living memory the roadway from the settlements on Baie des Chaleurs to Gaspé was built, so it is little wonder that in the isolated coves along the way the legends and traditions of another age lingered on and fabulous tales were told on long winter evenings.

The first railway venture in Gaspé Peninsula was begun here in 1886, the period when Canada was "railway-minded". It was to run from Matapédia to Paspebiac. It was twenty years before it got to its destination. In 1905 the second stretch of railway was begun and was to complete the line from Paspebiac to Gaspé. It managed to get there in six years but it broke the Charing Cross Bank of London on the way. It was a particularly difficult road to lay and when it was done there was very little to support it. Gaspé got its first telephone at the same time of construction and the Peninsula felt it had been lifted out of its solitude and had passed from its leisurely mode of travel by sail and by foot into the modern scheme of transportation and communication.

However, it takes more than a railway and a telephone line to modernize the tenacious French Canadian farmer and fishermen, and even their English speaking neighbors were proof against the spirit of frenzied speed. So although the South Shore has been a more enterprising and a slightly more sophisticated area than the North Shore, it is still a land of gentle moods and mellow leisure, just as its lands are gentler and its beaches sandier and its waters milder than those of the North Shore. Even the First World War did not bring many changes to Gaspé as a whole, but the Second World War with its air communication and the post war world's hunger for everything usable in reconstruction, have brought profound changes to the economic and social life of the Peninsula and one by one old customs are yielding to the awakening of Gaspé to modern life.

There is one more ghost ship common to all the Baie des Chaleurs so we may as well see it here. This legend runs that once upon a time a pirate ship was caught at its dastardly work in the Gulf and a fighting ship, whether of France or England no one knows, gave chase in time to save a peaceful merchant vessel which they were plundering. The pirates fled and making good use of the winds they got into the Baie des Chaleurs and hoped, under cover of night, to escape their pursuers. However the pirates' day of reckoning was at hand for the warship, sails spread like an infuriated bird, pounced on the pirate ship and raked it from stem to stern with shells. The ship took fire and limped on towards shore with every part of her ablaze. As she careened to her fate, burning swiftly down to the water's edge, the pirate crew perished. Now sometimes when a storm is brewing at sea, fishermen are prepared to see again the horrible phantom. Against blue-black storm clouds a square-rigged ship of an obsolete fashion dips and bows before the rising winds. Suddenly from stem to stern it breaks into flames and in that red light the ghostly pirate crew can be seen. As suddenly as it comes, it disappears again.

Just inside the Baie des Chaleurs, about three miles from Pointe Macquereau lies Anse au Gascon, a little bay scooped out of the sea wall, with a small protecting arm of rock and sand to protect it from the sea, and a gravel beach for the codflakes. Another four miles or so beyond Anse au Gascon is the harbor of Port Daniel. It is enclosed by two headlands, Pointe a l'Enfer to the east and the bold high land of West

Point across the bay. West Point is four hundred feet high, the loftiest part of this immediate shore. Between the two lies the famous harbor with five miles and more of beaches, its great barachois to shelter the fishing fleet and its safe anchorage for ships. Many of the ships that come to Port Daniel are schooners that load limestone from the quarries near the town. Much of the building stone used in Prince Edward Island comes from Port Daniel since that little island province has none of its own.

Port Daniel is a saw-mill center as well and the lank black smoke stacks indicate its chief land industry. The river bears down from the hills the rafts of timber that are cut and rolled down the mountain sides into the streams during the winter cutting.

Port Daniel began as a fishing station and it is still one of the chief colonies of fishermen in Gaspé. There is here an important freezing plant where cod and mackerel, salmon and lobster and other fish are prepared for big city markets.

For many years Port Daniel has been a popular stopping place for summer visitors because of its picturesqueness. Those who happen upon it at sunset linger there. When the tide is high the estuary is a shimmering bowl of water, dotted with lazy boats tugging at their anchors. When the tide recedes it leaves gleaming mud flats where barefooted fishermen dig for clams for bait and where patient horses with two-wheeled carts follow them to carry home the spoil. The bar is built over with little homes and shops and the "tickle" is spanned with a covered bridge. Across the sandbar runs the highway and the railway but the town sprawls all round the bay.

Port Daniel was named for Captain Daniel who was a friend of the Sieur de Champlain and who was in the king's service in the earliest days of the colony. One of his exploits brought him into conflict with the Scots of Nova Scotia. Among the baronets of Nova Scotia was Sir James Stewart of Kilkeith, a son of the Earl of Arran. He had impoverished himself in colonizing northern Ireland and he hoped to recoup his losses by colonizing Nova Scotia. In 1629 he took out sixty immigrants to Baleine Cove in Cape Breton and set them to clearing land and building cabins. They were brawny Scots in kilts and bonnets, willing to work for a chance at freedom and happiness. When Sir James saw how the forest melted before them he dared to dream of a feudal estate that would bring him honor and prosperity. But in the meantime Richelieu sent out another fleet to Quebec with colonists and stores and he put in command Champlain's friend, Captain Daniel. Somewhere on his way to Quebec, Captain Daniel fell in with a ship which carried news of this Scottish enterprise. Sputtering with wrath at the impudence of the Scottish aristocrat, Captain Daniel turned his fleet aside and set his course for Baleine Cove. There, sure enough he saw the Scots hard at work. Seven ships filled with Frenchmen was too formidable an enemy for sixty Scots, so Captain Daniel made the whole colony prisoners at one blow and carried off Sir James to his flagship in triumph. The French started off once more towards their destination at Quebec, only to hear from another wayfarer that the enemy had had better luck in the St. Lawrence and that Quebec was in their hands.

Whether or not Captain Daniel put in here then with his unlucky fleet we do not know but certainly this harbor was known as Port Daniel early in the seventeenth century. He is said to have taken to colonizing himself eventually at Ste. Anne's in Cape Breton, not far from the spot where he had ruined the hopes and plans of the Scots.

Port Daniel is testimony to the fact that Gaspé has no immigration problem. The mothers of Port Daniel have inherited the traditions of the King's Girls of the seventeenth century and whatever else they lack it is not affection for their swarms of bare-footed, bare-headed boys and girls. There is no great wealth in Port Daniel but the wealth of the spirit. There is poverty here that in a city slum would be morally degrading. Here in the clean sea air among a people who demand little of life but their daily bread and fish and a right to pray at the flower-decked altars of their favorite saints, it is socially deplorable but not as ugly as industrial poverty. At least the curé, whose coat may be faded and worn and who may smoke a homely pipe, gets into close touch with the realities of the life of his people as he sits on a woodpile and talks to them of their problems. The church here does not overlook its poor.

Between Port Daniel and Paspébiac was another long shore line always dreaded by fishermen and sailors in times of storm, for there was only one spot where the sailor could save himself from shipwreck and that was in the mouth of the little Rivière Nouvelle. Forbidding cliffs frowned all along the way and between the sea and the merciless rocks there was no hope of succor for mariners in distress. Those who made this country their home had to accept the possibility of tragedy. No man who earns his living on the sea has known when the sea will take him for her own. No woman knows when the sea will rob her of husband or son. Not a little home here but has at some time or other been touched by this grim drama of the sea.

In these towns many a home can produce some relic of a celebrated shipwreck. The sailing ship *Colbourne* was bound from England for Quebec with passengers and a valuable cargo, in the eighteen-thirties. The thirty-eight passengers included a number of woman and children. There were seventeen men in his crew. Included in its freight were forty boxes of golden guineas, a thousand to a box, on their way out to be used by the military for the support of British garrisons in Canada. It also carried the silver plate belonging to Sir John Colbourne of Upper Canada, the handsome veteran of the Peninsular Wars and a staff officer of the Duke of Wellington.

The *Colbourne* had been forty-five days at sea and one quiet night in October she was sailing along into what the captain thought was the Gulf of St. Lawrence. Actually the ship was off its course and was just inside the Baie des Chaleurs. A sailor in the crow's nest was keeping a night watch when not far ahead he saw the ominous curl of water breaking over fangs of rock. "Breakers ahead!" rang

173

out the warning and galvanized the crew into activity. Everyone who heard rushed to the gunwales peering into the darkness, even the women and children. It was too late to do anything. Blindly the ship plunged right on into the reef that ripped her oaken sides as if they were paper. In half an hour the ship was on her side, passengers and crew flung into the sea or into the limp shrouds that held her useless sails. It was cruelly cold and those who clung to the rigging and woodwork, swaying as the boat pitched about, were left to die of exposure. Those who fell into the sea and drowned were luckier. From Monday night until Saturday the great hulk, floated off the rocks at the next high tide, drifted about in the bay between Port Daniel and Anse au Gascon. Twelve of her unfortunates were rescued by fishermen but when everything had been done for the survivors that willing hands could do, the people along the shore watched the *Colbourne* with a very keen interest. She was a great ship with a fine cargo and it would be too bad if contrary winds carried her off and sank her beyond their reach. On Saturday they got together and sailed out to her, tied ropes to her broken ribs and towed her to the beach at Harrington Cove. When the tide went down they boarded her, took the pitiful bodies of the frozen dead from the rigging and gave them burial. When their duty to the dead was done they proceeded to rifle the wreck. There were trunks of unclaimed finery, taffeta frocks and satin slippers and wonders of all kinds for the womenfolk. Many of the boxes of guineas were retrieved. Some, it was whispered, disappeared mysteriously. The story goes, too, that those who took charge of the imperial money decided to count the guineas in each box before shipping it on to Quebec but that each time the gold was counted there were fewer guineas and so they gave it up and shipped it off uncounted. Furniture from the wreck went piece by piece into the little homes along the shore, to be handed down from generation to generation along with the story of grandfather's part in the wreck of the *Colbourne*.

One of the sailors saved from the ship that dark October was Joseph Ateson. He was taken into his home by one of the fishermen of Anse au Gascon and when he recovered he fell in love with the fisherman's daughter and decided that his travelling days were over. She married him and they settled down happily just where the sea had thrown him up into safety and a strange new life.

The very first white settler on the site of Port Daniel was a runaway French marine who married an Indian girl. The first English settler did not come until 1825.

A little more than six miles west of Port Daniel is the little English speaking settlement at Shigawake. The name of the river which flows out of the hills here is an Indian word, Shigawake, which is the Micmac description of this spot as "the land of the rising sun". The river was one of their favorite travelways when they came from their hunting grounds in the Shickshocks to fish in the Baie des Chaleurs.

# 20

## *The Autocrat of Gaspé*

IN THE quaint town of Paspébiac we have reached the capital of the Kingdom of Cod. Here, in its essence, is the romance of the fisheries, from its obscurity all the way through the feudal age of Charles Robin and his heirs.

The story of the fisheries of Gaspé divides itself roughly into four parts. First, there is the period of unwritten history when Viking and Basque and Norman touched the peninsula with the mystery of the unknown. Then there is the early French period when the fishing rights were passed from trading company to trading company until Nicholas Denys became seigneur of the fishing coasts and fought so valiantly for the colonization of Gaspé. The third period begins after the interlude of another war when Newfoundland and Nova Scotia were awarded to Britain. By this time France realized the blow to her maritime power was crippling and so set to work to make good in Gaspé her losses in the other fishing grounds of the Gulf.

In the next half century French enterprise was on the wane but nevertheless the Kings of France spent a million and a half pounds on the defences of Louisbourg in Cape Breton in the hope that the fortress would protect the Gulf from any further inroads by the British. France suffered more from the folly and corruption of her own people than from her enemies and the end of the Seven Years' War was foreordained by the selfishness and greed of those entrusted with the honor of France.

Once Louisbourg had fallen the British swept the Gulf so thoroughly of French power that from that day to this all France has had on this side of the Atlantic are the tiny islands of St. Pierre and Miquelon in the Gulf.

Then came the fourth phase of Gaspésian history, and it took its color from an unexpected source. Among the adjuncts of the British crown for more than seven hundred years are a few islands in the English Channel of which the principal ones are Jersey, Guernsey, Alderney and Sark. They were once known as the Norman Isles and now we call them the Channel Islands. They came to the British crown not by conquest but as part of the Dukedom of William of Normandy. The Conqueror who re-inforced his slim claims to the English throne by a stout sword, made himself King of England. But in these little islands he was Duke of Normandy. Even today King George of England becomes the Duke of Normandy when he visits the Channel Islands. The Islanders will tell you that England belongs to the Dukedom of Normandy by right of conquest.

The history of the Islands is a very long one. Jersey is a corruption of the Roman name of Caesarea. Lying off the coast of Normandy the Islands naturally fell in time to that Dukedom and Norman laws and customs still prevail, for the Channel Islands make their own laws and maintain their own code of justice even today.

The Islanders have always been great seamen and fishermen. In the thirteenth century they fared as far afield as Iceland for fish and traded in both France and England. They have a tradition that Jersey fishermen first discovered the cod-laden waters of the Gulf of St. Lawrence and that it was on their reports that Cabot set out to "discover" the new land for King Henry the Seventh. From that day to this the Channel Islanders have fished in the Gulf. By 1522 so many British ships were fishing in the Gulf that several men-of-war were posted at the entrance to the channel every year to protect returning fishermen from French pirates.

So throughout the seventeenth and eighteenth centuries while France kept command of the fishing coasts on the mainland, the fishermen of the Channel Islands looked enviously in their direction. So far as they were concerned, the news of the conquest of New France was important chiefly because thereafter Jersey and Guernsey fishermen might take advantage of what their neighbors had lost.

On the other hand as soon as the French were ousted from command of Quebec those fishermen of Gaspé who had escaped the torches of Wolfe's men (for he left the Baie des Chaleurs untouched), and those who returned to the sites of their burned homes because they had nowhere else to go, found that although they still had plenty of fish, they had no markets. The English speaking merchants who came to Quebec after the Treaty of Paris turned to Gaspé as a field of investment but they had made little headway in organizing the fishing trade before there appeared on the scene a young Channel Islander who instituted the greatest single influence in all the history of Gaspé,—the Jersey fisheries.

It was in 1766 that a firm of Jersey merchants, Robert Pipon and Company, entrusted one of their young clerks with a commission to sail to Gaspé and look over the situation with a view to investing in the overseas fisheries. Charles Robin was only twenty-three years of age. He was flattered at the trust in his judgment and grasped the opportunity with the greatest of eagerness and goodwill. The merchants put at his service a little ship called the *Seaflower* and stocked her with goods to be used in trading with whatever fishermen might have dried cod to sell, or with the Indians for furs.

Charles Robin was the son of Philip Robin and Anne d'Auverge. He had been well educated and well trained in the business methods of the day. From the subsequent history of the fisheries we can imagine that he was a man of more than ordinary will power and concentration, ambitious to a degree, revelling in a war of wits and using his power like an absolute monarch.

The report of his first journey to Gaspé was an enthusiastic report on the possibilities of developing profitable trade. So the following year he was sent out again, this time with a bigger ship and more goods of trade. The *Discovery* was a vessel of 118 tons burden. On June 2, 1767, he dropped anchor at Paspébiac to found a venture that, like the Hudson's Bay Company in the northwest, took the whole of Gaspé in its grip and acted as feudal lord of the population for more than a century. In every fishing village in Gaspé the name Robin, Jones and Whitman testifies to the vision of Charles Robin of Jersey.

Paspébiac was an ideal location for the headquarters of the new enterprise. Its barachois was one of the greatest, if not the greatest, on the Gaspé coast. The shore was hilly and fertile. Unlike other fishing stations, there was no river flowing out of the land into the bay. This barachois was the work of the sea alone and a picturesque bit of work it was. Two great sand and gravel bars met almost at right angles, the apex pointing towards the sea. Each of the arms was a mile long. The bars were wide enough to provide for all the docks and fish houses and stores that the company would ever need. The tickle was near the shore to the west and gave entrance into a protected lagoon. Probably the hard headed young Jerseyman had little time to think about the beauty of the place and to his eye its chief virtues lay in the quality of its gravel, the breadth of its harbor and its proximity to the cod banks. He was a man of decision and energy and within twenty-four hours after he had landed his men at Paspebiac, he was off upshore again on the *Discovery* to Bonaventure Island "to make a proposition to the planters" and to meet William Smith. Smith was apparently his only rival in Gaspé. He had come down from Quebec as the agent of a firm of merchants with headquarters there but had left them to set up in business on his own account. Charles Robin persuaded him that he would be better off in the employ of the Jerseymen.

As Smith was well established among the Acadians and as they were by far the most populous and thrifty of the Gaspésians, Robin did a good stroke of business by appropriating all their trade by drawing Smith into his organization. His business at Bonaventure accomplished, he pushed on up the Baie des Chaleurs to round up the Indians as recruits for his enterprise. At Ristigouche he found them encamped in scores of birch bark teepees and burned with zeal to attach them to his cause. He had been provided with a letter of introduction to the chief of the tribe by the Roman Catholic priest at Bonaventure. No sooner had he landed than he hastened to find the chief and presented him with the note.

Now this old chief had been one of the converts of the French missionaries and had, moreover, been taught to read and write. He was very proud of all his acquired manners and customs, which he had adopted from his French neighbors. Among other things he had instituted the Christitan Sunday. And he had acquired a pair of spectacles.

The chief accepted the letter courteously, produced his glasses, adjusted them carefully and then proceeded to read. Then he informed his visitor it was Sunday and consequently he could transact no business until it was over. It was, however, a feast day, and Robin was pressed to join the tribe at meat. There was another white visitor, Surveyor Pringle, who sat on the chief's right hand, while Robin sat in the place at his left. Robin had no choice but to make the best of it. Business is business and much may be won or lost over the dinner table. So with the best possible grace he accepted the pewter platter of moosemeat. When Monday came the chief told him that all their furs were gone. He had come too late to profit by that trade.

Robin was not to have things his own way and opposition developed from a very logical quarter. Boston had always had an acquisitive eye on the fisheries of Gaspé and this invasion of the American shore—now British territory and so part of the American colonies,—by a Jerseyman who was no better than a Frenchman, in Bostonian eyes, was not to be tolerated.

Robin left himself open to trouble through a technicality. He had cleared from Jersey for Gaspé without putting into any British port for clearance papers and the Bostonians seized on this pretext as a means of ousting him from Gaspé. When he came back the third year, in 1768, H.M.S. *Glasgow* sailed into Baie des Chaleurs with orders to turn him out. The letter from Commissioner of Customs at Gaspé said that the Channel Islanders were "downright smugglers and villians". Since, in addition to his first mistake, he had not entered at the customs station in Gaspé Bay, he left himself wide open to the intrigue of the jealous colonists.

Both the *Seaflower* and the *Discovery* were seized at Paspébiac and all the goods the customs officials and naval officers could find. But Robin was not to be entirely outwitted. He had safely concealed enough goods to carry on his trading until the company in Jersey could adjust things. He moved to Arechat for the winter and lived in a little cabin turfed outside for warmth but nevertheless so cold that his barrel of beer froze within a foot of the chimney and his bread had to be thawed for half an hour before each meal. His brothers had joined him in the Gaspé trade and one of them he sent home to report on what had happened, while he himself stayed on the spot to consolidate the gains he had already made.

His persistence was rewarded and presently all opposition was ironed out. "Jersey fishing rooms" began to grow on all the best fishing beaches in Gaspé. The "fishingroom" like the old fishing stations described by Nicholas Denys, consisted of stages for the landing of fish, equipment for gutting, splitting and salting, flakes for drying, the cookhouse and cabins for the men, the house for the agent in charge and, above all, a great store house for the dried cod and the casks of cod liver oil.

Month by month and year by year, Charles Robin labored devotedly at the building of a great trading enterprise. He was a hard taskmaster. No abbot ever ruled his monastery with a more austere authority. The boys for the Gaspé trade were selected from only certain quiet parts of Jersey for they must not be "accustomed to town dissipations". They were earmarked before they entered their 'teens and were brought up with the idea that all their thought and energy must be directed to the welfare of the merchants and that their employers had feudal rights over their comings and goings. No man in the employ of the company was allowed to marry. Or at least if he did marry he had to leave his wife behind him in Jersey and tend to business with undivided attention. All the office routine was dictated by Robin. All the men's habits of living were made to conform with the best interests of the capitalists. All the equipment had to be uniform and its use unvaried. Even the menus were laid down by the autocrat of Gaspé. Yet in spite of the severity of this monastic life, the men bowed to the imperious ways of the Jerseyman and the fisheries flourished under the dictatorship of Charles Robin.

He roused jealousies and rivalries, of course, but he brooked no opposition to his will within his own realm. Year by year he rose in the estimation of the Jersey capitalists who congratulated themselves on their astuteness in putting the young man in charge of the venture. After ten years of ever mounting profits they gravely presented him with a gold watch in testimony of their approval.

However, events over which Charles Robin had no control were shaping in America. The English colonies were in rebellion. Robin had much to fear from them. His old enemies, the New Englanders, would welcome any chance to pounce down on his fishing stations and take over his well-established trade. If the Americans took Quebec his mercantile fate would be settled. He hung on, cheered by the news that Arnold and Montgomery had been defeated at Quebec and that the Canadian colonists were loyal. However, he was vastly uncomfortable while his ships were on the seas. American privateers were doing a ruinous business in the Atlantic and owners of trading ships were gloomy with anxiety once their cargoes were afloat.

Then one bright summer day while everyone at Paspébiac was hard at work, a startled cry went round that two strange ships were heading in together towards the barachois. Robin hurried down to the dock to stare across the bay. Sure enough, two rakish ships with every inch of sail spread, like great birds of prey were swooping towards the harbor. When they came near enough to be identified, the fishermen saw the new flag of the revolutionists,—the stars and stripes.

Privateering was pirating with authority from the state, whether the head of the state was a king or a president. A privately owned ship, with a crew of adventurers trained to fight, was granted letters of marque which authorized it to do whatever damage it could to enemy ships and property and to share the loot with king or president.

Robin was loading two ships, *The Hope* and *The Bee* with dried cod. They were unprepared to defend themselves and the station was at the mercy of the invaders' brass guns. The Americans had their way at Paspébiac. Its storehouses were looted and when the privateersmen had stowed away all they wanted on their own ships, they put prize crews aboard *The Hope* and *The Bee* and sailed away with them. The war had come to Gaspé.

Later, the Americans fell foul of two British ships of war, the *Hunter* and the *Piper* who captured the whole fleet. Robin was offered the chance to salvage his two ships, for the navy apparently considered its services deserved payment. The price he had to pay for the protection of the navy was so high that the Jerseyman decided to give up the Gaspé trade for the duration of the war.

With the close of the American Revolution came a great change for Gaspé. Charles Robin returned, this time to set up in business for himself. Several others had the same idea and a number of Jersey and Guernsey enterprises took shape at different points around the coast. Many of those who came to build up the fisheries had been privateersmen or perhaps just plain ordinary pirates. But with the end of the war there was a slump in piracy so trans-Atlantic fishing gave these men a chance to combine business and adventure and to put to use their skills as navigators. However, French pirates, or corsairs, were still to be reckoned with. So, when Charles Robin came back to Gaspé, as a precaution he came trading under French colors.

Back at work his energy seemed to be redoubled. In spite of the uneasy years, the breaking out of the French Revolution, the rise of Napoleon, the vast European campaigns of agression and conquest, in spite of the fact that five hundred British ships fell into the hands of French corsairs every year, Robin went his way shrewdly and when he retired in 1802 he had amassed a great fortune. He was the big business man of Gaspé, who saw rivals come into his field, coolly watched their rise and fall and went serenely on, never relaxing his grip, never conceding them the tribute of fear or panic, and one by one they admitted defeat and went ruefully out of Gaspé. Charles Robin was not granted a monopoly, he created it.

Rival firms set up fishing rooms at Bonaventure and at Percé. A London merchant named Schoolbred got land at Migouaska Point while Robin was retired from the trade during the war. Schoolbred carried on during that period and had his ships convoyed to England by men of war. But even Schoolbred seems to have disappeared before the relentless persistance of Charles Robin. One of his rivals began business with a fortune of twelve thousand rounds and lost it all.

The result of this wiping out of competition, unrestrained by laws made to protect the fishermen and their families, was a system of barter that practically enslaved the whole population. There was only one market in which the fishermen could sell and they could sell there only when they also bought there. They never saw money. They were allowed credit in the Robin stores and were provided with their necessities, equipment for their boats, clothing and food for their families. It was all charged against their catch of fish. The merchants fixed both buying and selling prices. Of course the fishermen were always in debt to the company for they were encouraged to buy so that their burden of indebtedness would drive them to industrious fishing. If by any chance they attempted to carry their cod to any new merchant setting up in business, they were summonsed for debt. As all they owned were the boats and nets, these could be seized and the fisherman and his family made absolutely destitute and without a means of livelihood. There was no private enterprise for the fishermen of Gaspé.

Robin was no worse than the average business man of the eighteenth century. The age of humanitarianism was just dawning and its light had not yet reached Gaspé. Justice for the working classes, the rights of man as an individual, fair pay for a day's labor, these were still largely theories, though potent ones, and those who were attempting to put them into practice were condemned as the reddest of red revolutionaries. But today if the business man is no longer allowed to enslave the fishermen, neither is the navy allowed to gouge the merchant for protecting his ships. It took four decades of war, spreading like a bushfire from country to country, to establish the rights of man. The eighteenth century overlapped the age of feudalism on the one hand and the age of democracy on the other, and any age that covers the transition of human consciousness from one set of ideas to another is one of turmoil and catastrophe and experiment. So Charles Robin was an expression of an older age, when the working man was without power or organization to protest or protect himself; even without the vision of what his privileges were, or his responsibilities to his children. "The duty of revolution" as the Chinese call it, had hardly been thought of.

Robin was not without his sense of feudal responsibility. Without him or someone like him who would have done the same thing, Gaspé fishermen would have had no market for their fish. It took a strong man and a strong organization to keep the shuttle of trade working across the Atlantic during those years from the close of the Seven Years' War to the close of the Napoleonic wars. Robin was one of those men with single-tracked minds who accomplish so much in the world of physical enterprise. There was no diffusion of interest to weaken his will. Everything in his own life and in the lives of those he employed was bent to the one purpose of putting dried fish, cod liver oil and furs into the markets of Europe. Life had no other values or significance for him.

He kept six commissioners in Gaspé, two at each of his principal stations. Every second year one of them went home from each agency to report to him, when he had retired to Jersey. His profits were enormous. For every thousand pounds worth of goods he sent to Gaspé, he exported three thousand pounds worth of fish and oil. Most of his trade was with the Mediterranean and South America. Then and always the best grade of fish went to Spain and Italy. The second grade went to Brazil and the third grade to the West Indies. From these places he brought back supplies such as rum and sugar and salt. In the Baie des Chaleurs alone there were eight hundred fishing boats in his service and the trade eventually rose to a value as high as eight hundred thousand dollars a year, in terms of eighteenth century values.

Charles Robin's only successful rival was one of his own men, trained in his own policies and techniques. David Labouthilier did not set up in business for himself until the eighteen-twenties, but thereafter he very neatly duplicated the enterprise of the pioneer. Until recent years Labouthiliers were the nearest rivals in Gaspé to the Robin fisheries. A century after Robin made his first trip in the little *Seaflower,* thirty-five hundred fishermen were employed by the Robin firm and twenty-five hundred by Lebouthiliers.

However, serious competition only began long after Charles Robin had handed over control of the fisheries to his nephews. Until that time he continued to rule with his iron hand. He fought every effort of the government, from the coming of the Loyalists until his retirement from Gaspé, to settle the country with agriculturists. Like the Hudson's Bay Company in the north and west, Robin saw in such settlement only an interference with the chief business of the times, fishing and "making fish". The Hudson's Bay Company complained that settlers would frighten away the fur-bearing animals. Robin said that settlers and their affairs would distract the fishermen from his cod. What he really meant was that enlightened men and women coming from the outside world, with "reading and writing and 'rithmetic", would give his fishermen some idea of what was developing in society where democracy and social responsibility were becoming familiar concepts. It was long after Robin died that the idea of co-operatives was born in 1848 among economically depressed working people who were beginning to understand a little bit about economics.

But the times were moving in the right direction in spite of Charles Robin. At last the government intervened in Gaspé and laid out the country into surveyed townships. Land was offered to the fishermen but Robin persuaded them that they did not need more than ten acres a piece. The simple men accepted what he said and asked only for ten-acre lots. When they got them they realized that they did not have enough land to do any profitable farming. Certainly they could not produce crops and provide pasturage for cows and sheep on such small patches. But the situation served Robin very well. They had more time to fish.

When the government proposed schools for the children of Gaspé, Robin protested vehemently. "Will education make them any better fishermen?" he demanded.

Charles Robin was a great merchant and a great organizer. His enterprise was one of the most remarkable in the industrial history of Canada in his time. He was a successful business man but he was a lonely and cheated man. In spite of all his wealth, all his power, in spite of the pride it gave him to worst his rivals and bend his inferiors to his will, he died declaring that if he had it to do all over again, he would do differently. He denied himself home and wife and children and all that he had won at such a cost he had to pass on to the children of others. The warmth of human companionship, the unpurchaseable affections, Charles Robin had to do without. He had the Midas touch but all about him was

as hard and unresponsive as gold. He lacked the vision to
see beyond his trim fishing stations, lacked the imagination
to picture the days when ships loaded with cod and neat
ledgers would pall upon him.

He was honest enough to admit his mistakes and at least
he realized what he had missed. As he grew older he sometimes found that prosperity became irksome and discipline
lost its savor.

"There's no slave in the West Indies," he wrote, "but what
has much more time to himself and enjoys life better than
I do. If I was clear of the business, all the treasures in the
world would not tempt me to undertake it again."

And so we leave Charles Robin, wealthy, powerful and
lonely. There is not a line or a word that records that he
ever won or earned anybody's love.

Paspébiac is still the headquarters of the great company
that he founded. After several changes it is known today as
Robin, Jones and Whitman. Its headquarters is no longer in
Jersey, but in Halifax. Here on the historic gravel bar are
the offices and stores of the company. Robin's own little
house still stands and is incorporated in the office building.
His great brass key is still in the massive lock in the door
through which he emerged to rule his empire of cod.

Above the great lagoon rises a wooded slope where the
home of the Robin manager overlooks the fishing room, like
a keep overlooking a baronial stronghold. It is a delightful
home surrounded by gardens and filled with memories and
souvenirs of nearly two centuries of a remarkable history.
Here are paintings of the Robin ships, painted in many a
distant port. Here is also a spirited canvas of the raid of
the American pirates. The feudal days are over and what
remains is the flavor of old traditions. Down below until
very recent years a big schooner swung at anchor, the last
lonely survivor of the sailing fleet that carried the name and
fame of Gaspé to the cod-eating countries of the world. If
the spirit of Charles Robin still roams where his dearest
wishes were fostered, he will feel familiar moods among the

cluster of red and white buildings of the fishing room. Here towers the great high gabled storehouse, where thousands of quintals of cod can still be stored. There is a little rounded window under the gable from which a watch was kept up the bay towards the sea to announce the arrival of ships. Now the railway does what the old ships once did, and there is no look-out in the window.

In the offices are quaint, old-fashioned desks and bulky tomes that speak most graphically of the Jersey traditions. The clerks are still, for the most part, Jerseymen, with old Norman names. There is a row of hooks from which hang bunches of huge old brass keys. They might open anything from seamen's chests to secret dungeons. Some of the buildings date to the eighteenth century. In one of the storerooms lie lengths of great chain, old anchors and little brass cannons that spat defiance at privateers and corsairs.

The discipline of Charles Robin still applies in the fishing room. Everything is snowy with whitewash, sweet and airy and spotlessly clean. There is an air at once quaint and efficient about the great barachois of Paspébiac, and quite essentially Gaspesian.

# 21

## Coming of the Loyalists

IT WAS on a little ship named *Gaspé* that the first act of violence in the War of American Independence took place. The *Gaspé* was a revenue cutter at Rhode Island. In running to intercept an incoming ship, in a search for dutiable tea, she ran aground. That night she was boarded by a Boston party, headed by "a respectable merchant" and in the fray that ensued the commander was wounded. A decade later the revolution was over and thousands of those who refused to become "subversive" and to join those who worked to overthrow the old form of government, found themselves unwanted and stripped of their possessions. They were the "die-hards" who could see no good coming out of change, but their very refusal to support changes at home thrust them out into such enormous changes abroad that their history is one of tests of courage and stamina and ingenuity in the lands that gave them refuge. They were Royalists in the eyes of the American revolutionists; they became Loyalists in Canada and were granted officially the right to add to their names the letters U.E.L.,—United Empire Loyalist,— to distinguish them from native Canadians or immigrants from the United Kingdom.

A good many of the Royalists left the new republic for England, and spent their lives pressing claims for their losses in the revolution. Others, more practical minded folks, moved up into Canada and set to work as pioneers to rebuild their fortunes. Many of them came to Gaspé.

It was a terrible uprooting of a people, analogous to the movement of "displaced persons" in Europe in our own day. The Royalists represented a class of property owners, for

the most part, for the colonists could and did obtain land
easily and cheaply. Any man of energy could make himself
independent of landlords in the American settlements. They
represented, too, the most conservative element in the population, loyal to tradition, instinctively averse to violence and
yet they were by no means as subservient or acquiescent as
the same class "at home" in the British Isles. The American
Tory was a more democratic type of citizen, with much
more progressive views on the rights of the individual in both
local and state government, than the British Tory, and this
they presently proved. Nevertheless, the British liberals of
that day were much more sympathetic to the revolutionists,
than were the American Tories.

The Royalists, or Loyalists, as they called themselves, were
not always as romantic as their historians have made them
out to be. The king's officers who tried to treat them as they
would have done Tory subjects at home, were very often
harassed by their very un-Tory demands. They wanted rewards for remaining Tories and frequently we see them pro-
nounced a very troublesome lot. The miracle is, however,
that with the slow-moving machinery of the eighteenth century and the chaos of the post-war years, that these displaced
persons were all fed and clothed and transported to settlement in new lands. "The waste lands of the Crown" in
Canada had to be explored and surveyed before the new
settlers could be released from their temporary encampments
where, like prisoners of war, men, women and children were
fed and clothed at the king's expense. Thousands of them
tramped the weary miles through the wilderness to Canada
seeking homes, while thousands more were transported by
sea to join their fellow refugees in the St. Lawrence regions.

After their hot tempers had cooled the Loyalists began to
realize all that they had lost. The pioneering work of generations had oftentimes been sacrificed to their loyaltty. Now
there was not a hope of retrieving a single acre. The rebels
were exultant. As the Loyalists had been driven out of their
homes or had fled from the fury of the mobs, their lands and

properties had been sold to raise funds for the prosecution of the war. Certainly the new Republic did not want them back demanding the return of their lands. In the shuffle everything had passed into the hands of new owners who were quite content with their bargains. So edicts of death were issued against the great landowners to prevent them coming back to their old communities; the little people knew they had no chance to argue their cases if they went penniless back to their former homes. Traditional loyalty to a king or a throne may be a dramatic emotion in times of crisis; even war may be exciting while the stimulus of righteous indignation and hope of victory sustain the victims, but in the reckoning of the cold dawn of peace, wills falter and high spirits ooze away.

All honor, then, to these quite human exiles and equally human administrators who found a way out of their difficulties and by providing for their own immediate needs, opened up the wilderness for settlement and drew around their new hearths all the traditions of peace.

The Baie des Chaleurs was one of those areas selected as suitable for the planting of the Loyalist colonies. At Quebec, an energetic and good-hearted little Swiss gentleman was the king's deputy. Governor Haldimand was a Gaspésian seigneur in his own right, for he had long since purchased the Seigneury of Pabos with an eye to future developments. Even King George the Third himself showed a personal interest in the Gaspé experiment and allowed eighty thousand pounds to be spent upon it, in laying out dream towns that never materialized. Douglastown was one of them. New Carlisle was another. Both were to become great ports and trading centers. Douglastown was named for its surveyor, Douglas. Vonder Veldon, who laid out New Carlisle got no such reward for his trouble, but he is remembered because of the log cabin he built and which still stands. Governor Cox used to make his home in it, presiding over the court in an upper room and attending church service there, too. He set up the whipping post conveniently nearby.

192

Nicholas Cox was an officer who had distinguished himself in service under Wolfe at the siege of Quebec. He stayed on in the colony and won a post on Governor Carleton's staff. When the Americans, ragged and hopeful, trudged up to Quebec and tried to emulate Wolfe by storming the town, in a snow storm, he helped to rout them and then rounded them up as prisoners. Presently he was appointed to a pretty sinecure as Governor of Gaspé with a tidy salary of a thousands pounds a year. There seemed at the time no need for the new Governor to rouse himself out of the comforts of old Quebec.

Twenty years had passed since he set out with Saunders' great fleet for Quebec. He had earned his repose and some of the sweets of patronage. Then one summer day he had a letter from Governor Haldimand, dated at the Chateau St. Louis in Quebec.

"Sir," said the Governor, "hearing that the settlers of Gaspé, within your district, have fallen into some distress and confusion, I find it necessary to direct that you repair by the first opportunity that offers to that place in order that, by your countenance and such interpositions as you shall find available, you may give them the best assistance which the times and circumstances will admit, to recover the inhabitants out of their apprehensions and to introduce as much order as may be effected among them. Your presence there will be likewise necessary in order to enable me from such observations as you shall from time to time furnish me with, to form such regulations as will be most advantageous to the people concerned in that Post and to the King's government."

There was a ship leaving for Gaspé in two or three days, the Governor informed him, and he was to be ready to depart with it. So in the early days of August, 1778, Governor Nicholas Cox packed up his horsehide boxes and gathered together his briefs and documents and sailed down the St. Lawrence to the rocky principality which had so unaccountably demanded that its governor should govern.

One of those who rose from obscurity to power by his shrewd wit, during the process of revolution was Justus Sherwood. Eventually he joined the governing clique in Upper Canada but while Cox was getting settled in Gaspé, Justus Sherwood was still a royalist spy.

In the early days of the revolution he was arrested and tried for espionage and sentenced for life to confinement in Sunbury Mines. "Before they could execute this shocking sentence," he writes in a memoir, "I had the good fortune to break away from my keepers and fly to the mountains." There in a few days he rounded up some forty Royalists like himself who were in great distress. He led them through the wilderness secretly over two hundred miles of lightly marked trails and brought them out at Crown Point where they offered their services to General Carleton. They were the first body of Americans from the revolting colonies to join the king's forces. Sherwood at once became a scout and a spy and for his services he was attainted by the revolutionaries and lost a thousand acres of land along the Susquehanna and many lots elsewhere as well as some twelve hundred pounds worth of other property.

As soon as the war ended Justus Sherwood was sent to Gaspé to look over the possibilities of settlement of the Loyalists in that region. He went by boat from Quebec and landed first in Gaspé Bay. At first glance he saw nothing promising in Gaspé. "The mountains by their barren appearance present to one's view the very picture of indigence," he wrote but when he had explored Gaspé Basin he found it a "very pleasant commanding place where codfish, lobster and salmon abound."

Percé roused him to a little more interest. "Percé is a very pleasant place, finely situated." He thought it an excellent place for fishing with two hundred acres of cleared land bounded in front by the sea and in the rear by "tremendous mountains".

"If this spot was regularly divided into equal parts it might form a very pretty town about a hundred houses. Pabos was an "exceedingly pretty place when one got into the Basin but the entrance was difficult". He saw in it an excellent millsite and a splendid opportunity to develop the timber trade, as well as the best trading place in the Gulf. Port Daniel was "a roadstead closely surrounded with mountains"; Paspébiac "the next best trading place to Pabos". Justus Sherwood may have been glorifying Pabos to please the Governor for Paspébiac had always been recognized as a better trading center than any other along the South Shore. Bonaventure he found to be "well settled and appears at a distance like a populous town".

At Ristigouche he found the Indian meadows so rich in hay that he exclaimed that "they are the largest and finest I know of in the world and would if properly tended afford many hundreds of thousands of tons of good hay". And all this was way back in 1783.

The land scout thought the country so good that he put in a request for a grant of lands that Robin also wanted at Paspébiac but he graciously modified his petition so that he would be granted only half the harbor at Paspébiac and the adjacent lands as far as Rivière Nouvelle. Robin asked for the whole area around as well as the harbor itself, and neither got what they asked.

In his report to Governor Haldimand, Justus Sherwood suggested that fifteen hundred families could be settled along the Baie des Chaleurs and two hundred at Percé and Gaspé. He also registered a protest against "designing traders" who kept the inhabitants in debt.

Acting on what information he had gathered about Gaspé and the maps of the surveyors, Governor Haldimand inserted his first advertisement of the Gaspé settlements in the *Quebec Gazette* in the following February and May, 1784. Those who wished to go to Gaspé to settle were asked to place their names with the military secretary to the Governor at Quebec and to hold themselves in readiness to be transported to the Baie des Chaleurs in the early summer. All applications had to be in by the ninth of May.

On the twenty-ninth of the month Governor Haldimand again wrote to Governor Cox.

"In pursuance of His Majesty's gracious intention of granting lands in the province as a provision and reward for such of his loyal subjects who have borne arms in support of his government in the late Rebellion," he said, "and in consideration of the great national advantage to be derived from the fisheries in the lower part of this province, I have used every means in my power to engage persons of the above description, artificers and discharged troops who are entitled to portions of land, to form settlements at the Baie des Chaleurs and other most eligible situations. And I hope that from your local knowledge of that country and your station therein, to command to your direction the distribu- of the lands to be granted, confident that your zeal for the King's service will induce you to use every exertion in your power by which benefit can be derived to the public and for the speedy and happy establishment of such of his Majesty's faithful subjects as wish to settle in that quarter."

Along with the letter went official papers, minute instructions, a veritable book of words to which Cox was to refer in every sort of emergency. Haldimand tried to be very fair, for he was an enlightened gentleman for his times and the lessons of the revolution had not been lost on him. His original intention had been to grant to officers the lots along the shore. But he thought better of it.

"Upon reconsidering the King's instructions," he wrote, "and the good effects such an evidence of impartiality must have," he ordered that all land grants were to be made by drawing lots.

"The inconvenience will be very trifling to the officers, their proportions being so much larger than those of the men, it will be in their power to exchange for front lots should any particular situation make it desirable." At the end of twelve months all grants must be settled or they would revert to the crown.

On the ninth of June the first embarkation from Quebec

for Gaspé made quite a flutter in the little capital. The chief migration of Loyalists was up the St. Lawrence to the new townships in Upper Canada. The little fleet of exiles sailing eastward was a novelty and the terraces and quays were lined with the curious and the well-wishers as the little fleet got under way. There were two brigs, the *St. Peter* and the *Polly,* a sloop the *Liberty,* a hoy called *St. Johns* and four whale boats. It was a motley little armada but it carried men and women of stout, even if heavy, hearts and little children who from infancy had known nothing but hardship and tales of war. There were three hundred and fifteen settlers, a hundred and twenty-nine men, a hundred and thirty-two women and the rest children. The ships were heavily laden with supplies to take care of them for three months.

Late in July, thirty-six men of the 84th Regiment were sent down to join them and in the autumn twenty-four more, so that altogether three hundred and seventy-five Loyalists were placed on the land in the Baie des Chaleurs that first year of settlement, 1784.

The June fleet made good time in its sail down the river and landed in Gaspé on the eighteenth of June,—nine days sail. At Gaspé, Governor Cox met them and welcomed them to their new home. He accompanied them when they went on a few days later to the Baie des Chaleurs. But it was by no means a holiday jaunt. The old officer found them a sorry lot to handle. They dawdled along the South Shore, landing here and there to look over the land available but "they would agree to nothing".

However, after furious arguments and all sorts of good and bad suggestions, agreement was finally arrived at and the colonists landed to draw lots out of a hat, for their lands. The first things to be done were the building of cabins and the planting of potatoes. It was early enough to get in a crop to eke out the government rations.

Governor Cox chose as the site of the new Loyalist town a spot between four and five miles west of Paspébiac. It was called New Carlisle. Today New Carlisle is still a Loyalist town and three-quarters of its population are descended from the original inhabitants. It never became the great city that its founders dared to dream about.

It was a fine spot for a backwoods village. The site of the town was elevated and beautifully wooded. Below was a long sandy beach. There was no river here and no bridges to be built, but there was excellent soil for cultivation, a forest rich in game and nearby were freshwater lakes teeming with trout. It was a healthful district, a great point in its favor, for many pioneer communities suffered from ague and other fevers when the land was low or infested with mosquitoes. It might be lonely, but it was also very lovely, and if they kept their hearts high with hope, they could feast their eyes on as fine a countryside as any one of them had left behind in the rebel states.

However, there were disadvantages. Haldimand intended that the Loyalists should engage in the fisheries both for their own benefit and for the advantage to the state of a well-established fishing population. But to the east lay the Jerseymen at Paspébiac who resented this addition to the population. And to the west lay the Acadians who gave them as sour a welcome as Paspébiac but with better reasons. These older inhabitants were quite naturally jealous of the advantages with which these Americans were equipped. The state was paternal towards them and everything was on their side from the lieutenant-governor of Gaspé to the crown itself. The newcomers put on ridiculous airs as long-suffering patriots, thought the old Gaspésians. The rivalry between the old and the new groups reached the point where Haldimand had to appoint a sheriff and a justice of the peace, to lay down a heavy hand on unnecessary lawlessness.

The chief duty of Cox was to keep the Loyalists at work, providing against the winter ahead. They were given everything they needed for a start, building materials, tools, clothing, farm implements. Seeds were available to every family and that first summer gardens were planted with onions, Dutch cabbages, turnips, carrots, beets, marrowfat peas, radishes, water cress and parsley. The women had an allowance of woolen cloth and linen, so much for each child, so much for each adult. Given a genuine desire to settle down to pioneering and the ambition to make good, the Loyalists had more than a fair start in the new country.

The habits of conflict are hard to overcome. The king's favorites felt that the country belonged to them by right of loyalty, for the lessons of adversity had not taught them respect for the rights of others as it might have done. The exasperated Haldimand discovered within a few weeks that they were trespassing on those fine hay meadows of the Micmacs along Ristigouche Bay and preparing to bring on themselves all the problems of an Indian war. He had to intervene to reassure the Indians and to threaten punishment for any one, old inhabitant or newcomer, who invaded the rights of the Micmacs.

There were other things, too, to harass the good Governor. Schoolbred, the English fish merchant, was holding large areas of unoccupied land along the coast, which he refused to yield. He intended to hold them for speculation until the Loyalists had made the land valuable. Haldimand had to intervene. Then he discovered that Charles Robin was irate and was making urgent claims to Governor Cox.

"Mr. Robin's claim is too vague," Haldimand decided, "to admit of any material inconvenience to the immediate settlement of the Loyalists." But he could see that things were becoming complicated for Governor Cox. "You will need aid for the government of the motley society you are employed in settling."

As an assistant to the busy Governor, Haldimand appointed Henry Law of New York, one of the most energetic of the Loyalists. He was born and bred to the sea and had served in the Indian trade. At the outbreak of the revolution he was offered the chief command of the rebel navy but refused it "with fixed contempt and unspoken resolution" as he put it very neatly. He, too, like Justus Sherwood, was condemned for life to Sunbury Mines. He, too, escaped, and rounded up as many pilots as he could trust along the coast, and made off to Canada. A cargo of mahogany that belonged to him was siezed by the British in New York and used to build barricades. By one of the little ironies of war, because the mahogany was used by his own side and not by the enemy, he could get no compensation for it when he put in his claim for losses, at the end of the war when the Loyalists billed the king for property lost in the revolution. Captain Law was a bachelor and perhaps for that reason he was free to act as scout and messenger for Governor Cox and as a reward for his services he got the official post of deputy governor.

The fishing rights of the Loyalists were the cause of no small part of the difficulty. Captain Hugh O'Hara of Gaspé was friendly to the government and from long residence in the country he was able to advise both Cox and Haldimand. He was very anxious to see Haldimand prevent a fishing monopoly. He had seen the trend of Charles Robin's enterprises in the years before the revolution and he knew the Jerseyman was back to plunge more eagerly than ever into the building up of a vast monopolistic system of trade. He urged Haldimand to see that the fishing beaches were reserved for the accommodation of the local residents so that the fishermen who came from the Channel Islands, or from Quebec, for the summer months, would not crowd the colonists out of the fisheries.

Haldimand paid careful heed to those who knew the country better than he did. He laid down rules so that not even the Loyalists could play the dog in the manger. Every man was given an area of beach for his flakes and landing place, but if he did not use them, or allowed a year to pass idly, they were siezed and a value placed on the equipment he had on the land, and it was passed along to some one else. Speculation in beaches was to be regarded as a cardinal sin. Any part of a beach not required by the local fishermen was to be open for the use of newcomers. The conditions were fair enough and considering the press of the thousands of details, of requests and complaints and suggestions, showering upon the desk of stout little Governor Haldimand that summer of 1784, the care he bestowed on Gaspé spoke volumes for his energy and capacity.

However, it did seem like rubbing salt into an open wound when the Loyalists, not six weeks in their new homes, found that at St. Peter's Point, at Bonaventure River, and Bonaventure Island, their late, detested enemies, the American rebels, had come to take their share of the Gaspé fisheries. Their rights in the fisheries were provided for under the treaty of peace, they declared, and set busily to work building stages and flakes and setting their lines on the banks about the coast.

The Loyalists were furious. Having lost everything to the rebels, they settled down to begin all over again only to find themselves confronted by the very people who had impoverished them. Off they sent their protest to Governor Haldimand at Quebec.

Haldimand acted swiftly. Admiral Douglas at the Halifax station was informed of what was afoot, and a British warship sailed up to Gaspé to send the Americans back home to read over their treaty with a little more care.

Shipments of arms and munitions were sent down to Cox to distribute to the Loyalists. With their help they stocked their larders with wild game. They had trout, salmon, mackerel and cod, dried and salted. Their potatoes were coming up and the peas were in bloom. Considering the time they had been at work, the colony seemed to be flourishing. But in spite of this there was more and more trouble.

"I am concerned," writes Governor Haldimand to Nicholas Cox, "to find that you have so many ill-disposed persons among the Loyalists and that the officers whose examples and precepts should influence the lower people to an observance of regularity and good order, should be the most troublesome." Cox was told he might use his power in the curtailment of provisions as an effective inducement to good hehavior. The colonists of the Baie des Chaleurs, he pointed out, had already had twice as much in the way of tools and other provisions as the colonists in Upper Canada.

Meantime, Charles Robin, outwitted by Haldimand, and still demanding a complete monopoly of the beach at Paspébiac, wrote over his head to the King. His petition was sent back to Haldimand. Haldimand had the good sense not to retaliate. "In regard to Mr. Robin," he wrote, "there is no doubt that from the progress he has made in the fisheries as a public good, he merits encouragement, but as the same time every stretch towards the monopoly of lands at a settlement, which will most probably become extensive, must be guarded against."

In the fall Mr. Longmore, a surgeon's mate at the military hospital in Quebec, was despatched to Gaspé to look after the Loyalists, the first medical man to make his appearance among the fishermen.

There are innumerable tragedies and romances hidden away in the papers relating to the exodus and the settlement of the Loyalists. Haldimand's voluminous correspondence was carefully filed away for reference and is a treasure store for the historian of those times. When the king set up a commission to hear the claims of the Loyalists for losses sustained at the hand of their enemies or in the service of the crown, each claimant had to put in writing the story of his services and an inventory of his losses. The petitions remain mute testimony to the uprooting of a people. The proceedings of the commission, neatly inscribed with patient quills, in great volumes, seem to bring back to life once more the strange task of those eighteenth century gentlemen.

On one hand, the king's pocket was not bottomless, and he had a war to pay for as well as his loyal subjects to compensate. On the other hand, even patriots are human. Pine chairs had a way of turning into mahogany settees as they sat down to recall what their losses had been. The bent forks and the battered knives looked, over the distance, like family plate; every little cottage was the mansion of a prosperous land owner. Even big estates had a way of stretching into principalities. It was hard to prove the claimant right or wrong. The Republic of the United States was a long way off and the Commission had no access to its records and archives. The claimants had to call in old neighbors to testify to their honesty. For the most part the claims were plain and authentic enough but there was enough of proved fraud to put the commission on its guard. So the many had to suffer for the few and the commission often bewailed the fact that though it wished to be kind and just it also had to be watchful. The claims they adjusted ranged from a few pounds to one of more than half a million pounds, and another for nearly three hundred thousand pounds. Sir John Johnson laid claim to compensation to the amount of a hundred and three thousand pounds and he was awarded thirty-nine thousand. The sum total of claims paid was £2,613,260. The claims submitted totalled £8,943,658. Years were consumed in the consideration of the petitions and the final payment to the scattered Loyalists at home and abroad.

Chief among the Loyalists to settle at New Carlisle were the members of the Man family. Isaac Man, senior, was jailed several times for his loyalties before he was banished on pain of imprisonment for life if he returned to the rebel states. His home was at Stillwater, New York, where he had land worth four thousand pounds. His petition for claims is a pathetic document, for in it he set out the dear possessions he had lost, "a large Turkey carpet . . . a looking glass . . . mahogany chairs . . . brass fenders . . . candle sticks . . . four feather beds . . . a library of law, divinity and other books . . . silver plate . . . household linen". He was born in New York and was a colonel of militia and a judge of the inferior court when the war broke out, a gentleman of very considerable importance in his little world. He claimed losses of £4,595. The commission awarded him £285. He had no documents to prove the value of what he had lost.

His son, Isaac Man, junior, was in business with him at Stillwater. In 1776 he was jailed at Albany for his obstinacy in supporting the royal cause. The next year he succeeded in getting away and joined Burgoyne's army. After a little while his superiors sent him off to join Jessup's corps. "He has suffered much in prison and is a genteel lad, and fit for an officer," was the way the matter was summed up. In his claim for compensation he mentioned a feather bed and furniture worth twenty pounds, as well as a sword worth ten pounds. Altogether his claim came to eight hundred pounds. He was awarded £78. It was assumed that his family was amply provided for as Isaac Man, senior, had a pension of thirty pounds a year.

These were two of the men who brought their exiled women to the Baie des Chaleurs to make new homes. Colonel Man was one of the leading men among the Loyalists and in recognition of his abilities he was made sheriff of the district until his death nineteen years later, at the age of seventy-three. He lies among the pioneers at New Carlisle.

Captain Azariah Pritchard was one of the Welsh Loyalists of Gaspé. He had owned a ship that was captured by the rebels and he owned a grist mill that was confiscated. Thereupon from a passive loyalty he turned to an active one and spent the rest of the years of revolution as a spy and a guide in the country round about Lake Champlain. His father and brother were revolutionists. He rose to the rank of Captain in the King's Rangers and he was an officer on half pay when he chose to join the settlers in the Baie des Chaleurs. He laid claim to compensation of more than two thousand pounds. He had to content himself with £450. Captain Pritchard built a grist mill with what little fortune he had left and ground the first flour for the pioneers.

As time went on the animosities died out and hopes rose higher in the hearts of the newcomers. Gaspé was "the best country for a poor man", they agreed, as they harvested their crops and turned their cod on the flakes. By November of the first year they had exported twenty-five thousand quintals of cod. The Baie des Chaleurs colony prospered so well that in 1785 Governor Cox moved the seat of his government from Gaspé Bay to New Carlisle. A new era had opened in the history of the peninsula.

# 22

## *Vice-Regal Memories*

THE road from New Carlisle to Bonaventure lies through fine agricultural country and long established farms. The road skirts Pointe Bonaventure, crosses the River Bonaventure and brings us into the historic settlement of the same name. The name itself is one of the oldest in Gaspé and comes from a ship which sailed into this little harbor in 1591, commanded by Sieur de la Cour-Pré-Revillon.

It is a lovely bit of country with red stone cliffs, a river with a broken barachois and mud flats and, far inland, many little tributaries where game fresh water fish abound. On the sea front there are long beautiful beaches for bathing and there is also a board walk on which the citizens love to take their evening strolls. The town is a favorite resort for visitors from the Upper St. Lawrence who come back year after year to enjoy its leisurely hospitality, to hunt for game in the nearby forests and to haunt the salmon pools in the hilly, river-freted interior.

The Gaspé Road runs close to the sea as it takes us out of the Bonaventure countryside. The next village on our way is little St. Siméon. Its church with a shapely tower faces the sea and is a landmark for many miles around. Of course the citizens of St. Siméon fish for cod but they do not depend on it entirely for a livelihood. This is a farming township, proud of its herds of cattle. A great deal of butter is shipped inland to the city markets.

The land has become so gentle that we no longer face the steep climbs of the rest of Gaspé, so we leave the village by merely ascending a hill and come out on top of a headland. There before us, in the lap of the hills, is a lovely scene. The headland we are surmounting is known as Black Cape, a powerful, brooding promontory of volcanic rock. Along its summit the village of St. Charles de Caplan spreads itself. There are pleasant water trips in this vicinity and one of them is round the point of Black Cape.

There is dispute about the name of Caplan and there seem to be a choice of explanations, one as good as the other. There was, it seems, an Indian by the name of Caplan camping on the river nearby when the first settlers came. The river was named for him. However, newcomers seldom adopted Indian place names and were even less inclined to name them for their Indian neighbors. Then it is said that the settlers spoke of the vicinity as Cape Land and it was written down as Caplan by the French. Still others say that there was plenty of bait, known as caplan or capelan, in the river and along the beach. Whatever the truth of the matter may be, the river and the village now bear the name of Caplan.

These hills have something of the charm of the Laurentians, with their rounded peaks and wooded sides, changing with the changing light and shadows of the day. Along the skyline little gothic peaks of pine fret the overhanging blue. Scooped out here and there from the forest are the latest of the fields won from the woods, patient little fields fighting against the encircling growth of the wilderness.

New Richmond grew up around the settler's home at the mouth of the Cascapedia rivers. It is a town spread along the sea shore. The Petite Rivière Cascapedia winds and twists its way down from the mountains about three miles west of the Rivière Cascapedia proper. Down this river came the first of those who crossed the peninsula by way of the Shickshocks, for it is the gateway to the mountains and now also the gateway to a mining country that lies in the heart of the Shickshocks.

The rivers flow onto a beautiful bay enclosed on one side by the Black Cape and on the other by the Capes of Maria. This is a remarkable bit of country. Up the valleys we can see broad, sloping land, smooth with generations of good ploughing and harvesting, crisscrossed by rail fences, but as gentle and kindly a country as we have seen in all Gaspé. It has a rural pattern of land long settled.

New Richmond boasts the deepest area of cultivation in Gaspé, for her farm lands run ten miles back into the valleys. It is largely an English-speaking community and if there is nothing else to testify to the history of New Richmond but its Presbyterian church and graveyard, they would speak for themselves. Both are obviously Scottish and very Presbyterian. There is an air of self-respecting, granite religion about the place that always hides a deep vein of sentiment, if not romance. The little church is old and quaint and its setting is lovely, by the sea shore, with a tall, thin screen of trees between it and the quiet graves and the wind of the bay. The church yard is as well kept as a garden, for there is a reverence here for those who came and laid low the forests with their pioneering hands.

New Richmond was named for the Duke of Richmond, the unfortunate Governor who came out shortly after the Napoleonic wars, to rule from Quebec. He was a friend as well as an officer of the Duke of Wellington. He rode across the field of Waterloo in his train when that famous battle was ended. It was the Duchess of Richmond who gave the famous ball on the eve of Waterloo in Brussels,—"there was a sound of revelry by night",—during which the alarm came and British officers rushed away to battle and many of them to death. The Duke was a man of tremendous energy and he loved to get around the country he was trying to govern. On one of his journeys he was bitten by a pet fox and died a terrible death of hydrophobia.

The Big Cascapédia is a famous salmon stream and winds for eighty miles among the Shickshocks. In the old days, forty miles of the river were reserved for the use of the vice-regal family and many of them came here for their holidays and to fish for the game salmon. One of the best known of the vice-regal visitors was a young daughter of Queen Victoria. Princess Louise, Duchess of Argyle, was an artist, both painter and sculptor. In Kensington Gardens in London is a seated figure of her mother, that came from her studio and there is a replica of it at the Victoria College in Montreal. She made a romantic marriage with the Marquis of Lorne who later on became the Duke of Argyle. It was considered a most extraordinary thing for a daughter of the Queen-Empress to marry "beneath her" but the queen wisely consented, although the Marquis of Lorne must have been considered lamentably modern in those severe Victorian days. He had very liberal political views, dabbled a little in the arts and sciences and was himself an author. While they were in Canada, during his term as Governor-General, he founded the Royal Society of Canada, and Princess Louise, working discreetly through her husband, founded the Royal Canadian Academy. In her widowhood Princess Louise went to live for many years in old Kensington Palace. She lived to be a very old lady, probably given much to memories, and so perhaps sometimes in that old London home she recalled the silver dapples of sun on those cool salmon pools of the Cascapedia where she once sketched while her husband fished, and thought happily of the hours in the birch woods where the green and golden light played around her while she ate her picnic lunches so long ago. Princess Louise lived until 1939.

The little town of Maria, and the great Capes of Maria, commemorate another vice-regal lady, a notable little figure in the history of Quebec, Lady Dorchester. Somehow this only memorial to her in Canada seems oddly at variance with herself and her story and so it must have been a curious mischance. She was everything that this rugged headland is not,—petite, sophisticated, elegant.

Guy Carleton was one of General Wolfe's favorite officers. A serious young man, he took soldiering very much to heart, and after distinguishing himself at Quebec, he eventually went back to the Canadian capital as Governor-General. King George the Third had no use for Guy Carleton. Carleton had been heard to say things that, repeated at court, rasped the King's ears. He was not going to allow him to join the expedition to Quebec. Young General Wolfe had the audacity to oppose the royal wishes, and, strangely enough, the king bowed to the young man's demands. Guy Carleton got his appointment on Wolfe's staff. The time was to come when Carleton saved Canada for the English crown by preventing the Canadians from joining the American rebels. When Guy Carleton came back as Governor-General of Canada he was Lord Dorchester.

With all his fighting and governing, Lord Dorchester had had little time for romance. Now he was getting on in years, he had a distinguished title and no little influence. But he had no wife. On a visit to England he became very interested in a daughter of his friend, Lord Effingham. He conferred gravely with her father and received his permission to propose marriage to her.

The young lady was very fond of him. She probably regarded him as an extra uncle. She was startled and dismayed when he heard his proposal. She left him in tears and going into the garden found her sister, Maria, and a companion, sitting there. She sobbed out to them that she had refused "the best man in the world". "The more fool you," said Lady Maria severely.

The companion repeated the little phrase to the lady's father and he repeated it to Lord Dorchester. It surprised him. Probably it flattered him and soothed his wounded sensibilities. He proposed again and with better luck. Lady Maria decided to become Lady Dorchester.

As it happened it was an excellent arrangement. Lady Maria was an aristocrat to her finger tips. She had been educated in France and trained at the court of Versailles in the last luxurious years before the revolution. She held her slim little body as regally as if she was Marie Antoinette, and she knew how to wear the picturesque and voluminous crinolines of her day to perfection. When Lord Dorchester brought this paragon of all the French virtues to the Chateau St. Louis, Quebec was charmed. The Queen is dead; long live the Queen. No doubt little Lady Dorchester did a lot to fan the fires of enthusiasm for royalty and vice-royalty after they had died out in the rebel colonies to the south, and while they were being quenched in the blood of the French revolution.

A township, new about the time of their arrival, was named Carleton for the Governor and the old village of Tracadigache was re-named for him also. As a gesture of tribute to his lady the great capes were named for her and eventually a little town adopted the name also.

Three of the delicacies of Maria are lobster, plaice and eels. At Maria is an Indian reservation where some of the Micmac tribe, turned farmers, now that the days of trapping and hunting are over, cultivate their little farms.

# 23

## *Evangeline's People*

W EST of the Capes of Maria we run into the shores of Tracadigache Bay with its great triangular barachois, around which lies the town of Carleton. Tracadigache is an Indian word meaning "the home of the herons" and the bay was one of the places explored by Jacques Cartier more than four hundred years ago. The mountains lying northwards are known as Tracadigache Mountains and the great dome towering over the town and barachois is Carleton Mountain. The hike to the top is a pleasant one and will pay returns in fine views and long vistas of the surrounding countryside.

When the Loyalists settled along the bay, the settlement at Tracadigache became the focus of their activities and in gratitude to the man who had supervised the expatriation of of the royalists from New York, and who was Governor-General of their newly adopted country, they changed the name to Carleton.

When they came it was already a well settled and highly cultivated countryside. The story behind it is one of the most familiar as well as one of the most tragic in our history, for almost everyone knows something about the Acadians who planted hereabouts their wealth of traditions.

The Acadians are quite a distinct and folk-proud branch of the Canadians. They are descended from colonists brought out from France in the sixteen-thirties by Sieur de Razilly, who came to govern Acadia for the Company of One Hundred Associates, of which he was a partner. The Acadia to which they came and whose name they took as their own, was a vast kingdom with scarcely defined limits. It was generally conceded to consist of what is now Nova Scotia, New Brunswick and Gaspé. When it suited their purpose its kings, now French, now English, stretched its boundaries one way or another.

It was to Acadia that the Huguenot trader, Sieur de Monts, turned to found a trading post in 1604, after his friend and agent, Sieur de Champlain, had explored its coasts and the Lower St. Lawrence. De Monts' little colony at Port Royal, or what is now Annapolis Royal, was the first permanent settlement in what is now Canada. While the French were experimenting there the first English colonists were settling at Jamestown and in Virginia. But when Champlain a few years later on decided on Quebec as a more desirable place for a post and settlement, Port Royal lost its original importance. All eyes turned to Quebec, much more dramatically placed in the shadow of Cape Diamond on the St. Lawrence.

The rollicking King of France, Henry of Navarre, who fought like a tiger for the throne of France, and was said to have been carried there "on the points of Huguenot swords", died too soon for the good of his Huguenot explorers and colonizers. Evil times fell upon them. Sieur de Monts was relieved of all his privileges in Acadia. A lady wanted his lands and they were granted to her in the name of the child king who succeeded Henry the Fourth.

The lady who comes into our history as the owner of the whole coast line of North America from Gaspé to Florida was the Marquise de Guerchville. France overlooked the fact that there were already English colonies to the southward, so that the lady could have the distinctiy pleasurable thrill of looking at the map and imagining herself mistress of an enormous new sea kingdom.

The Marquise de Guerchville is the heroine of one of those rare anecdotes of French court history in which virtue vanquishes a royal heart. The Marquise was a famous beauty, wealthy and witty and an ornament to the royal circle. Wicked old Henry of Navarre, who gives so much color to the stage of French history, with his frankly piratical eyes which gleam even out of his portraits, quite naturally fell in love with the lovely Marquise. And quite naturally he let the lady know how he felt about it. Henry stormed and won Paris but the lady was impregnable in her haughty virtue. To Henry's practiced importunities she made her famous reply:

"Sire, my rank, perhaps, is not high enough to permit me to be your wife, but my heart is too high to permit me to be your mistress."

Perhaps Henry had heard remarks something like that before, for he did not lose heart.

He knew that the Marquise lived in regal magnificence in her chateau at La Roche Guyon, so he organized a hunting party in that neighborhood. As was the privilege of kings, he sent a messenger to the chateau to inform the Marquise that he and his suite would do her the honor to spend the night under her roof.

At the end of a day's hunting, and in a sprightly royal humor, King Henry turned his horse's head down the road to La Roche Guyon. As they came through the woods to the walls of the castle he saw that candles blazed in every window and there was evidence that nothing had been left undone that would do him honor. The lady was there at the door, gracious and beautiful and hospitable. The king was shown to his rooms and smiled in secret satisfaction. When he had refreshed himself he sallied forth to meet his hostess. To his consternation he discovered she had fled. She was bound, he was told, for a neighboring chateau in her travelling coach and the message she left for his majesty told him that she preferred to quit her roof while another ruled under it. The king took the hint and saved his amorous adventuring for less troublesome quarters.

However, the lady, unlike most virtuous ladies, had her reward. The king made her a lady in waiting to his queen, Marie de Medici. "Here is a lady of honor who is indeed a lady of honor," he said significantly as he presented her.

Now, apparently as she grew older, the Marquise grew more and more virtuous and more and more ambitious. When the Jesuits wanted to find someone who would further their plans for the American missions they found the very person in the Marquise de Guerchville. She secured a grant of all the Atlantic coast and nominated the ardent and vigorous Jesuits to Christianize the Indians in place of the poor and gentle Recollets who had been doing their best with the Micmacs at Port Royal.

The Marquise de Guerchville played only a short part on the stage of Gaspésian history, for Argall came up from New England in 1613 and put an abrupt end to her missions. Presently King James carved Nova Scotia out of Acadia and gave it to Sir William Alexander. But finally Acadia went back to the French and the Company of One Hundred Associates sent out a Governor to settle it with farmers and traders and fishermen and missionaries to the glory of God and the King of France.

When Sieur de Razilly sailed out to govern Acadia, its population consisted of four tiny settlements,—the post of Charles de la Tour at Cape Sable, Captain Daniel's at Ste. Anne's not far from the site of Sydney, the remnants of a Scottish settlement at Port Royal, and a trading post on Miscou Island, at the entrance to Baie des Chaleurs.

Razilly's instructions were to eject every British subject in Acadia and to plant French colonists in the most promising quarters of the great wilderness. He began by establishing a colony of his own at La Havre and continued by encouraging emigration of intelligent and enterprising farmers.

To that movement of Sieur de Razilly's to people Acadia the race of Acadians owe their origin. They took the great new lands to their hearts and in return the land prospered them, and imprinted on them new characteristics that they bear to this day in spite of all the sorrows and struggles they were doomed to face. For three-quarters of a century the Acadians tilled the rich virgin land of Nova Scotia. They built steeped-roofed houses that from generation to generation took on more of the comforts and civilities of gracious living. With patience and steady effort they built up the fertile mud flats of the tidal rivers with cribwork and created the famous dykelands of Acadia. To this day the dykelands of the Acadians add to the richness and the beauty of Nova Scotia, and over the areas where they developed their tidy settlements there is a brooding sense of their presence to these times which not even generations of new comers can dissipate.

The year 1713 saw Acadia, or that part of it which covered Nova Scotia, but not Gaspé, transferred for good to the rule of the British crown. Acadians suddenly found themselves British subjects. They were shrewd and land-loving, more loyal to their Acadian homes than to distant France. Left to themselves they might have settled down eventually to reconciliation with their new fortunes, but those in France and New France, who hated the English and who grieved over the loss of the colony, sent agents and emissaries among them to keep their memories fresh, to be-devil the English and to instill a panicky fear of the new rulers and what they might someday inflict on a subject race. Of course the agitators eventually brought down the very evils they had created in imagination. The Acadians refused to take the oath of allegiance to the crown, the crown officers became suspicious of the Acadians, and year by year antagonism and resentment grew and flourished. As a matter of fact, the British were patient. It was only when the Seven Years' War was imminent that their resentment of the Acadian posititon ripened into action. In 1755, forty-two years after Acadia became a British colony, when the greater part of the Acadians were in fact born and bred as British subjects though still maintaining their allegiance to France, the British administrators decided upon an expulsion of the dangerous population which might rise, to a man, imbued with the fanatic patriotism of a national minority, and strike from the back while England was engaged in a life and death struggle with France in America.

216

It was a day and age in which many things were justified that our more recent humanitarianism finds revolting. War is never commendable under any circumstances. Today we can sympathize with both sides in an unhappy situation. A rich and hostile population was an element to fear, and, on the other hand, the Acadians knew that after a long history of resistance and political conflict, there was no hope, in the shadow of war, of lenience from their rulers. The wiser of the Acadians prepared for voluntary migration from the lands of their forefathers.

There were at the time ten thousand Acadians in Nova Scotia. Some of them were very rich. Some of the far-sighted turned everything they could into gold, sold their farms and set off to live under the French flag for which they professed so much ardor. Some of them went to Prince Edward Island. Some went farther afield, with their household goods, their farm implements and their cattle crowded into broad-beamed little sailing ships,—they went to the Baie des Chaleurs. Of the ten thousand in Acadia, six thousand were afterwards expelled, another thousand escaped to the woods and made their way eventually to other settlements. About three thousand went into voluntary exile.

How many came to Baie des Chaleurs we do not know but the number was considerable. Very shrewdly they chose lands in the vicinity of Tracadigache, not unlike the lands they left behind them. They loved the soil. They must have sighed for the fat lands they had left but they set sturdily to work to create new homes and new fields. The little log cottages were as nearly like the farm houses of Acadia as they could make them. They dug wells and planted apple trees and tended their cattle as diligently as their forefathers had done in the wilderness that had come to blossom like the rose. Presently their meadows were lying like dusty gold under the autumn suns of Gaspé, their barns bulged with the harvests, and to the vespers that rang, sweet and gentle, over the new settlement, they responded with the same prayers of gratitude and praise. And well they might. Many of those who waited until they were driven out of Acadia wandered for long unhappy years throughout the strange colonies along the Atlantic coast, only to find their way, some of them, up to Gaspé long after Tracadigache had become a smiling land.

But the bitter irony of the situation made itself clear when the Seven Years' War ended and the Acadians of Gaspé found themselves once again under British rule. Perhaps they had learned a lesson, perhaps now that France had been vanquished and the fleur de lys flew over only two little insignificant islands in the Gulf, the British could afford to overlook a lot and regard the Acadians merely as good farmers and settlers. Certainly as soon as the English speaking business men got down to trading in the new colonies, it was here they sent agents to develop trade and commerce. A few years later after the War of the American Revolution, when so many British were in turn expatriated, Justus Sherwood was astonished when his tour of inspection brought him to this vicinity. As far as he could see from his ship the little homes clustered along the roadway, with their attendant barns.

Well might the colony grow for the Acadians were a prolific people. There is the record of one of them, Grandpere Forest who, when he died, counted among his descendants three hundred and eighteen Gaspésians. A true patriarch was Grandpere Forest.

The Acadians of Bonaventure did not take their second transplanting to British rule without striking a blow for their old allegiance. During the Seven Years' War many a privateersman that preyed upon the British ships in the Gulf hailed from the Baie des Chaleurs and was manned by Acadians. Occasionally they were chased home by irate British ships and on occasion they came to disaster at the hands of their intended victims.

The Acadians have always been intensely proud of their descent and their traditions. They were a self-conscious people and when they settled in Gaspé they brought all their pride and prejudice witth them. Indeed they showed a distaste

218

for their neighbors that persisted until recent times. They considered themselves socially a step above the Gaspésians whether they were French Canadian, Channel Islands or the Pasby Jacks as the descendants of Norman and Basque fishermen and Indian women were called. Generations passed before the Acadians would intermarry with any of them.

These were the neighbors to the west that the Loyalists discovered when they settled in New Carlisle that first summer of 1784. The exiled Americans, it would be expected, might have a deep sympathy with the Acadians and an admiration for what they had accomplished since their expulsion. Curiously, that sympathy was entirely lacking. Like the Acadians they had wandered far from their homes, their enemies were in possession of the acres their forefathers had taken from the wilderness and they were about to begin all over again. Yet instead of taking heart from the excellent example of the Acadians, the Loyalists looked, as Justus Sherwood had looked, at those long fields, at the cows browsing so contentedly in the deep meadows, at the whitewashed houses with their broad chimney stacks and realized how desirable they were. So they proposed to Governor Cox that he should expel the Acadians and put the Loyalists on their lands!

The suggestion was actually forwarded to Governor Haldimand who found it revolting to his sense of justice. No wonder he began to think of the Loyalists as a motley crew. The suggestion was not entertained for a moment by any of the authorities, but the Acadians must have known what was in the minds of the newcomers and it was a poor basis on which to build up a neighborly spirit.

However, the times of tension were over. The new government of Canada was entirely friendly to the thrifty Acadians. Governor Haldimand was a great admirer of the Acadians and their ways. When Governor Cox wrote to tell him that some Acadians were anxious to move down the shore and settle on Haldimand's seigneury at Pabos, Haldimand wrote:

"I have not yet decided with respect to Pabos and as I shall probably sell or settle it all at the same time, I should be sorry to disappoint any of the Acadians by placing them there at present, but if I should settle it I shall certainly prefer them to any other people."

The little town of Carleton boasted the first post office in Gaspé, way back in 1796. Before that the mails came only once a year from Fredericton by courier and the only way of communicating with Gaspésians between mails was by messenger or by the chance fortune of travellers bound that way. It was 1819 before Douglastown had a post office, too. By 1829 there were actually two or three mails every winter. The first government mail carrier from the Upper St. Lawrence was Noel the Indian, who came down through the Matapédia Valley with his pack on his back, sometimes on foot, sometimes by canoe, sometimes on snowshoes. How eagerly the Loyalists must have watched for him, hungry for news of scattered friends and relatives and the mending of their broken fortunes.

Long before the coming of the Loyalists, Philip Robin, the brother of Charles Robin, settled in Tracadigache and brought with him Jersey willows to plant. They have spread all along the coast.

# 24

## Battle of Ristigouche

THE Baie des Chaleurs comes to an end at Migouaska Point. Beyond lies Ristigouche Bay in which, much to his annoyance, Jacques Cartier realized there was no way open to China at this point.

The Ristigouche and Matapédia Rivers meet to flow into this glorious estuary, fourteen miles long, enclosed on every side by hills. The bay varies from half a mile wide, between Cross Point and Campbellton, New Brunswick, to three miles at its widest part. Navigation ends at Cross Point but little boats can sail up the winding channels of the estuary.

The cliffs at Migouaska Point are famous among geologists and they have been named the Hugh Miller Cliffs in honor of a great Scottish geologist. In no place in the world is there a greater wealth of fossil fishes and small sea creatures than in these red stone cliffs. Specimens from them have gone to museums all over the world.

The land about Migouaska once comprised the seigneury of John Schoolbred, a London merchant who engaged in the fishing here in the eighteenth century. There was not a settler on it when the Loyalists came and he introduced methods of land speculation by holding it for the increased values the land would have when the newcomers had made the country prosperous.

One of Napoleon's old army surgeons, Dr. Labillois, was one of the nineteenth century colonists on this part of Gaspé and a strange place it must have been to him after his army experience in France.

Beyond Magouaska Point the Gaspé Road frequently leaves the water's edge and runs inland through woods and farmlands. Off the road, just before Cross Point is Pointe à Bourdeau, the focus of a large settlement of French Canadians who came here from the Upper St. Lawrence in the seventeen-fifties and formed a colony which they called New Rochelle. For three miles along the shore, in true French Canadian fashion, the steep-gabled cottages stood while the colonists laid out their fields in ribbon strips running back into the hills. By the time of the fall of Louisbourg in 1758, New Rochelle had become quite an important place.

When Wolfe came with his ships and men to steal the fishermen's nets and burn their huts, as he put it ironically, for some unknown reason he left the Baie des Chaleurs almost unmolested. He must have known about New Rochelle, but he sent no one here to set torch to their dwellings and their barns and their fish houses.

The following year the siege of Quebec accomplished the task Wolfe had been sent out to do. New France was in British hands, although Levis still held out a forlorn hope in Montreal. Much depended upon which side got reinforcements first in the spring. If French ships of war with transports of troops and supplies sailed up the river to Quebec, the hard-pressed British garrison, depleted by hardship and disease, could scarcely hope to hold out. If British ships arrived first, the kingdom that Wolfe had conquered would be saved and all New France would see the red flag of the British replace the lillies of France.

As everyone knows, the British ships got there first. But all the time French ships were on the way. When they found that by going on to Quebec they would only run into a net, they turned back. Most, if not all the fleet, put in to Baie des Chaleurs, sailed the length of it and came to anchor off Pointe à Bourdeau. The shore was fortified. The place names still carry the memory of those old defences, Ruisseau a l'Officier, Point a la Batterie, Point a la Garde.

What was New Rochelle thinking as it watched these ships at anchor under its feeble defences? There were four great warships, twenty-two schooners with troops and supplies, and many smaller ships. Everyone was discussing the disaster, the fate of the fleur de lys, debating what next to do, in which way lay the least of the evils.

Meantime the British had heard news of where the French ships had gone. A little fleet of five men-of-war under the command of "Foulweather Jack" was sent off to hunt them out. "Foulweather Jack" in ordinary parlance was Admiral Lord Byron who gave the world the son who was, of all his line, to be known simply as Byron.

The British ships sailed down to the end of Baie des Chaleurs with every flag flying and all their guns yelping for prey. There between the hills the last naval battle of the Seven Years' War was fought for six long days. The four French ships of war were demolished. Thirty Frenchmen were killed. All the supply ships fell prizes of war. It was a battle bitterly contended and in the course of it two hundred houses in New Rochelle were destroyed and the settlement laid waste.

So ended the war that fixed the status of French and English in America. By driving the French from the new world, the British prepared the way for the revolution of the American colonies. It was the colonists who wanted the Frenchmen driven off their northern flanks. Once that was done they had no need for the protection British army and navy could give them. Free from danger from the north, the colonists got down to the business of rebellion. For fifteen years all the Atlantic colonies were under British colonial rule. Then came 1775 and the Declaration of American Independence.

Quantities of shells have been dug up along the shore and in the garden of the monastery at Cross Point mounds of them can be seen to this day.

Cross Point is the site of the old seventeenth century mission to the Micmacs. Canadian Indians have been granted certain Reserves as Indian territory, in the course of their treaties with the Canadian government. Most of the tribes have annual grants of money and gifts in recognition of their treaties. This is one of the Reserves where four or five hundred families live on their little farms with their own schools and religious leadership.

The word Micmac is derived from the Indian word Migmagig meaning "the country of fellowship". Such was the Gaspé of these intelligent and philosophic red men. The missions to the Gaspésians had many ups and downs. First the Recollets attempted to Christianize them, then the Jesuits took over and when they had abandoned the field as hopeless, the Recollets tried again. All of them at one time or another worked here at Cross Point among the pagans.

After the Ristigouche mission had been abandoned for some years and the old monastic buildings had fallen into decay (probably between the British conquest and the French Revolution), the fortunes of war once more gave them life. A hundred and forty French priests, exiled from France at the point of the revolutionary sword, found refuge here in the tumbledown mission buildings. Judging by the death toll they must have been ill and hopeless before they crossed the sea for sixty-seven of them died.

In the course of time Capuchins settled down to revive the interrupted mission work.

The Micmacs clung persistently to their language and their customs. Their traditions were very dear to them but they looked back gratefully to that old missionary, Father LeClercq, who had devised for them a written language of symbols which they had found of extraordinary value in communication. Father LeClercq went back to France. The mission fortunes ebbed and flowed, years passed when there was no one to teach them their prayers. But the language of symbols they cherished.

In the middle of the eighteenth century a missionary named Abbe Maillard discovered these symbols still in use and made use of them; a century later Father Christian Kauder, born in Luxemberg and much travelled in the Catholic missions, was sent to Tracadie to rest in broken health. There, in his unaccustomed leisure he discovered the Micmac alphabet. Some friends in Austria became interested in his discovery and had a set of Micmac type cut. Presently they published a catechism, a prayer book and a book of meditations and a book of chants. Unfortunately when these were being sent to the Micmac missions many of them were lost at sea. Some survived the journey and even today, though they are rare and valuable, they are to be found among the Micmacs.

The Micmac mission at Cross Point today is represented by a fine monastery of the Capuchins and a great church. The church here is dedicated to Ste. Anne, a favorite saint among the Micmacs. Within it is large and lofty and quite austere with snowy walls and unpainted woodwork. It was on June 24, 1910, that the Micmacs celebrated the first baptism to Christianity among the Indians of Canada. It was on that day in 1610 that old Chief Membertou and all his family were received into the church by the Recollet missionaries at Port Royal, with all the ritual and ceremony at their command. Membertou took the name of Louis, for the King of France, and all his family adopted royal names as symbols of their new estate.

The Micmacs were a part of the Ottawas and there were small groups of them throughout Acadia. There are as many now as there were three and a half centuries ago. They were never friendly to the English colonists and in Gaspé a Micmac still calls an American a "Bostonnais". At the time of the American Revolution, Count d'Estaing, vice-admiral of France, published a proclamation in Boston, offering the Micmacs certain rewards if they would rebel against the British and join the rebels. Although he represented the French to whom they had so long been attached, he also represented the Bostonnais whom the French had taught them to mistrust and fear and fight. So they declined his enticements and remained true to their new allegiance.

In the courtyard of the Capuchin monastery is a quaint old well. The well head was brought from Brouage, the home town of Sieur de Champlain, by Dr. John Finley of New York who was then a lecturer at the Sorbonne in Paris. It stood for centuries in the gardens of the Recollet Monastery in Brouage where Champlain must have talked over the American missions, for when he brought missionaries to New France, he selected the gentle Recollets. Over the well perhaps Champlain and the monks talked of that strange land so far away where he dreamed of building a New France.

Over the well is a little turret and within is painted this story of its origin and also a memorial to the exiled priests interned in the abandoned convent when the last of the French kings went to the guillotine.

Here in this modern monastery, with its ancient gardens and its memorials to the past, the spirit of old France still walks beside these men with shaven heads and rough gowns, in sandals and with girdles of clinking, wooden rosaries.

# 25

## *The Matapédia Valley*

THE way home lies through the Matapédia Valley. Ninety-five miles of highway runs through the wooded hills and by the quiet lakes that lie among them.

Across the river lies New Brunswick and the waters on both sides of the boundary line are famous among salmon fishermen the world over. One of the world's greatest salmon fishing clubs is located at Matapédia and if cod is king among the Gaspésians to the east, salmon holds undisputed sway over this part of the country.

When we leave Matapédia we come into something different. The first fifty-three miles of roadway follow the river to the lake in which it has its source. This is the lowest pass through the mountains that lie between the Baie des Chaleurs and the St. Lawrence. It divides the Notre Dame Mountains from the Shickshocks. From the town of Matapédia to Lake Matapédia, the road rises five hundred and twenty feet.

The road we travel follows the ancient Indian trail, a portage from the St. Lawrence to the Baie des Chaleurs over which the tribes travelled for many centuries before the white men came. We are apt to think of Canada in terms of our own settlement and exploration, forgetting that the white men of the seventeenth and eighteenth centuries who ventured farther and farther westward, moved over the travelways of the Indians, and with their guidance and advice. A history of portages in Canada would open a new chapter in our history and give us a new sense of our relationship to the people who lived on this continent for unrecorded centuries before the Europeans wakened from the lethargy of the Dark Ages of Christianity in Europe, and became the restless, energetic, colonizing creatures with which we are familiar. So when Frenchman and Englishman alike came to this country their success in exploration depended on their ability to win the collaboration of the red man who could show the ancient travelways over which, in time, the new-comers built roads and railways. So this is one of the Indian portages that became in time an explorer's trail and at last the path by which colonizers and pioneers plodded in to seek free land. It is always the pioneer, land hungry and hard working, who opens up the country to other political and commercial uses. Homesteaders are still at work hereabouts doing just that thing. At last this became a postroad and the first mails were carried over it on foot. For twenty-two years in the middle of the nineteenth century dogs carried the mail bags that grew bulkier with every year as more and more colonists found the country good and fertile. At Lake Matapédia the trail also branched and one road ran to Metis and another to Matane. When this forest road became a highway of sorts it was known as the Kempt Road. Now it is part and parcel of the Gaspé Road.

The Matapédia Valley is not the least interesting part of the road. Those who like to recall the days of the pioneers, who remember with admiration and respect the historical tasks they did so well, will see along this road as though in a sort of panorama, every stage of pioneer life just as it was in the days of the French regime, or when the Loyalists came into Gaspé. Or, indeed, in the days of the great depression of the nineteenth century when British emigrants, driven out of a land of evictions and machinery and potato famine, came to Canada to begin again.

Half a century ago this valley was unknown except to hunters and travellers and the faithful mail carriers. When the Kempt Road was built the government built log refuge stations along the way for the safety of those who, at their peril, attempted to cross the peninsula. In 1833 the first settler, Pierre Brouchu (he deserves to be remembered by name), went into this wilderness and cut a space in the forest for his home. For six years he was its solitary inhabitant. Twenty-five years later there were only eight settlers up and down the length of the river. In 1860, a colony of Acadians came over from Prince Edward Island and brought with them a new era of development for the Matapédia Valley.

Today along the highway new townships are opening up and French Canadians from the over-crowded lands of the upper province are coming here to begin again with virgin land just as their ancestors of a dozen generations ago did around Quebec and Montreal.

Beside the roadside here and there are the little clearings. Here is one in which the trees have lately been cut away but the stumps still stand. The trunks have been used to build a cabin. On every side except where the clearing faces the road, the forest presses in upon the little home. There is the pioneer, young and brawny, biting into the trunk of a silver birch with his axe. In the doorway stands a young woman, strong and hopeful and friendly, watching the day by day labor of clearing. In and out among the tree stumps runs a child who will someday inherit the farm that has not yet taken form except in the mind of the colonist.

Farther on you will come upon another clearing and this time the stumps are gone and there is a field of grain and a stack of golden hay and a cow browsing under the trees. The woods have been pushed back a little farther and the worst of the struggle is over, for now the settlers can grow enough to live upon until more fields are cleared, more trees cut and sold.

Presently the clearings will have become pleasant farms with fenced fields that climb up and over the hills and drop down on the other side. The tiny cabins will have become cow sheds and brave new houses will stand in the middle of the farmyards.

By the time we arrive at the tableland around Lake Matapédia we are in a rich and prosperous farming country, where plenty proclaims itself in big barns and where the church has come to guard its little flocks. Churches with slender spires point heavenward lest the farm folks, with their eyes upon their furrows, might forget whence comes the warmth and rain to reward their work.

So in fifty-odd miles we have had a living picture of pioneer life, all the way from the thick virgin forest lands to the completely conquered fields and meadows of the second and third generations.

For thirty miles after leaving Matapédia the road follows the river where the famous pools lie and where from each side, tributary streams, each with their secret hordes of salmon, come out of the hills. In all that distance there is not a village of any kind. The first we come upon is less than half a century old and it lies off to one side, on the other side of the river. This is Causapscal, or to give it its parish name, St. Jacques-le-Majeur de Causapscal. It takes the name of Causapscal from the river which joins the Matapédia here. The town is a center from which many hunters and fishermen reach their camps and lodges, some on pack-horses, some on foot.

In this vicinity we travel for some time beside Lac aux Saumons, or Salmon Lake. The mountains climb on each side of the road, breaking into seas of green. The roar here is not that of the breakers, but of the winds in the trees. Over the hills the lights and shadows move swiftly on a windy day that keeps the clouds moving overhead. Great blue-purple patches of shade are chased from horizon to valley by the melting gold of the sunlight. This is a lovely piece of the road and worth time off for a little thought.

Lake Matapédia, the source of the river, is the largest lake in the region. It is fifteen miles long and was once a famous salmon spawning ground before the lumbering industry was established in the district and saw mills went up along its banks. From Lake Matapédia to Baie des Chaleurs there are many big private fishing preserves. Big industrialists and financial men from American and Canadian cities keep camps here, which explains why Jean Baptiste in the clearing and the men from Wall street and St. James street are such oddly assorted neighbors.

When we leave Lake Matapédia we begin the descent to the St. Lawrence, for the great lake is on the height of land. From now on our road drops towards the level of the St. Lawrence and runs through a fine agricultural area where farming is done on a much bigger scale and where dairying is one of the chief industries.

At this last step of the journey, before we say farewell to the Gaspé Road, there are still two interesting things to notice, in addition to the sudden and superb view of the St. Lawrence that comes as a grand finale to this pageantry of the peninsula. After spinning along the highway between green fields, it is as though a curtain was raised on an unexpected setting. High above the wide, blue river we seem to hover. Like some titanic sapphire it lies, set in a frame of hilly shores. Ahead the road lies as straight and smooth as a golden ribbon and below, along the water's edge, the houses of a village lie.

It is as though Gaspé has kept this last impressive glimpse as a farewell gift, a handsome gesture of dismissal, just to prove that for all its lavish wealth of landscapes and seascapes, its largess is not exhausted. This last scene is not by any means the least. Gaspé knows how to speed the parting guest.

Then, as though a signature scrawled on the canvas by the artist, these last few miles sum up Gaspé's geological history. As we drop from level to level from Mont Joli to Ste. Flavie we have a striking example of the marine terraces that characterize all Gaspé. We pass over four of these, each indicating a sea level, a beach at one period in the unwritten history of the slowly rising coast.

Still another quaint fact about this bit of road concerns its churches. St. Joseph de le Page is a tiny village less than four miles from Ste. Flavie, but it has its own little church with its inevitable silver spire. Its next neighbor is Mont Joli, a much bigger and richer neighbor with a bigger church

and a high bell tower. Then at last comes Ste. Flavie not
much bigger than its hill top neighbor, St. Joseph. But Ste.
Flavie had a famous church, too. Every mariner that sails
the St. Lawrence knew these three places, because the spires,
mounting one above the other, fell into a straight line which
was one of the St. Lawrence landmarks for St. Lawrence
navigation. So the man on the bridge as he sails up or down
the great river glances towards the Gaspé shore for the three
spires. Not long ago the church of Ste. Flavie was burned
to the ground and the old landmark made incomplete. But
on the foundations of the old church a new one is being built
and so before long, the St. Lawrence navigator will again
discover the old familiar three spire line by which to check
his course.

So we leave them one by one behind us and drop swiftly
and perhaps a little reluctantly down to the river's edge.
There are other little villages and other fields of golden stubble
and other autumn roadsides dripping gold and scarlet, other
little churches with shapely little steeples along the road, but
those we have left belong to Gaspé.

# Index

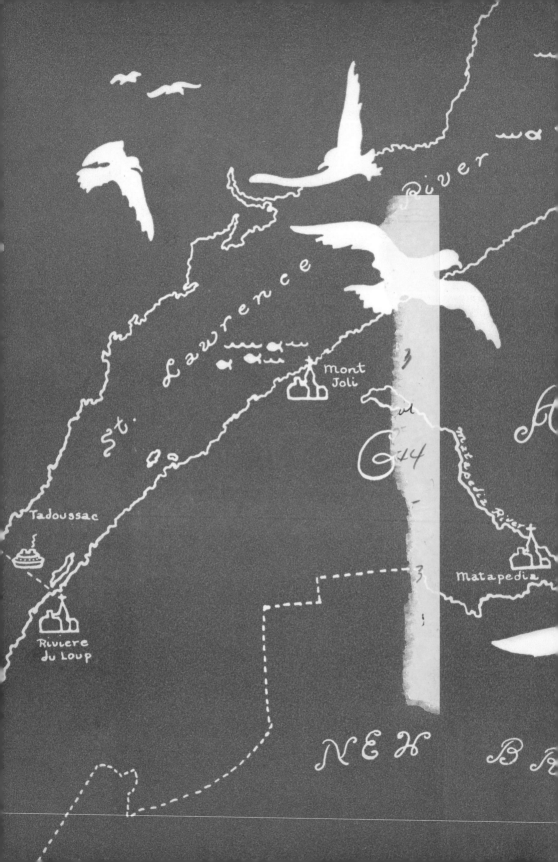